Biosecurity in the Global Age

Biosecurity in the Global Age

BIOLOGICAL WEAPONS, PUBLIC HEALTH,

AND THE RULE OF LAW

David P. Fidler and Lawrence O. Gostin

STANFORD LAW AND POLITICS
An Imprint of Stanford University Press
Stanford, California

Stanford University Press
Stanford, California

Printed in the United States of America on acid-free, archival-quality paper

Library of Congress Cataloging-in-Publication Data

Fidler, David P.
 Biosecurity in the global age : biological weapons, public health, and the rule of law / David P. Fidler and Lawrence O. Gostin.
    p. cm.
 Includes bibliographical references and index.
 ISBN 978-0-8047-5029-5 (cloth : alk. paper)
 1. Biological warfare--Prevention. 2. Biological weapons--Law and legislation. 3. Bioterrorism--Prevention. 4. Public health laws. I. Gostin, Larry O. (Larry Ogalthorpe) II. Title.

UG447.8.F54 2008
363.325'3--dc22

                         2007031119s

Typeset by Bruce Lundquist in 10/14 Minion

TABLE OF CONTENTS

LIST OF TABLES AND FIGURES

Tables

Figures

LIST OF ABBREVIATIONS

AHG	Ad Hoc Group
APEC	Asia Pacific Economic Cooperation Forum
BARDA	Biomedical Advanced Research and Development Authority
BSL	biosafety level
BTCC	Biological Threat Characterization Center
BWC	Biological Weapons Convention
BWPP	BioWeapons Prevention Project
CBM	confidence building measure
CBW	chemical and biological weapon
CDC	Centers for Disease Control and Prevention
CIA	Central Intelligence Agency
CWC	Chemical Weapons Convention
DHHS	Department of Health and Human Services
DHS	Department of Homeland Security
ECDC	European Centers for Disease Prevention and Control
EPA	Environmental Protection Agency
FACA	Federal Advisory Committee Act
FAR	Federal Acquisition Regulations
FEMA	Federal Emergency Management Agency
FOIA	Freedom of Information Act
G7	Group of Seven

G8	Group of Eight
GHSI	Global Health Security Initiative
GOARN	Global Outbreak Alert and Response Network
GPHIN	Global Public Health Information Network
HIV/AIDS	human immunodeficiency virus/acquired immunodeficiency syndrome
ICRC	International Committee of the Red Cross
IFFIm	International Finance Facility for Immunization
IHR	International Health Regulations
ISR	International Sanitary Regulations
ISU	Implementation Support Unit
NATO	North Atlantic Treaty Organization
NBACC	National Biodefense Analysis and Countermeasure Center
NBFAC	National Bioforensic Analysis Center
NGO	nongovernmental organization
NIH	National Institutes of Health
NSABB	National Science Advisory Board for Biosecurity
PEPFAR	President's Emergency Plan for AIDS Relief
ProMED-mail	Program for Monitoring Emerging Diseases
PPP	public-private partnership
PSI	Proliferation Security Initiative
SARS	severe acute respiratory syndrome
TOPOFF	Top Officials
TRIPS	Agreement on Trade-Related Aspects of Intellectual Property Rights
UN	United Nations
UNDP	United Nations Development Programme
U.S.	United States
VEREX	Ad Hoc Group of Governmental Experts
WHA	World Health Assembly
WHO	World Health Organization
WMD	weapon(s) of mass destruction

ACKNOWLEDGMENTS

We would never have been able to complete this book without the contributions and kindnesses of many people. We particularly thank Barry Kellman for sharing with us issues, ideas, suggestions, and his passion for getting people to see the problem of biosecurity in new ways. We also owe a debt of gratitude to Ben Berkman for reading drafts of the manuscript and always providing helpful feedback. J. J. Welling provided us with timely and accurate help in researching specific issues covered in this book. The editors at Stanford University Press have been patient with us, and we appreciate their willingness to allow us the time we needed to finish this book. Finally, we thank our families for enduring yet another project that has often occupied our time and attention.

David P. Fidler
Bloomington, Indiana

Lawrence O. Gostin
Washington, D.C.

Biosecurity in the Global Age

1 INTRODUCTION

The Challenge of Biosecurity
in the Twenty-First Century

I. THE UNFOLDING POLICY REVOLUTION OF BIOSECURITY

In the first years of the twenty-first century, the United States and the rest
of the world have endured shocks, crises, and fears captured in the haunting
images, words, and events that define our turbulent times—September 11th,
Al Qaeda, weapons of mass destruction, USA PATRIOT, axis of evil, SARS,
quarantine, HIV/AIDS, Guantanamo Bay, Abu Ghraib, Darfur, bird flu. This
troubling lexicon captures pressing dangers individuals, countries, and the
international system face today.

Some of these dangers are not new, such as war, tyranny, and torture. They
represent recent manifestations of age-old threats to human dignity, national
security, and international peace. Other dangers combine, however, to create
new threats to individuals, countries, and the global community with few, if
any, precedents. This book focuses on one of these new dangers—the threat
infectious diseases pose to human life, the security of states, and international
political and economic stability. In short, the world confronts a serious biosecurity threat.

The argument that something called *biosecurity* has emerged as a new issue
in national and international politics may be greeted with skepticism because
states addressed challenges posed by biological weapons and naturally occurring infectious diseases for most of the twentieth century. The Geneva
Protocol banned, for example, the use of bacteriological agents in warfare in
1925 (Geneva Protocol 1925). States established international health organizations tasked with cooperation on infectious diseases in the first decade

of the twentieth century (Rome Agreement 1907; Weindling 1995). In addition, international cooperation on infectious diseases dates back to at least the mid-nineteenth century (Goodman 1971; Howard-Jones 1950; Howard-Jones 1975).

The emergence of biosecurity as a policy concern connects, thus, to historical efforts made to address biological weapons and infectious disease epidemics. What has transpired recently, however, represents a policy revolution, the implications of which are still unfolding and are not yet fully understood. So much of such importance has happened so rapidly with respect to the challenges of biological weapons and infectious diseases that synthesis presents a daunting challenge. This book takes up the challenge and explores the emergence of biosecurity as a critical policy area in the first decades of the twenty-first century.

II. MAIN ARGUMENTS OF THE BOOK

We argue that biosecurity encompasses threats from both biological weapons and naturally occurring infectious diseases. The policy revolution that biosecurity represents requires integrating two policy realms previously separate from one another—security and public health. We stress the importance and difficulty of this integration strategy throughout this book. Integrating security and public health requires changing entrenched perspectives and practices and building new, sustainable governance approaches to threats posed by pathogenic microbes.

As discussed more later, our argument about integration touches on one of the many controversies that surround biosecurity. Traditionalists in both security and public health resist weaving these new areas together. The integrative task is, however, critical. Approaching this task forthrightly forces both security and public health leaders to re-think their approaches to the challenges of governance convergence. One of the most important of these challenges involves the role of the biological sciences in the pursuit of biosecurity. We argue that the development of the biosecurity challenge requires supervision of the biological sciences as part of the integration of security and public health.

The policy thrust for such supervision comes from worries that malevolent actors may transform scientific advances into weapons of mass terror and destruction. We acknowledge the prudence of these worries and accept the need for oversight to prevent or deter misappropriation of scientific progress for evil ends. The dynamics of oversight cannot, however, sacrifice science's critical function in improving humanity's health on the altar of narrowly construed notions of national security.

As illustrated by the novel challenge of balancing scientific freedom and security fears, the integration of security and public health requires policy makers to engage in complex decisions often characterized by a lack of complete information. We argue that, in such an environment, embedding biosecurity policy in the rule of law becomes critical. Whether the issue is the supervision of science for security and public health or another of the myriad challenges biosecurity presents, the governance framework provided by the rule of law approach serves as a lodestar for biosecurity policy.

Our belief in the rule of law does not mean we claim that this approach always provides the "right" response. The choices biosecurity threats force policy makers to confront are too complex and contingent for any approach to be foolproof. We do assert, however, that the rule of law philosophy of governance provides a tested methodology for policy formulation and execution that allows material interests to be pursued without losing sight of core normative values.

The integration of security and public health within the rule of law raises the problem of achieving these ends in a world increasingly characterized by globalization. We argue that effective biosecurity policy has to involve globalized forms of governance. As with many policy areas transformed by globalization, security and public health can no longer view the world through the state-centric lenses of national governments and intergovernmental coordination. Governance mechanisms have to reflect the malevolent and benevolent roles non-state actors play in world politics.

Crafting effective globalized governance for biosecurity is, however, difficult. The enormity of the challenge often tempts people to revert to traditional governance approaches, especially retrenchment into narrow conceptions of a nation's self-interests in security and health. As the book explores, these backward-looking reversions have a powerful logic that flows from the sheer difficulty of making globalized governance work coherently. We acknowledge this difficulty but maintain that biosecurity, even narrowly defined, cannot be achieved and maintained in a sustainable way without robust globalized governance efforts.

The book develops these arguments in greater detail, but, before launching into systematic analysis, more introductory context for the biosecurity policy revolution would prove useful to readers. We have designed this book to be useful to different academic and policy disciplines, so establishing some baseline understanding with our readers on key themes is useful. The next sections of this chapter accomplish this objective by exploring the concept, controversies, and key challenges of biosecurity policy in the early twenty-first century.

III. THE CONCEPT OF BIOSECURITY

We generally define *biosecurity* to mean society's collective responsibility to safeguard the population from dangers presented by pathogenic microbes—whether intentionally released or naturally occurring. With respect to the malevolent use of microbes, our use of the term *biosecurity* is not novel because many experts have used it to describe efforts to defend against threats from biological weapons and biological terrorism. These threats are indeed primary subject matter for biosecurity policy, and Part I of this book addresses the threat of violence perpetrated through biological means, or what Kellman has called the perpetration of bioviolence (Kellman 2006b).

Our approach to biosecurity includes, however, more than the development and use of biological weapons. Biosecurity concerns two intertwining strands of pathogenic threats that include biological weapons and naturally occurring infectious diseases. Biosecurity is as much about public health as arms control because of the dangers infectious diseases pose to human societies in the twenty-first century. We agree, "Biological security . . . must address both the challenge of biological weapons and that of infectious disease" (Chyba 2001, 2349), and "We need to pay much closer attention to biological security" to build "an effective global defence against bio-terrorism and overwhelming natural outbreaks of deadly infectious disease" (UN Secretary-General 2004, viii). Understanding the threats of naturally occurring infectious diseases and biological weapons "is critical to formulating an effective biosecurity policy" (Grotto and Tucker 2006, 1). The threats presented by biological weapons and natural disease epidemics weave together to form an interdependent policy challenge the likes of which we have never seen before.

Acknowledging interdependencies in policies on biological weapons and infectious diseases does not mean that all infectious disease outbreaks are biosecurity problems. Many infectious disease events remain localized, low-impact outbreaks. To include these infectious disease issues within the scope of biosecurity wrongly equates this concept with public health generally. The biosecurity concern is with infectious disease outbreaks and problems, whatever their source or origin, that could potentially disrupt the normal functioning of societies.

Societal disruption is not, of course, a concept capable of precise measurement or prediction because too many factors are involved. Infectious disease outbreaks can powerfully affect the human psyche in ways that extend beyond statistics on death and illness. Even harms that are small statistically can generate destabilizing effects within and among societies. The social, economic, and political disruptions caused by the anthrax attacks in 2001 and the outbreak of severe acute respiratory syndrome (SARS) in 2003 illustrate the disruptive potential of even low morbidity and mortality events.

Our approach to biosecurity deviates from traditional policy perspectives on what "security" means. Security has historically been concerned predominantly with threats of military violence by one state against another state. In our view, the least pressing biosecurity concern involves the possible use of biological weapons by one state against another state. Although our concept of biosecurity includes the potential for inter-state use of biological weapons, we recognize as security concerns possible biological attacks perpetrated by non-state actors—bioterrorists—and the transnational threat presented by naturally occurring disease epidemics.

Expanding the notion of security beyond its conventional paradigm has proved controversial, whether the focus of the expansion involves pathogenic threats, environmental degradation, or other candidates for new security challenges (see more later). Threats of military conflict by one state against another remain security concerns, as worries in the United States about China's growing military power, North Korea's claimed possession of nuclear weapons, and Iran's alleged pursuit of nuclear weapons suggest. Conventional wisdom about security does not, however, provide sufficient guidance when we consider the spectrum of serious threats posed by infectious diseases.

The frequency and intensity with which bioterrorism and the specter of contagious pandemics have appeared on U.S. national and homeland security agendas indicate that significant real world developments inform our analysis (White House 2002; Office of Homeland Security 2002). In its latest *National Security Strategy,* issued in March 2006, President George W. Bush's administration again conceived of "public health challenges like pandemics (HIV/AIDS, avian influenza) that recognize no borders" as a national security problem related to globalization (White House 2006a, 47). The Bush administration argued that the risks to social order from naturally occurring disease epidemics can be "so great that public health approaches may be inadequate, necessitating new strategies and responses" (White House 2006a, 47). One of these new strategies and responses is to conceive of naturally occurring infectious diseases as security threats, as we do in our definition of biosecurity.

As subsequent chapters discuss, the real challenge is not justifying the shift away from conventional wisdom on what security means. Rather, the task involves how best to balance the need to protect against the proliferation of biological weapons and the perpetration of biological attacks by terrorists and the need to address threats presented by naturally occurring infectious diseases. Calibrating these aspects of biosecurity constitutes a policy challenge wholly unlike previous security tasks, such as how much political détente and how much nuclear deterrence the United States needed to address the Soviet threat during the Cold War. This unprecedented task also affects traditional understandings of public health, as the position of the Bush administration in its latest *National Security Strategy* demonstrates.

IV. THE CONTROVERSIES OF BIOSECURITY

The emergence of biosecurity has generated significant controversies at virtually every level and step of analysis. For that reason, the terrain of biosecurity policy is a conceptual and practical minefield, making it a very politically charged arena of debate. The disagreements begin with attempts to define security in ways that include more than inter-state military violence. Efforts to include naturally occurring infectious diseases within security thinking form part of a larger controversy about redefining security, especially national security, away from its traditional state-centric, military-biased perspective. This conventional perspective has been particularly strong in the United States because "traditional definitions of U.S. national security have focused almost exclusively on the potential of violent attack by other countries on the United States, its citizens, and its vital overseas interests" (Bergen and Garrett 2005, 1).

Many security experts are leery of expanding the traditional concept of security to include new types of threats from non-state actors or transnational phenomena. In some respects, this wariness is warranted because discourse on new security threats often threatens to collapse notions of security with notions of governance (e.g., as happens with the concept of human security). In other respects, security traditionalists are fighting a losing battle. The terrorist attacks of September 11th laid to rest the debate whether non-state actors really represented national security threats to the United States. With the traditional state-centric framework penetrated, policy space has opened for considering the potentially disruptive effects of transnational, nonmilitary phenomena. The Bush administration's willingness to include threats from naturally occurring infectious diseases repeatedly in its national and homeland security strategies suggests that a sea change, however controversial, has indeed occurred. Leading nongovernmental analyses also reflect this sea change (Grotto and Tucker 2006; Ikenberry and Slaughter 2006).

In addition to disagreements about what threats security policy should address, many other controversies have accompanied biosecurity's emergence as a new policy endeavor. Debates rage, for example, about what type of security threat bioterrorism really presents to countries today. Some, such as former Senator Bill Frist, have argued that bioterrorism constitutes one of the most serious existential threats to U.S. national security in the early twenty-first century (Hirschler 2005). Other analysts challenge this assessment and assert that bioterrorism is not one of the most pressing issues facing the United States or the world today (Leitenberg 2004, 2005).

This controversy contains many issues on which experts diverge. Are terrorists really interested in developing biological weapons and engaging in biological attacks? How easy is it for terrorists to weaponize pathogenic microbes and use biological weapons effectively? Should scientific freedoms be curtailed to ensure that peaceful research and development do not inadvertently facilitate the malevolent use of microbes? How much can policies pursued to defend against biological weapons also be productively exploited in addressing threats from naturally occurring infectious diseases? What is the right way to govern events that are characterized by low probability but potentially extreme consequences? These questions and others force policy makers and scholars to confront hard choices in an environment permeated by uncertainty concerning risks and benefits.

Controversies also appear when biosecurity policy turns to infectious disease epidemics. Many public health practitioners and experts have viewed with skepticism and concern the "securitization" of public health. Such attitudes suggest that conceiving of public health as a security issue poses dangers for public health's mission of protecting and promoting population health. A key danger is that a security focus will force public health to concentrate resources and personnel on rare events (e.g., a bioterrorist attack or highly contagious pandemic) at the expense of tackling health problems that cause the great death and illness in populations daily. For example, some public health experts have expressed concern that initiatives focusing on communicable diseases divert attention away from the growing global toll that non-communicable diseases cause (Yach, Leeder, Bell, and Kistmasamy 2005).

Throughout the book, we take up many of the most serious controversies that make biosecurity policy important, intriguing, and unsettling. Our approach will not make everything fall magically into place and thus transform the controversies of biosecurity into the mere teething pains of a nascent transition to a new policy consensus. Having experienced the rough terrain of biosecurity in our professional work, we are mindful of the limitations of our analysis. We do aim, however, for this book to help biosecurity policy move beyond the disaggregated, disjointed, and dysfunctional jumble of controversies that now overshadows this emerging area of governance.

V. THE CHALLENGES OF BIOSECURITY

The deeper we delved into the controversies of biosecurity, the more aware we became that behind the sound and fury of disagreements lurked deeper issues—what we identified as the central challenges of biosecurity. These challenges drive the structure and substance of our arguments in this book because they make transparent the foundations on which effective and sustainable biosecurity policy and governance must be built. Too often in our work on this book we have sensed ourselves unable to see the forest of biosecurity for all the trees—the proliferation of proposals, projects, policy wonks, and polemics on how to make the United States and the world safe from biological harm. The more frenzied the biosecurity debate became, the more convinced we were that these challenges give the frenzy underlying focus and direction. Identifying and unpacking these challenges may, for many readers, be more valuable than the recommendations we make on pursuing them.

The main arguments of this book briefly described earlier capture these four central policy challenges. Effective biosecurity policy and governance requires, nationally and globally, the integration of security and public health, supervision of science for security and public health, embedding biosecurity policy in the rule of law, and globalizing governance for biosecurity. This section explains these challenges in more detail and emphasizes not only their importance but also the difficulty of achieving these objectives.

A. Integrating Security and Public Health

We argue that biosecurity will not be achieved within and among countries without effective integration of the policy worlds of security and public health. Whether the threat comes from biological weapons or naturally occurring disease epidemics, biosecurity policy confronts the task of integrating security and public health. As indicated earlier, skepticism and concern about such integration exists in both the security and public health worlds. The worry is perhaps greatest in public health, given the imbalance of power and resources between security bureaucracies and public health agencies. We understand these public health fears, which, as later chapters explore, are not unfounded. We maintain, however, that integration of security and public health is not only practically but also normatively necessary in seeking better biosecurity.

In many respects, the emergence of biosecurity flows from the collision of two policy spheres—security and public health—previously not connected or related. The distance between conventional security thinking and traditional public health activities is reflected in foreign policy conceptualizations of security as representing the "high politics" of international relations and of public health falling within the category of "low politics" (Fidler 2005a). Even within "low politics," public health was at the margins—really low politics—because it was largely considered a technical, nonpolitical, and humanitarian endeavor (Fidler 2005b). The gap between public health and the theory and practice of national and international security has historically been enormous.

Even in the area of biological weapons, policy demonstrated no serious consideration of public health. Security approaches to biological weapons involved either deterrence (e.g., having biological weapons capabilities to respond in kind to biological attacks) or arms control (e.g., prohibiting development and use of biological weapons). If public health arose in these contexts, it caused problems. For example, international legal prohibitions on biological weapons development contained in the Biological Weapons Convention of 1972 (BWC) could not ban all research on, and uses of, biological agents because peaceful research activities were necessary for health purposes, namely basic research on pathogens and applied research on antimicrobial drugs. Similarly, national and international public health systems operated without serious reference to security concerns about the proliferation and use of biological weapons.

The biosecurity challenge of integrating security and public health is colored by the historical reality that these policy endeavors operated in distinct worlds of unequal significance. Security activities were highly political and generously funded, but public health was politically impotent and starved of resources. The emergence of biosecurity as a policy concern suggests that this separation no longer exists and is no longer tenable.

The restraints that prevented use of biological weapons during the Cold War do not necessarily have the same strength in the post–Cold War era. Non-state actors, moreover, seem even less likely to abide by international rules and norms restraining development and use of biological weapons. For rogue states and non-state actors, the scientific challenges of producing biological weapons are receding with rapid advancements in microbiology and biotechnology and the global dissemination of these advances.

At the same time, the resurgence of naturally occurring infectious diseases has stimulated new understandings about how states and populations should perceive their security. The HIV/AIDS pandemic, for example, made the international community face the reality of microbial-related destruction of populations, economies, development prospects, and military power and preparedness. Such destruction came to be seen as having not only public health but also international and national security importance (Feldbaum, Lee, and Patel 2006; Garrett 2005a; Security Council 2000). The global political and economic shock of SARS and the portents of avian influenza and an influenza pandemic have further opened the eyes of political leaders to the nexus between security and public health. For example, the UN Secretary-General's High-level Panel on Threats, Challenges and Change (2004) prominently featured the need to improve public health as part of its vision for comprehensive collective security.

The collision of security and public health has destroyed the policy silos in which governments engaged in these endeavors and produced the need to create synergies in the new relationship between security and public health. The challenge of integrating security and public health arises from this synergy requirement. Integrating security and public health requires fundamental conceptual and practical changes in both areas to strengthen connections between them. Expanding the concept of security to include infectious disease threats requires substantial improvements in public health infrastructures. Investments in national and international biosecurity make little sense without upgrading public health systems. Investments in laboratories, surveillance, data systems, and public health workforce capabilities frequently aim to create "dual use" capacities for defense against biological weapons and against disease epidemics. Biosecurity means having both security and public health firmly planted in the realm of the "high politics" of foreign policy and international relations.

For its part, public health can no longer remain separated, by desire or design, from security policy and its attendant power politics. What public health does has always mattered to individuals, states, and the international community, but biosecurity has heightened the political importance of the public health endeavor. Being on the agenda of national and international leaders involves, however, political questions, pressures, and dynamics that public health rarely faced historically.

Moving security and public health from silos to synergies has not proved easy, and the integration challenge will remain a constant feature of biosecurity. Integrating security and public health involves overcoming the weight of distinct policy histories and the ever-present jealous guarding of traditional bureaucratic turfs and funding streams. Security communities may fear the loss of resources and control as public health emerges as politically important. Public health practitioners and experts may develop anxieties about the securitization of policies for protecting population health. Beyond such fears and anxieties await problems generated by a lack of shared experiences and a common culture between those responsible for security and those overseeing public health.

The difficulty intensifies because the low probability of both biological weapons attacks and socially disruptive epidemics may lull politicians into complacency that biosecurity was yesterday's problem or the responsibility of some future government. The integration of security and public health has to be sustainable over decades and thus needs to be grooved deeply into the structures, interests, and practices of governments at the highest levels nationally and internationally.

B. Supervising Science for Security and Public Health

The second central challenge of biosecurity involves the need to supervise science in the new relationship between security and public health. We argue that such supervision should be part of biosecurity policy nationally and globally. The supervision of science becomes critical when policy moves in the direction of integrating security and public health. The supervision issue arises from security's concern about the dangers created by the rapid development and dissemination of ever more powerful scientific knowledge and capabilities. Ignoring these dangers would be imprudent from a public health perspective, let alone a security one. How such supervision unfolds is more critical than whether it should, if one accepts the need to integrate security and public health.

The policy challenge of supervision revolves around choices that have to be made with respect to three principles: scientific innovation, scientific freedom, and the open dissemination of scientific research. The collision of the policy worlds of security and public health includes a clash of cultures with respect to the enterprise of science. Biosecurity has to sort out this clash in a way that facilitates the sustainable integration of security and public health.

Traditionally, security policy has attempted to harness and control scientific research and development. The basic strategy was to allow science to innovate in ways that would increase the power of the state vis-à-vis rival states (e.g., through government-funded research) and to deny such rivals access to new technological capabilities (e.g., through export controls). National security policy on nuclear technology illustrates this approach. The United States encouraged advances in nuclear weapons technology as part of deterrence against the Soviet Union, but it also tried to prevent such technology from reaching the Soviets or other countries that presented a potential threat to the United States. As a result, the United States imposed strict regulations and oversight on nuclear technologies under scientific investigation in the United States. In short, security policy conventionally viewed the principles of scientific innovation, freedom, and open dissemination in the nuclear realm as part of the larger zero-sum game of international power politics.

By contrast, public health operated under an entirely different perspective on the pursuit of science. Advancing the cause of population health has traditionally supported maximizing scientific innovation, freedom, and open dissemination of research. The objective was the proverbial "marketplace of ideas" through which the best concepts, approaches, and technologies would emerge for the betterment of health. The scientific communities feeding research into public health developed deep commitments to the principles of encouraging scientific innovation, expanding scientific freedom, and broadly sharing the fruits of scientific endeavors. These commitments have found support too in the larger principle of the freedom of expression, which constitutional law in many countries and international law recognize as a civil and political human right.

The coming together of security and public health as policy endeavors forces both areas to look again at their respective traditional approaches to the scientific enterprise. The zero-sum instincts of security policy have to confront the reality that the biological sciences are not like nuclear research and thus cannot be regulated as nuclear technologies have been. Preventing the malevolent use of scientific advances requires more complex and sophisticated thinking than the "command and control" used for nuclear technologies.

Similarly, public health's assumption that scientific innovation, freedom, and dissemination are unquestionably public goods has confronted the specter of potentially devastating externalities arising from uncontrolled, cavalier, or misappropriated scientific exploration. Is every experiment really a good idea, regardless of its potential to be exploited for evil ends or to cause damage through unintentional release of dangerous by-products of the research? Does it make sense to deny or discount the contributions scientific openness could make to governments or terrorists potentially interested in acquiring biological weapons or engaging in biological attack? At the very least, these and similar questions have made the public health community realize that its devotion to the scientific enterprise now operates in a very different, and perhaps more dangerous, environment.

The challenge for biosecurity policy is to achieve a regime for supervising science that contributes to security without hobbling science's potential to improve human health. Finding this balance is fraught with difficulties to which no one has easy answers. As this book explores, the scientific and political realities of today's world require careful calibration of security and public health objectives with respect to scientific innovation, freedom, and open dissemination of research.

C. Embedding Biosecurity Governance in the Rule of Law

The third challenge of biosecurity involves ensuring that integrating security and public health and supervising science occur within the framework of the rule of law. We believe that this framework is critical, especially with respect to dramatic policy changes connected with security fears and interests. The rule of law in the United States and other countries often has an uneasy relationship with the exigencies of national security. Security claims require substantive and procedural scrutiny to prevent executive discretion from eroding political and philosophical commitments to the values grounded in the concept of the rule of law.

As lawyers, we understand that the phrase "rule of law" is often used as a ritual incantation that those chanting rarely explain. The concept of the rule of law is indeed abstract, complex, and laden with normative values. Traditionally, the rule of law refers to a philosophy of governance: Formal legal rules, rather than the arbitrary whims of politicians and leaders, govern the exercise of political power in societies. Hence, Americans are fond of asserting that they live under "the rule of law, not the rule of men."

As a philosophy of governance, the rule of law focuses on four objectives: (1) ensuring that governance actors are properly empowered through law to take actions necessary for the defense and welfare of populations, (2) protecting individual rights and liberties in the exercise of government authority, (3) pursuing natural and distributive justice in public policy, and (4) creating transparent and accountable forms of governance.

We believe that the rule of law philosophy of governance should inform biosecurity policy. As Chapter 6 explains, the rule of law approach facilitates adequate empowerment of government actors to address biosecurity threats and disciplines the exercise of government power to ensure the protection of individual rights. The rule of law approach also ensures that principles of nondiscrimination, procedural due process, distributive justice, and transparency and accountability remain pertinent to biosecurity discourse.

This stance places our analysis right in the middle of a central challenge for biosecurity policy: How to maximize governance by formal law of the integration of security and public health and the supervision of science in a politically fragmented, globalized context. This challenge has a number of layers.

To begin, the rule of law gains most of its currency as a governance philosophy within states. When the rule of law mantra leaves the hierarchical, unitary governance context of a state and enters the anarchical, divided world of international relations, its strength wanes. Historically, international law has not governed the behavior of states in the sense projected by the rule of law philosophy of governance. International politics has most often been characterized by dominance of the great powers rather than by states' adherence to the supremacy of formal rules of international law. We understand all too well that biosecurity governance, especially given its globalized nature, could fall into traditional patterns of great power machinations, which historically have not been characterized by the rule of law.

Within domestic and international law, the rule of law has had its greatest struggles in the context of states pursuing their security. When governments are determined to take certain actions to protect their national security, they often ignore rules of law that obstruct or complicate such actions, or manipulate such rules to provide legal cover. The post–September 11th war on terrorism has provided many examples of tension between national security imperatives and rules of domestic and international law. The rule of law challenge in biosecurity policy requires confronting these tensions rather than pretending they do not exist.

Although law and public health have had a long and critical relationship, the notion of the rule of law is not commonly associated with public health activities. The contributions of domestic and international law to public health achievements are often underappreciated (Fidler 2000; Goodman et al. 2006; Gostin 2000). Thinking about embedding biosecurity policy in the rule of law requires elucidating how and why law is critical to the public health functions required to meet the threats posed by pathogenic microbes.

The rule of law is not merely concerned with the supremacy of formal law in governance activities. This philosophy of governance also connects to the desire and need for justice. The rule of law seeks not just procedural but also substantive justice. When biosecurity policies are designed and implemented, a rule of law approach encourages that attention be paid to questions of whose security and whose public health are being protected. Biosecurity governance can become the plaything of the great powers, and it can be a source of unfair and unjust resource allocations that weaken security and public health for many populations over generations. Biosecurity governance creates questions of distributive justice, the answers to which will have profound implications for security and health around the world.

D. Globalizing Governance for Biosecurity

The fourth challenge of biosecurity policy concerns organizing governance of transnational threats through a political structure dominated by sovereign states. We argue that effective biosecurity policy requires globalized governance of biosecurity threats. Globalized governance involves activities at national, international, and global governance levels. Although definitions of "global governance" vary, what distinguishes global governance from international governance is the involvement of non-state actors. In other words, international governance is governance by and among states.

Global governance involves not only states but also non-state actors, such as nongovernmental organizations, multinational corporations, philanthropic foundations (e.g., Rockefeller and Gates Foundations), and public-private partnerships (e.g., Global Fund to Fight AIDS, Tuberculosis, and Malaria).

Our emphasis on globalized governance concerning biosecurity reflects our sense that governing the integration of security and public health has to involve the efforts of state and non-state actors. The challenge of supervising science illustrates this point. Many experts on the relationship of developments in the biological sciences and the potential proliferation and use of biological weapons acknowledge that a critical governance actor is the individual scientist, who probably does not work for, or on behalf of, any government. Raising awareness of potential dangers of biological research among the community of scientific researchers treats this community as a front-line governance actor and resource.

As noted earlier, the political structure of sovereign states affects the challenge of embedding biosecurity governance in the rule of law, but the effect of this political framework on biosecurity is more comprehensive. Integrating security and public health, supervising science for biosecurity, and embedding governance in the rule of law require governance structures and processes. The threats of biological weapons proliferation, biological attack, and infectious disease epidemics are largely transnational problems. The global governance challenge arises because humanity largely confronts the borderless nature of terrorism, scientific advance, and pathogenic microbes through a border-filled political world that fragments jurisdiction over virtually all essential security and public health functions.

The challenge of responding to transnational threats through sovereign states is not, of course, new. For public health, globalization is not a novel phenomenon. Classic public health mantras include "germs don't recognize borders" and "germs don't carry passports." Public health experts have long understood that the international mobility of people, animals, and products makes pathogenic microbes a transnational threat. A message in the mantras is that humanity's division into sovereign states rarely, if ever, materially slows the spread of infectious diseases. Governance responses have to be built, however, on the fragmented foundation provided by a system of independent, sovereign states where borders still matter politically and legally.

The answer most often given to the mismatch between the nature of transnational problems and the political structure of international relations is to encourage better, deeper, and stronger international cooperation between states. This approach essentially attempts to supplement national governance responses with international governance, or governance by and among states. Such cooperation is, of course, necessary, and our book identifies instances where international cooperation should be pursued, however difficult it might be. Although international governance is necessary, we do not believe that it is sufficient for effectively meeting the biosecurity challenge. We accept the need to build globalized governance mechanisms to achieve sustainable biosecurity in the twenty-first century.

Contributing to the challenge of globalized governance for biosecurity are the disparate historical experiences of security and public health with national and international governance. For differing reasons, security and public health have predominantly been national governance functions. Certainly, international cooperation has been a part of these policy areas, but such cooperation has historically been weak. The unwillingness of states to relinquish sovereignty over policies connected to their basic survival and power has long plagued international cooperation on security matters. National security was too important, for example, to leave to the United Nations or to arms control agreements. International cooperation on health has long been plagued by the opposite problem, namely the status of public health as a mere humanitarian endeavor of little consequence to the balance of power and security of states.

The biosecurity challenge involves, thus, moving two policy areas toward globalized governance in a context characterized by weak international cooperation and weak international institutions. The daunting nature of this task may create incentives for policy makers to prefer what appears to be the easier route—concentrating on the state and its individual resilience in the face of biosecurity threats. Why "forward deploy" resources and assets for globalized biosecurity governance when the weakness of international institutions and international cooperation make such investments unlikely to produce sustainable results? This question implies that the prudent strategy is to "harden the target" of one's state rather than build globalized governance castles in the air.

Although we recognize the difficulty of globalized governance for biosecurity, we are convinced that such governance plays a role in the strategies to pursue in achieving biosecurity. At relevant points, the book analyzes the most prominent challenges of globalized governance and attempts to provide our understanding of how globalized biosecurity governance should be constructed and sustained.

E. Summary of the Concept, Controversies, and Challenges of Biosecurity

We have introduced the reader to important aspects of the debate about bio-security and attempted to shed light on our main arguments about this emerging area of policy and governance. Defining the parameters of biosecurity constitutes an analytical first step, and we outlined how we define and conceptualize biosecurity as involving threats from both biological weapons and naturally occurring infectious diseases. Our approach does not settle the larger controversies about how broadly "security" should be stretched conceptually. We focus, instead, on the interdependent policy tasks that arise when contemplating governance of pathogenic threats. The historical separation of security and public health, even in the context of biological weapons, is simply no longer tenable as a basis for policy choices.

Nor do we pretend that our approach neatly resolves all the politically charged and acrimonious controversies that afflict biosecurity deliberations. Indeed, we do not believe that some of these controversies can be resolved because of the lack of certainty involved with anticipating low probability/high consequence events involving microbial agents. The controversies are, however, indicators of the complexities and difficulties attending the central challenges of biosecurity policy, which we have identified as integrating security and public health, supervising science for security and public health, embedding biosecurity policy in the rule of law, and globalizing governance for biosecurity.

The normative arguments we make produce a daunting agenda for biosecurity policy and governance, one that has made us pause at times to consider whether we are too ambitious in our approach. We have tried to calibrate our ambition in such a way that produces a biosecurity regime that makes us more secure in ways that are consistent with our values. The unprecedented policy revolution biosecurity represents calls for ambition in policy and governance, even if the nature of our ambition proves unpersuasive to the reader.

VI. STRUCTURE OF THE BOOK

We organize our analysis in three parts. In Part I, we focus on the biosecurity threat posed by biological weapons. Chapter 2 provides an overview of the historical and contemporary problems biological weapons represent, and it includes analysis of the techniques and technologies of biological weapons and of past experiences with arms control efforts on biological weapons. Chapter 3 then examines strategies for preventing and responding to the development and use of biological weapons that go beyond the traditional arms control approach. Chapter 3 also focuses on biodefense as a response to contemporary threats from biological weapons, including the implications biodefense creates for the relationship between security and the principles of scientific innovation, freedom, and open dissemination.

Part II looks at the biosecurity threat that naturally occurring infectious diseases pose. Chapter 4 explores the collision that has occurred between the worlds of security and public health because this collision has significantly changed both policy areas. Chapter 4 also delves more deeply into the theory and practice of public health to enrich analysis of the manner in which security and public health policies are becoming intertwined. Chapter 5 then focuses on the implications of the convergence of security and public health and on the requirements for effectively integrating them in biosecurity policy.

Part III examines the complex relationships between biosecurity policy, the rule of law, and globalized governance. Chapter 6 considers the challenge of embedding biosecurity in the rule of law. The chapter explains what we mean by the rule of law and why the rule of law is important for biosecurity policy. The chapter then delves into the specific elements of the rule of law philosophy of governance and how they relate to the governance challenges presented by biosecurity. Chapter 7 explores the relationship between biosecurity and globalized governance. It looks at how comprehensively the globalized governance challenge affects biosecurity, and the chapter digs conceptually into why it proves such a difficult task. Chapter 7 also examines the proliferation of new governance initiatives that have appeared in the biosecurity context and tries to identify patterns at the national, international, and global governance levels. These patterns, we argue, provide some signposts for the creation of a mechanism for globalized governance for biosecurity.

The final chapter reviews the book's analysis in terms of the concept, controversies, challenges, and choices presented by biosecurity's emergence. We acknowledge that our vision for biosecurity imposes significant burdens on private and public actors around the world, but the burdens are commensurate with the nature of the pathogenic threats facing world politics. Although the burdens should not be ignored, they should not overshadow the opportunity that biosecurity governance represents for twenty-first century humanity. We see in biosecurity a glimpse of how governance of the world's problems in the twenty-first century might unfold—a glimpse that presents us with momentous choices that may well mark how history remembers this century.

BIOSECURITY AND BIOLOGICAL WEAPONS **Part I**

2 THE PROBLEM OF BIOLOGICAL WEAPONS

I. INTRODUCTION

The rise of the biosecurity challenge owes much to the growing security and public health concerns about the threat the development and use of biological weapons pose. Although biological weapons have been a feature of international relations since the early twentieth century, the past decade has seen fears about them increase with each passing year. The anthrax attacks in the United States in 2001 elevated these fears and helped make biological weapons a higher security and foreign policy priority for the United States and other nations. Skeptics responded to this heightened importance by arguing that policy makers and experts were hyping the threat unnecessarily, creating distortions in making and implementing policy.

The attention biological weapons have received underscores this threat's centrality to thinking about biosecurity as a policy and governance challenge. The importance of the biological weapons threat has increased the scrutiny of, and the stress upon, prevailing governance mechanisms designed to address the threat, namely the arms control approach embodied in the Biological Weapons Convention (BWC 1972). This chapter examines the biological weapons problem in light of the dramatic changes affecting actors, technologies, and norms in this area. The chapter's objective is to provide the reader with a sense of the problem biological weapons represent in the early twenty-first century.

We begin with an overview of the biological weapons problem. Our analysis stresses the tensions created by a situation characterized by controversies about the threat and understandings that the stakes concerning biological weapons development and use are very high for countries and the global community. The chapter then looks at how changes in the actors relevant to the biological weapons problem make the problem more difficult. We next consider biological weapons technologies to illustrate the complexity of this field and to communicate concerns that many experts have about future development of the threat.

Finally, the chapter explores the history of attempts to govern the biological weapons threat. We focus on the basic norms prohibiting biological weapons development and use found in arms control treaties, particularly the BWC. This history indicates that traditional approaches embodied in arms control treaties no longer provide an effective foundation for addressing the problem of biological weapons. The world confronts, thus, a growing problem of biological weapons with approaches that are not adequate for the task of governing the threat.

II. THE BIOLOGICAL WEAPONS PROBLEM:
INTENSE CONTROVERSY, PROFOUND CONSEQUENCES

Pathogenic microbes have played significant roles in humanity's history (Diamond 1997; O'Neill 1977). Different periods saw humans or germs getting the upper hand. The Black Plague devastated fourteenth-century Europe. Microbes traveling with European explorers decimated native populations in the New World. Cholera epidemics in the nineteenth century frightened populations and jolted governments to recognize their responsibilities for their public's health. The twentieth century witnessed unprecedented victories against infectious diseases, such as the global eradication of smallpox, and alarming vulnerabilities to pandemic diseases, such as HIV/AIDS, SARS, and virulent strains of influenza.

Humanity's struggle with infectious disease has, however, a more sinister side that reveals efforts by armies, governments, and terrorists to develop and use biological weapons. Biological weapons are instruments of bioviolence, which Kellman (2006b) defines as acts that inflict harm through the intentional manipulation of living microorganisms, or their natural products, for hostile purposes. History records various infamous actual or alleged biological attacks, including the catapulting of diseased corpses over the walls of a besieged city in the fourteenth century, the distribution of blankets contaminated with smallpox to Indian tribes in the eighteenth century, and the gruesome biological weapons experiments conducted on prisoners of war and civilian populations in the twentieth century.

In the early twenty-first century, these incidents seem scientifically primitive and morally repulsive. Unfortunately, the problem of biological weapons is today well beyond catapulted corpses. In 2001, letters laced with anthrax became weapons of death, illness, and terror in the United States. Advances in microbiology and biotechnology combine with a radically different political context to confront our moral revulsion at weaponizing disease with complex and arduous policy and governance responsibilities.

Just how serious the biological weapons problem is, however, remains controversial. Debates rage about the possibility and probability of state or terrorist use of biological weapons. Questions proliferate: What is the real risk of a biological attack by a state or terrorist? How difficult is it for a state or terrorist to make an effective biological weapon? Why might states or terrorists undertake to make such a weapon? Don't governments, communities, and individuals have more serious threats to worry about than hypothetical scenarios of biological weapons proliferation and use?

Disagreements about the answers to such questions permeate biosecurity discourse. The past decade produced an avalanche of meetings, workshops, articles, books, and policy wonks focused on biological weapons and, more specifically, biological terrorism. Despite all the frenetic activity, agreement has not emerged about how much of a threat biological weapons in the hands of states or terrorists constitute. In this environment, analysis easily degenerates into polemics, and methodologies often transform into theologies.

More interesting perhaps than the raging debate is the fact that the debate continues to rage. The controversy lives on and grows more intense because of the increasing seriousness of the threat and the intended and unintended consequences of policy responses. Biological weapons have long been lumped with nuclear and chemical weapons in the category of weapons of mass destruction (WMD). Of these WMD, policy makers most fear nuclear and biological weapons. Detonation of a nuclear device or release of a contagious pathogen would disrupt social order and stability nationally and globally. In short, the stakes for proliferation and use of nuclear and biological weapons are extremely high.

Between nuclear and biological weapons, biological weapons have advantages that enhance concern about their proliferation and use. Compared with nuclear weapons, biological weapons are easier to manufacture because the necessary materials are more accessible and less expensive. In addition, the "footprint" required to make and move a nuclear weapon is larger and more detectable than are the parallel activities related to biological weapons. By this comparison with nuclear weapons, we do not imply that making and using a biological weapon is as easy as some commentators suggest. Actually, the difficulty of making and using a biological weapon produces policy options for preventing proliferation and use.

Policy interest in biological weapons has also been intense because they offer advantages in their use compared with nuclear weapons. Unlike detonation of a nuclear device, which would cause immediate physical and radiation damage and leave clues about the origins of the nuclear material, use of a biological weapon could unfold over days in a process invisible even to the trained eye of the epidemiologist. This process could occur in multiple places simultaneously if the perpetrator released the microbe in different geographic areas.

Many days could pass before authorities determined that certain morbidity and mortality trends were linked with release of a biological agent. By this time, the perpetrator would in all likelihood have disappeared, increasing the difficulty of establishing responsibility for the crime. For example, the U.S. government still has not identified the perpetrator(s) of the 2001 anthrax attacks.

In September and October 2001, the United States—still reeling from the September 11th tragedy—experienced two rounds of attacks involving anthrax disseminated in letters mailed through the U.S. Postal Service. The first anthrax-laden letters were sent to media outlets in the United States, and the second round of letters went to the offices of two U.S. senators. Initially linked to international terrorism, experts later came to believe that a domestic source perpetrated the attacks because the anthrax strain used (the Ames strain) was the strain used in U.S. biodefense activities. The attacks killed five people, infected twenty-two others, caused thousands of people to take antibiotics to prevent potential exposure to the anthrax from causing disease, shut down parts of the federal government for decontamination, and led to many false alarms and hoaxes around the country. The attacks also spurred the federal government to scale-up significantly its efforts on bioterrorism.

The FBI's massive criminal investigation into the anthrax attacks has, however, produced no indictments, arrests, or investigatory breakthroughs. Controversially, the Justice Department identified Steven Hatfill, an American virologist and biological weapons expert, as a "person of interest" in the investigation. The federal government never charged Hatfill with any crime related to the anthrax attacks, and Hatfill filed a lawsuit against the U.S. government to receive compensation for the damage to his reputation and professional career the investigation caused.

The criminal investigation has produced no leads that indicate who was responsible for the attacks. Newspapers reported at the end of 2005 that the FBI was downsizing its investigation. Media stories in the fall of 2006 suggested that the FBI no longer believed that the anthrax used in the attacks came from a U.S. military facility, which widened the potential scope for suspects. In December 2006, members of Congress criticized the FBI's handling of the case and its refusal to brief Congress in response to congressional oversight requests. As of this writing, the mystery of the Amerithax attacks was not close to being solved.

Fortunately, the perpetrators of the anthrax attacks did not use a contagious microbe. Use of contagious pathogens as weapons would achieve something no other weapon can—the ability to replicate and spread. Chemical and nuclear weapons cannot spread their harm much beyond the range of their initial dispersal. Given globalization's intensity, a biological attack with a highly contagious agent has the potential to infect the world. Although developed countries might be able to contain a contagious outbreak if early detection, response, and mitigation measures work effectively, much of the developing world probably could not contain a highly contagious pathogen because of weaknesses in public health infrastructures. Beyond the death toll, fear, and panic such an attack could produce, the aftermath of this kind of global biological attack could profoundly affect world politics.

Whether contagious or not, biological weapons are terror weapons. They spread disease and infect people with fear. Fear of contagion could foster a sense of vulnerability that exceeds any person's or community's actual epidemiological risk of infection. The anthrax attacks in the United States in 2001 triggered such fears for many Americans, who suddenly experienced great anxiety about the commonplace task of opening their mail.

In short, the political, economic, and social consequences of the development and use of biological weapons are deadly serious. This situation does not mean governments must subordinate every other governmental responsibility to the prevention of biological weapons proliferation and use, but the consequences of the biological weapons threat suggest that governments individually and collectively would be recklessly imprudent to ignore the possibility of the spread and potential use of biological weapons.

III. STATES, TERRORISTS, AND THE FOG OF BIOSECURITY

As skeptics argue, hypothetical descriptions of what might happen shed little light on what is the actual risk of biological weapons proliferation or use. In other words, biosecurity policy should not be driven by vulnerabilities highlighted by worst-case scenario-ism but by coldly calculated assessments of the actual threat. Such assessments are, however, difficult given the incomplete and often politicized information used to allege that certain states or terrorist groups have the intent and capability to engage in biological weapons development and use.

Many such allegations assume nefarious intent merely from the existence of pharmaceutical or biotechnological expertise or capacity. We see capability to make biological weapons in rival states and worry that our enemies are plotting microbial malevolence against us. Members of terrorist organizations who have any training in biological sciences easily become sinister figures, pursuing monstrous forms of microbial life to wreak havoc on innocent populations.

Hardheaded calculations of the actual risks biological weapons proliferation and use pose must, of course, get beyond figments of anxiety-laden imaginations. Almost immediately, however, the simplicity of these caricatures of biological evil begins to look attractive against the messy, non-transparent, shifting, and devilishly complex reality of biosecurity. In such a context, perspective is easy to lose.

A. States and Biological Weapons

Turning first to potential state interest in biological weapons, most states, except those least economically developed, have the scientific and technological capabilities to make biological weapons. Most states have access to the tool kit needed to make biological weapons because most of the pathogens, technology, and expertise are used for peaceful purposes. Most states have not, however, pursued biological weapons and are unlikely ever to do so. Among those states that are known to have developed biological weapons, or that allegedly are doing so currently, a common rationale appears to be to develop biological weapons as a deterrent capability.

Biological weapons connect to a number of deterrence scenarios. First, a state could develop biological weapons to deter a rival state from using its biological weapons. Such bio-deterrence operated after the adoption of the Geneva Protocol (1925). The Geneva Protocol technically only prohibited the first use of biological weapons in armed conflict among states parties. As this chapter discusses later, the Geneva Protocol did not prohibit states parties from developing biological weapons, and these capabilities could be used (1) to deter other states parties from first-use of biological weapons, and (2) in second-strike retaliation should first-use occur.

Second, biological weapons create deterrence possibilities for weaker states facing military threats to their security and survival. States that confront enemies possessing superior conventional military power might find biological weapons useful in deterring such enemies. For example, most states alleged to have, or be interested in, biological weapons today (e.g., Iran, North Korea, and Syria) face adversaries that biological weapons might deter. This rationale may also help explain Saddam Hussein's long-standing interest in biological weapons (Pearson 2006).

Strategic deterrence does not illuminate, however, the Soviet Union's development of its offensive biological weapons program in the 1970s and 1980s. The Soviet Union accelerated its offensive program after the United States unilaterally abandoned its offensive capabilities at the end of the 1960s (Hart 2006). The Soviets were not, thus, seeking to deter possible U.S. biological attacks. Nor was the Soviet Union facing conventional military inferiority vis-à-vis the United States and its NATO allies that biological weapons could help redress. Further, the program was very secretive and could not deter the United States and its allies, which knew little about the effort.

The limited nature of contemporary state interest in biological weapons development resonates with the general normative position that such weapons are illegitimate instruments of statecraft. Today, governments alleged to be engaged in biological weapons efforts never attempt to justify these activities or defend the right of states to engage in biological deterrence. This sense of illegitimacy was not always the case, as illustrated by the belief many countries had that bio-deterrence was justified under the Geneva Protocol.

How much of this sense of illegitimacy flows from the international legal prohibition on the development and use of biological weapons, and how much results from state calculations that biological weapons are not useful instruments of state power, remains controversial. Whether this controversy needs to be settled is not clear because the current situation does not point to a resumption of biological arms races among the great powers under the guise of strategic bio-deterrence.

The real threat to biosecurity from state activities concerning biological weapons may actually be more complex and more difficult to address. As explored in the next section, state concern about terrorist interest in biological weapons increases state involvement with activities related to defenses against biological weapons, or biodefense. Such activities may include conducting secret research on biological weapons agents to develop defensive countermeasures (e.g., vaccines, antibiotics, sensors).

One state's expanding biodefense efforts may make other states nervous for two reasons. First, these other states might believe they should also be scaling up biodefense research because the threat might be greater than they perceived. Second, distrust among states may develop about what is actually taking place under the guise of biodefense. The international political context for biosecurity could deteriorate without a biological arms race involving stockpiles of germ weapons taking place. The race instead would involve state competition to stay on the cutting edge of what is possible to achieve with the biological sciences. States could "ramp up their own R&D activities as a hedge against technological surprise and the unpredictability of future adversaries—a 'keeping up with the Joneses' effect" (Grotto and Tucker 2006, 43). We return to this policy challenge in Chapter 3.

B. Terrorists and Biological Weapons

As noted earlier, questions remain about how much the international legal prohibitions on the development and use of biological weapons affect state calculations. Consensus exists, however, that the prohibitions have little relevance to terrorists and criminals who might be tempted to engage in biological attacks. The constraints that shape state interest (or lack thereof) in biological weapons do not apply to non-state actors. Terrorist or criminal motivations will not necessarily be constrained by instruments and approaches designed to apply the taboo on use of disease as a weapon against states.

These motivations mean that terrorist groups do not need to replicate military-quality biological weapons to engage in bioterrorism. The development threshold is, thus, lower from a scientific and technological point of view. Advances in, and global dissemination of, scientific knowledge on pathogenic microbes increasingly brings this descending threshold closer within reach of non-state actors. Contributing to this lower threshold is the recognition that the state-centric levers of bio-deterrence, in-kind retaliation, and systemic moral opprobrium do not necessarily affect the calculations of the terrorist.

The threshold on use of biological weapons is also different. The only example of offensive use of biological weapons by a state against another state was Japan's use of biological weapons in China in the 1930s and 1940s (see later for more detail). Otherwise, states have avoided crossing the biological Rubicon in their armed conflicts. This state-centric logic of restraint has little relevance to terrorist groups, who willingly kill civilian populations to advance extremist views. Whatever logic of restraint exists with respect to terrorist interest in biological weapons is murky and unstable, which raises fears that terrorists might commit biological attacks. The anthrax attacks in 2001 have left, for example, the United States with more questions than answers about how and why this act occurred. These unanswered questions breed fear of the unknown and, perhaps, the unknowable.

We want to know how significant are the threats of terrorist-sponsored proliferation and use of biological weapons. Historically, we know that terrorists have not been avid bioweaponeers or practitioners of biological attacks (Carus 2000). Whether the past proves an accurate guide for the future is hotly debated. We know that the scientific and technical difficulties of developing a biological weapon are decreasing and will continue to decrease as more advances in microbiology and biotechnology are made and spread globally. The speed and scope of such advances are, of course, not presently known. Most experts agree, however, that the trajectory of scientific developments is not making biological weapons harder to create and use.

We also know that our societies are vulnerable to terrorist attacks, particularly attacks involving biological weapons. Experts in bioterrorism repeatedly emphasize how unprepared even the most developed countries are for biological attacks. The lessons learned from simulated attacks reinforce concerns about the vulnerabilities of societies to biological weapons use.

Skeptics of terrorist involvement with biological weapons challenge assertions that bioterrorism is a clear and present danger. In the fog that permeates this aspect of biosecurity are the shadows we perceive cast by real bioterrorists, or are they phantoms of our fear-laden imaginations stimulated by a pervasive sense of our vulnerability? In this context, the fog of biosecurity is thickest where the political stakes seem highest. The challenge is neither to overreact nor to underreact to the threat of bioterrorism. No precedents exist to guide the judgments governments have to make in this fog.

C. The Complexity of Policy Related to Biological Weapons

Achieving security against the proliferation and use of biological weapons has always been complicated. The complexity of the contemporary threat is, however, greater than previous historical periods. The increasing vulnerability of societies, combined with the opportunities that progress in the biological sciences produces, rightly creates unease among policy makers responsible for protecting their populations from violent attack. The terrorist problem changes the structure and dynamics of the biological weapons threat. Unilateral, secretive state responses to the perceived bioterrorist threat may corrode inter-state relations and increase opportunities terrorists have to secure access to biological weapons. Badly done, biosecurity policy—in the name of the universal condemnation of using disease as a weapon—could enhance the prospects for biological weapons proliferation and use worldwide.

Concern exists, however, that badly done biosecurity policy is what is happening today. Critiques come from different perspectives and by no means converge harmoniously, but they point to growing unease at the directions policy on biological weapons is going. At relevant points, this book examines aspects of policy on biological weapons that prove problematic and controversial, such as the analysis later in this chapter and the next about the BWC's future. Chapter 3 also considers policy and governance challenges that fall outside the traditional arms control approach.

In many respects, the concerns raised about current trends in biosecurity policy highlight the gap that exists between the universal condemnation of using disease as a weapon and the dysfunctional national and international governance systems dealing with biological weapons. Given the policy revolution that biosecurity represents, we would expect governments and governance processes to experience wrenching transition periods during which ineffectiveness and inefficiencies reign. We fear, however, that biosecurity governance is not emerging from its transition period in ways that will materially reduce the threat of biological weapons.

Having a sense of the stakes and complexity of the threat of biological weapons provides a glimpse into the problem biological weapons present today. A glimpse is not, however, sufficient. We must go deeper, and this chapter's next two sections accomplish this objective. We begin by looking at technologies and techniques associated with biological weapons. This analysis exposes the dangerous diversity of biological weapons and the daunting problems this diversity generates.

We then consider the norms against the development and use of biological weapons enshrined in international law. We argue that the traditional arms control approach can no longer be the exclusive regime for strengthening the normative framework against development and use of biological weapons.

The chapter concludes by assessing the strengths and weaknesses of the norm against the development and use of biological weapons. The norm is actually both stronger and weaker in the early twenty-first century, and exploring this paradox provides the lead-in for Chapter 3's analysis of the new world of biological weapons governance.

IV. BIOLOGICAL WEAPONS TECHNOLOGIES AND TECHNIQUES

A. Defining What Constitutes a Biological Weapon: The Complicating Role of Intent

The range of biological agents that states or terrorists could develop into biological weapons is extensive and unfortunately expanding. This range perhaps makes biological weapons the most diverse of any category of weapon. Whether a biological agent is dangerous is not, however, what makes the agent a biological weapon. Fittingly, defining what constitutes a biological weapon is difficult. The definition of a biological weapon helps shed light on the complexity of addressing the threat such weapons present.

The leading definition of a biological weapon appears in Article I of the BWC, which provides

> Each State Party to this Convention undertakes never in any circumstances to develop, produce, stockpile or otherwise acquire or retain:
>
> 1. Microbial or other biological agents or toxins whatever their origin or method of production, of types and quantities that have no justification for prophylactic, protective or other peaceful purposes;
>
> 2. Weapons, equipment or means of delivery designed to use such agents or toxins for hostile purposes or in armed conflict.

For many experts, the BWC's definition proves difficult to apply because the intent of the actor in question rather than objective criteria of fact is the controlling factor. A microbe is a prohibited biological weapon unless the holder can justify the type and quantity of the microbe possessed as falling within a permitted prophylactic, protective, or other peaceful purpose. The BWC does not define these permitted purposes, but they have commonly understood meanings.

Development of vaccines and antibiotics against biological agents falls under the prophylactic exception. Conducting research on pathogens to develop defensive technologies (e.g., sensors, protective military equipment) and countermeasures (e.g., vaccines, antibiotics) represents a protective purpose. Other peaceful purposes could involve research into the microbiology of biological agents that adds to our understanding of the agents and of microbial life forms in general. Considerations of intent, thus, permeate the definition of what constitutes a biological weapon. This situation creates problems for knowing whether a government or non-state actor is developing a biological weapon before the state or terrorist actually uses it.

A government military research facility possesses the plague bacteria. Are these bacteria biological weapons? Whether they are depends on why the research facility possesses these microbes. The government would likely argue that it is conducting defensive research to develop methods to protect its troops from possible plague attacks. Its intent relates to a protective purpose the BWC permits. But, how do we know that the protective purpose argument reflects the actual intent and actions of the government? If the government possesses tons of plague bacteria, then this objective quantity indicator would suggest that the bacteria have no justification for protective or any other peaceful purpose.

Without objective evidence, however, deciphering benign from malevolent intent proves difficult, if not impossible. Intent is only easy to detect after behavior reveals the real motivation. The same problem arises with respect to non-state actors (e.g., pharmaceutical companies, biotechnology companies, academic research departments, agricultural industry) and their possession and use of biological agents. How, amid all the rapidly expanding peaceful uses to which private enterprises employ biological agents, are we to detect potential development and use of biological weapons?

When developing biosecurity policies, we need to distinguish legitimate from illegitimate activities before the biological weapon is developed and perhaps used. This need partly motivated the attempt in the latter half of the 1990s to create a BWC inspection and verification regime so that states parties could detect malevolent intent earlier. The failure of this effort, and its ramifications, which we discuss later, helps reinforce the policy priority of preventing opportunities for malevolent intent to exploit microbial life.

This prevention challenge may stimulate policy motivations that require scrutiny. First, governments may tighten regulation on private sector activities, such as scientific research, to prevent them from inadvertently helping states or terrorists develop biological weapons. Movement in this direction might create tensions between peaceful scientific research and the exigencies of security.

Second, the difficulty of identifying behavior that may violate the prohibition on biological weapons development could encourage governments to become more aggressive in their biodefense research, which they justify as legitimate because the intent is defensive. Scaled-up biodefense activities may threaten to erode the norm against the development of biological weapons because every government will claim that any biological work it conducts is legitimate because its intent is defensive. This dynamic would exacerbate the problems the definition of what constitutes a biological weapon already faces.

B. Making and Using a Biological Weapon

1. Biological Weapons Agents

If a state or terrorist wants to develop and use a biological weapon, certain steps have to be completed: The state or terrorist has to select the agent, obtain it, weaponize it, and disseminate it. Completing these steps effectively is not easy, even for state-sponsored programs. Each step has complexities, and understanding them helps convey the message that biological weapons development and use demands significant resources, technical skill, political commitment, and infrastructure and support.

The list of possible biological agents that could be used as weapons is extensive, and the list gets longer when the potential for agricultural warfare and terrorism are considered. Annex 1 contains the U.S. government's select list of biological agents and toxins access to which the government regulates for biosecurity purposes. The select agent list does not, however, convey the technical and epidemiological complexities these agents and toxins present to a potential bioweaponeer in obtaining, weaponizing, and disseminating them. These complexities mean that each agent or toxin would, in effect, require its own research and development program, a costly proposition that places a premium on the selection of the agents or toxins to be pursued.

Biological weapons programs operated by states in the past reveal sustained interest in a handful of biological agents and toxins. At the top of this list sits anthrax. U.S., Soviet, and Iraqi bioweaponeers considered anthrax optimal for offensive military programs. Seed stocks of *Bacillus anthracis* are easy to obtain from laboratories or even from nature because it is common in grazing animals (e.g., sheep, cattle, and goats). Inhaled, the anthrax spore multiplies and releases toxins that are lethal if antibiotic treatment is not timely. A small amount of anthrax disseminated effectively has tremendous killing potential. Anthrax is not, however, contagious and cannot spark an epidemic. A vaccine of disputed efficacy and side effects is available. These features also make anthrax attractive for bioterrorism, as the 2001 anthrax attacks in the United States attest.

Other biological agents and toxins that have featured in state biological weapons programs include the plague bacterium (*Yersinia pestis*), hemorrhagic fever viruses (e.g., Ebola, Marburg, Lassa, and Rift Valley fever viruses), tularemia (*Francisella tularensis*), and the neurotoxin botulism (*Clostridum botulinum*). Table 2.1 describes these biological agents and why they raise biosecurity concerns.

Although long considered biological weapons agents, each of these traditional agents has drawbacks that raise questions about how interested non-state actors would be in them. For example, plague bacteria are sensitive to heat and ultraviolet radiation, do not survive long outside a host, are difficult to manipulate and disseminate as an aerosol, and are susceptible to widely available antibiotics. Tularemia bacteria prove difficult to culture using standard culturing techniques. Botulinum toxin poses challenges for aerosol dissemination, the most likely exposure method of interest to terrorists. Hemorrhagic fever viruses are difficult to handle and propagate and kill with such rapidity that human-to-human spread is unlikely absent unsanitary clinical or mortuary conditions.

At present, the most nightmarish biological agent is smallpox (*Variola major*). Smallpox is highly contagious because it transmits through airborne droplets, and the disease is quite lethal in unvaccinated populations (see box). Ironically, the smallpox nightmare results from one of the greatest public health triumphs in history—the eradication of smallpox as a naturally occurring infectious disease. Before its eradication in the late 1970s, smallpox held little interest for biological weapons purposes because of high levels of effective vaccination in military and civilian populations. The Soviet Union's interest in smallpox as a weapon developed approximately at the time the smallpox eradication campaign was virtually complete. With most of the world's population no longer protected by vaccination, the use of smallpox as a biological weapon would be a global catastrophe. The presence of large populations of people in the developing world with immune systems compromised by HIV/ AIDS and other diseases would feed the fury of a smallpox pandemic.

Table 2.1 Descriptions of Various Traditional Biological Weapons Agents

Agent	Basic Epidemiological Description	Biosecurity Features of the Agent
Botulinum toxin	Toxin made by the Clostridium botulinum bacterium causes botulism, a rapid muscle-paralyzing disease, which often leads to death unless antitoxin and clinical care (e.g., ventilation) are administered soon after ingestion of the toxin. Botulism is not contagious.	Botulinum toxin is a biological weapons concern because the toxin is extremely potent and lethal and is rather easily produced and transported. Botulism can be caused by contaminating food or through aerosolizing the toxin.
Plague	Plague is a disease caused by the Yersinia pestis bacterium. The disease appears in two forms—bubonic and pneumonic plague. Bubonic plague is caused by human infections from bites of fleas associated with rodent species. Bubonic plague is not contagious. Pneumonic plague occurs through inhalational of the bacterium dispersed in respiratory droplets emitted by infected animals or humans. Pneumonic plague can be contagious. Antibiotics and medical care, when applied early enough after infection, are effective.	Yersinia pestis can relatively easily be obtained and readily produced in significant quantities. The contagiousness of pneumonic plague underscores the danger of aerosolized plague as a weapon. However, effective weaponization of plague bacteria proved challenging during the Cold War.
Tularemia	Tularemia is a disease caused by the Francisella tularensis bacterium. Human infections can occur through insect bites, handling of infected animals (e.g., rodents, rabbits, and hares), ingesting contaminated food or water, or inhaling the bacteria. Tularemia is not contagious and can be effectively treated with existing antibiotics.	Tularemia bacteria are found in nature, can be isolated and grown in quantity, and are highly infectious. Aerosolization of the bacterium is the most likely weapon use, but producing an effective aerosol weapon from the tularemia bacteria has proved difficult for state biological weapons programs.
Hemorrhagic fever viruses (e.g., Ebola, Marburg, Lassa, and Rift Valley fever viruses)	Hemorrhagic fever viruses cause various diseases that produce bleeding under the skin, in internal organs, and from body orifices. Death rates vary by virus but reach 90 percent in the case of the Ebola virus. These viruses are found naturally around the world and usually are transmitted to humans by animal or insect vectors. Human-to-human transmission can, however, occur with some of these viruses through contact with contaminated blood or bodily fluids. Treatment is mainly limited to clinical care because antivirals have limited effect and no vaccine exists for most of these viruses.	Aerosolized hemorrhagic fever viruses would constitute fearsome biological weapons because of the morbidity and mortality they could cause, the lack of antiviral treatments or vaccines, and the fear the hemorrhagic symptoms of these diseases would cause. Aerosolization has been shown possible but, as with plague and tularemia, difficult to achieve.

SOURCES: CDC 2001a, 2003, 2004, 2005; Center for Biosecurity 2005a, 2005b, 2005c, 2005d

Concerns that some of the former Soviet Union's smallpox stocks are un-accounted for and may have been diverted enhance the frightful potential of smallpox as a biological weapon. Advances in genetic engineering also create worries that bioweaponeers could re-create the smallpox virus in a laboratory, making it unnecessary to have access to the tightly protected remaining samples of the virus. These fears influenced the decision not to destroy the last two of-ficial samples of smallpox held in Russia and the United States (Koplow 2003).

The ferocity of smallpox may also be a reason why states and non-state actors interested in biological weapons might avoid this pathogen. The choice of a biological agent will depend on many factors, but key among these is the purpose the weapon is intended to serve. Using smallpox could only serve the most extreme, fanatical, or apocalyptic ends. This scenario is not, however, true for all biological weapons, but thinking about intent in relation to small-pox highlights the need to consider why states and non-state actors may find biological weapons useful.

2. Motivations to Develop and Use Biological Weapons
States might be most interested in biological agents to use against enemy mili-tary forces. Effectiveness would depend, however, on such use being credible and effective. To achieve these goals would require a sophisticated biological

---

SMALLPOX AS A BIOLOGICAL WEAPON

"Why is smallpox feared as a biological weapon?"

Several factors fuel the concern of smallpox as a biological weapon:

· it bears a 30% case-fatality rate;
· there is no treatment once symptoms begin;
· it is physically disfiguring for those who survive;
· it is spread person-to-person; and
· very few people in the United States have been vaccinated since 1972, leaving the population vulnerable to an attack.

Since there are no symptoms at the time of exposure, a clandestine release of smallpox would likely not be detected until sick people begin showing up at doctor's offices and hospitals, roughly 7–17 days after the attack. Although the disease is not contagious during the incubation period, exposed individuals may travel, spreading the disease to many geographical areas from one source."

SOURCE: Center for Biosecurity 2005e

---

weapon that could serve tactical military needs quickly while not endangering friendly forces, be durable enough to work in varying atmospheric and weather conditions, and not be easily rendered ineffective by enemy countermeasures (e.g., vaccines). Even if a biological weapon meets these requirements, an enemy's ability to retaliate with conventional or other weapons would weaken the credibility of the biological threat.

The purposes terrorists might have for biological weapons span a more unpredictable range of possibilities. For a terrorist, biological weapons might be useful for killing large numbers of people, causing widespread economic disruption, or causing fear and panic in a population. The terrorist does not face the same demands of precision, control, speed, durability, and credibility a state faces in contemplating military use of biological weapons. The terrorist typically does not need to discriminate between combatants and civilians or to have the agent work swiftly in those it infects. The terrorist would welcome lower performance thresholds because, compared with a state, he or she will likely be constrained by scarce financial resources, limited technical expertise, small supplies of weapon-grade agent, and the need to conceal his or her activities.

A key potential difference between state and terrorist motivations concerns use of contagious agents. From the state's perspective, contagious pathogens make risky weapons because of their potential to infect its own troops, civilian populations, and countries not involved in the conflict. For the terrorist, contagious agents offer advantages for causing damage and fear in target populations. With a contagious agent, victims themselves become munitions, allowing the weapon to replicate and transmit itself. Terrorists might not want the blowback a contagious attack could create for their cause, but expecting terrorist groups attracted to biological weapons to conform to conventional rational calculations would be a dangerous policy premise. This reasoning helps explain why policy makers have remained concerned about smallpox as a potential bioterrorist weapon.

3. Weaponizing a Biological Agent

A state or terrorist that has selected a biological agent still must obtain the agent and weaponize it. The complexity and difficulty of these two steps depends on the characteristics of the agent chosen. Smallpox would be easy to weaponize (e.g., infect a few humans) but extraordinarily difficult to obtain. Anthrax, plague, and tularemia can all be relatively easily found in nature or in laboratories doing peaceful research, but effective weaponization of these and other agents proved a difficult challenge that severely tested the well-funded biological programs of the Cold War superpowers. Weaponization also proved too difficult for the bioweaponeers in the Japanese apocalyptic cult Aum Shinrikyo, which experimented with anthrax, botulinum toxin, cholera, and Q fever, but failed to weaponize them effectively (Olson 1999). Aum Shinrikyo turned instead to chemical weapons and stunned the world with its sarin gas attack on the Tokyo subway system in 1995, which killed 12 people and harmed nearly 1,000 others.

Weaponization is the greatest technical challenge and involves making sure that the agent has the intended effect when used. Weaponization is largely a dissemination challenge that requires matching an agent's characteristics with an appropriate dispersal methodology. Biological agents can be disseminated in many ways, including aerosol delivery, explosive devices, water supplies, food or other types of products or inanimate objects (e.g., medicines, blood, posted letters), and insect, animal, or human vectors.

The technical hurdles for effective aerosol delivery (e.g., appropriate particle size, concentration of particles in the aerosol, stability and survivability of the particles in varying environmental conditions) are significant. In different ways, explosive devices, water supplies, and product contamination dilute the impact of biological agents by destroying the agents, producing low agent concentrations, or limiting the scope of population exposure. Terrorists might, however, select these dissemination techniques because their intent is to terrorize rather than to kill people. Vector dissemination requires that the host efficiently transmit the biological agents to target populations, and this host-agent compatibility requirement limits the range of agents that could be spread through this method. In addition, use of some vectors, such as insects, to spread biological agents would raise problems with control and reliability of agent transmission.

This overview of issues related to defining, making, and using a biological weapon communicates the bewildering dangers, diversity, and difficulties that biosecurity policy faces. This summary tended, however, to reflect on what has characterized the biological weapons threat in the past rather than on what the threat may look like in the future. To capture this aspect of the problem, we need to understand how the threat from biological weapons might change over the next decades.

C. Darkening Horizon? Future Biological Weapons Threats

We have already focused on one aspect of the biological weapons problem that differs from the Cold War context—the threat of development and use of biological weapons by terrorists. To what extent non-state actors have been, are, or will be interested in biological weapons continues to be debated. An important part of the context for these debates involves the rapidly shifting possibilities for biological weapons development provided by the global dissemination of advances in the biological sciences.

Is biosecurity policy facing a cascade of new biological agents and diseases made possible by capabilities being discovered, refined, and applied through microbiology, genetic engineering, and biotechnology? Is the peril in such scientific progress imminent or illusory? Do advances in the biological sciences thicken the fog of biosecurity and make it more likely that we fear the presence of bioterrorists behind every shadow and uncertainty the fog produces?

Experts debate questions like these without consensus yet being realized. Genetically engineering new pathogens that can be effectively weaponized would be an undertaking currently beyond the abilities of many governments let alone terrorist groups, even assuming states or terrorists wanted such a capability. We cannot ignore, however, the rapid changes occurring in the biological sciences and how new scientific capabilities might affect the threat of biological weapons during the next few decades. In terms of weapons, the twentieth century was the century of physics, culminating in the arsenals of nuclear weapons states. The twenty-first century may be the century of biology with potentially profound implications for how we construct sustainable biosecurity policies.

We mention here only a few concerns raised in relation to the increasing scientific ability to manipulate microbial life forms. A frequently voiced worry focuses on the power genetic engineering creates for the bioweaponeer. Genetic engineering could allow states or non-state actors to alter the genetic structure of traditional agents, such as anthrax and plague, to augment or moderate their lethality or their physiological impact, to make them resistant to antibiotic treatments, to circumvent existing vaccines, and to enhance the agents' stability and survivability. Soviet bioweaponeers experimented with such techniques long before the current concerns about advances in genetic engineering (Hart 2006). As scientists sequence, probe, and unlock the secrets of the genetic codes of microbes, more opportunities to hide dangerous genes in germs for malevolent purposes are created.

The now infamous Australian mousepox experiment reveals that transferring genes between microbes can inadvertently enhance pathogen lethality. In 2001, Australian scientists modified the virus that causes mousepox in an effort to develop contraceptive vaccines that would sterilize mice and rabbits without killing them. When administered to mice through a vaccine, the genetically modified mousepox virus killed 60 percent of the vaccinated mice, a lethality rate much higher than unmodified mousepox. Further investigation revealed that the inserted gene switched off part of the mice's immune system, making them more vulnerable to the mousepox virus.

The publication of the mousepox experiment caused controversy because it revealed the dangers of genetically engineered microbes. The controversy deepened when scientists in the United States replicated the Australian mousepox experiment, produced greater lethality in the modified mousepox virus, and conducted similar genetic modification experiments on the cowpox virus, which—unlike the mousepox virus—can infect humans.

Defenders of such research argued that these types of experiments were needed to help the United States prepare countermeasures against genetically modified biological weapons. The Australian mousepox experiment, and its aftermath, raised questions about how much oversight certain types of biological and biotechnological research should receive from scientists or government authorities.

Another example of unintended results occurred when British scientists created a hybrid pathogen, dubbed "dengatitis," by combining the dengue fever and hepatitis C viruses (Arthur 2001). This experiment sought to decrease the number of laboratory animals required to test a hepatitis C vaccine, but it produced a new, hybrid pathogen that may have posed a serious threat to human health if accidentally or malevolently released outside the laboratory.

The potential for manipulating microbes that genetic engineering creates has raised the frightening possibility of ethnic-specific biological weapons. Once believed scientifically impossible, some experts have argued that, given the exponentially increasing capabilities of gene sequencing and the unraveling of the mysteries of the human genome, the prospect of the creation of a virus or bacteria that affects a particular ethnic population is moving from the realm of science fiction to science possibility (British Medical Association 1999, 2004).

Science is also equipping states and non-state actors with the ability to re-create viruses and bacteria from scratch. U.S. scientists created, for example, the poliovirus in a laboratory (Cello, Paul, and Wimmer 2002). As more pathogen genomes are sequenced and shared globally, synthetic replication of microbes, perhaps including smallpox and virulent influenza strains, are increasingly possible. The genetic sequence of the influenza virus that caused the 1918 pandemic flu has, for example, been published and the virus reconstructed (Taunbenberger et al. 2005; Tumpey et al. 2005). Controversial experiments involving the reconstructed versions of the 1918 virus have been conducted on mice (Kash et al. 2006) and primates (Kobasa et al. 2007). Synthetic replication provides one way to overcome difficulties of getting access to pathogenic agents from nature, regulated civilian laboratories, or protected military facilities.

Future possibilities may also extend into the synthesis of new microbial life forms capable of engaging in different functions, from consuming polluting substances to producing antimicrobial drugs. For example, the Artemisinin Project seeks to use synthetic biology to create microbes that produce the antimalarial drug artemisinin, which is increasingly in demand as the malaria parasite develops resistance to other antimalarial drugs (Artemisinin Project 2006). Scientists also see molecular nanotechnology as a future growth area because "nanotechnology will alter our relationship with molecules and matter as profoundly as the computer changed our relationship with bits and information" (Foresight Nanotech Institute 2006). Although exciting benevolent uses beckon, capabilities unleashed by synthetic biology and molecular nanotechnology could also be used to craft new a generation of biological weapons.

Predicting how advances in the biological and other sciences will affect the prospects for developing and using biological weapons is impossible because too much remains uncertain, unknown, and even unknowable. Against that backdrop, the tendency is to look backward for guidance about the future. With respect to biological weapons, the past may not be the best guide for the challenges biosecurity policy will face in the twenty-first century. We have left the context where bio-deterrence between the great powers dominated and have entered an unstable political and scientific environment where the problem of biological weapons has no real precedents to guide policy.

V. BIOLOGICAL WEAPONS AND ARMS CONTROL: THE DEVELOPMENT AND DILEMMAS OF INTERNATIONAL NORMS ON BIOLOGICAL WEAPONS

Grappling with the problem of biological weapons in the emerging political and scientific environment requires understanding the norm against the development and use of disease as a weapon. The norm's story in the twentieth century revolves around arms control—the attempt to ban the development and use of biological weapons by states through international treaties. The tale is sobering and leaves those concerned about biological weapons in the twenty-first century with doubts about the contributions the arms control approach can make in the new biosecurity environment.

A. From Geneva to Nixon: Emergence of the Norm Against the Use of Biological Weapons

The problem of biological weapons is a modern problem directly connected to the progress of the biological sciences. Disease has been associated with war and conflict for millennia, and, as mentioned at the beginning of this chapter, history records examples of military forces trying to use disease as a weapon. Such historical anecdotes are interesting but do not provide much insight into the biological weapons threats we face today. War's ability to spark and spread infectious disease among troops and noncombatant populations has been far more important in the historical relationship between war and disease than biological weapons.

The shift from disease as merely a devastating by-product of war to disease as an intentional weapon of war begins to occur in the wake of the slow but steady triumph of the "germ theory" of disease in the late nineteenth and early twentieth centuries. Before the acceptance that microorganisms caused infectious diseases, scientists and physicians debated the causes of diseases, such as cholera, plague, and yellow fever. Miasmists, who believed that such diseases arose from unsanitary local conditions, argued against the contagionists, who believed that these diseases spread from community to community (Howard-Jones 1975).

This debate raged largely over the value of civilian quarantine policy, especially the economic burdens quarantine policies created for international trade and commerce, but the scientific discoveries that produced and proved germ theory opened potential new military opportunities for the use of disease. The ability to isolate, culture, and experiment with microorganisms made possible by the work of Louis Pasteur, Robert Koch, and others began to allow humans to develop better strategies against the age-old scourge of infectious diseases. But these new scientific skills also created the potential for the development of entirely new kinds of military weapons.

The military, political, and moral challenges biological weapons present appeared during World War I, the first major armed conflict in which more scientific application of biological agents for military purposes was considered. German secret agents allegedly infected horses and cattle destined for use by Allied forces in Europe with anthrax and glanders (Guillemin 2005). These attempts had no impact on the course of this armed conflict. In World War I, chemical rather than "bacteriological" weapons proved the more effective use of scientific advances for the purpose of war. Nevertheless, World War I raised the question whether political and moral constraints on the use of disease as a weapon would change as scientific capabilities improved.

The 1920s witnessed developments that brought this question to a head. Further scientific advances encouraged some military experts, such as Auguste Trillat of France, to argue for more systematic exploration of the military potential of biological weapons. The interest in harnessing the biological sciences for military applications connected with other movements in military thinking, such as the development of theories of air power and total war. A leading interwar air power theorist, Italian Giulio Douhet, advocated strategic bombing of the enemy's civilian populations with conventional and unconventional weapons to produce shorter conflicts (Douhet 1921). The advent of air warfare meant, "Even before it was technically possible, the idea of planes spreading invisible clouds of germs over enemy factories and cities stirred the imaginations of the military-minded scientists who conceived the first biological weapons programs in the years leading to World War II" (Guillemin 2005, 6).

States demonstrated awareness of the potential threat biological weapons might present when they included a prohibition on the use of bacteriological weapons in the Geneva Protocol of 1925. (See Annex 2 for the text of the Geneva Protocol.) The Protocol's main objective was to prohibit the use of chemical weapons, but states extended the prohibition to include biological weapons. This initial application of international law to biological weapons requires close attention because states chose to hedge their biological bets under the Geneva Protocol in three ways.

First, the prohibition on use only applied to conflicts between states parties to the Geneva Protocol. The prohibition did not apply in war between a state party and a country not party to the Protocol. Second, the Geneva Protocol contained no restrictions on states parties conducting research, development, production, and stockpiling of chemical or biological weapons. The Geneva Protocol did not affect the ability of states to see where scientific advances would take biological weapons.

Third, many states formulated reservations to the Geneva Protocol in which they reserved the right to use chemical and biological weapons in response to an adversary's first use of such weapons (Roberts and Guelff 2000). In essence, the Geneva Protocol became a "no first use" agreement backed by deterrence supplied by the ability to develop and deploy chemical and biological weapons. This outcome became a recipe for arms races because deterrence only worked if adversaries had credible abilities to retaliate in-kind to a first use of chemical or biological weapons. The Geneva Protocol's international norm against the use of biological weapons was, thus, legalistic in application and limited in scope. It expressed a shared repugnance for chemical and biological weapons but did not allow repugnance to stand in the way of prudential power politics.

The Geneva Protocol's gossamer quality became evident in the 1930s and World War II when Japan, which was not a state party to the Protocol and thus not bound by its prohibition on use, experimented with and used biological weapons in its military campaigns in China (Barenblatt 2004). At the center of these efforts was the infamous Unit 731 in Harbin, China, where Japanese military forces experimented on prisoners with plague, cholera, hemorrhagic fevers, and even some sexually transmitted diseases. The Japanese military also conducted field testing and aerial dissemination of biological agents against Chinese cities and populations.

The horror of the Japanese use of biological weapons during World War II did not lead to a renewed postwar effort to shore up the Geneva Protocol's norm against the use of biological weapons. Many states, including the United States, continued and sometimes expanded biological weapons programs they began before or during World War II. The United States was sufficiently eager to learn what Japanese scientists and doctors had learned in their experimentation on prisoners in China that it granted them immunity from war crimes prosecutions in exchange for information. This unseemly episode characterized the mood that prevailed during the next few decades concerning biological weapons—it was best to keep the anthrax powder dry, just in case.

The details of the various biological weapons programs pursued by states in the decades after World War II until the late 1960s can be found in other works (Wheelis, Rózsa, and Dando 2006). For our purposes, a few themes emerge from this period. First, virtually all biological weapons programs involved both offensive and defensive research and development. This situation was consistent with the underlying objective of bio-deterrence that gave the Geneva Protocol's prohibition on use whatever bite it had. Second, the programs were generally highly secretive, which leavened bio-deterrence with sufficient uncertainty to keep adversaries suspicious of each other and committed to continuing their own biological weapons research.

Third, the programs brought the full arsenal of expanding scientific knowledge and capabilities to bear on making effective biological weapons and defenses against them. Fourth, although bioweaponeering made progress, the determined application of modern science did not produce biological weapons that military strategists and planners rushed to embrace. Military skepticism of biological weapons, which was present from the 1920s, continued despite extensive efforts made by governments to weaponize biological agents for military purposes.

Ironically, the renaissance for the crimped norm against the use of biological weapons in the Geneva Protocol began when the United States, one of the premier bioweaponeering states of the Cold War, unilaterally determined in 1969 that biological weapons had little if any military utility and thus no place in U.S. military doctrine. President Nixon's decision to terminate unilaterally the U.S. offensive biological weapons program had nothing to do with U.S. legal obligations under the Geneva Protocol because the United States had not ratified the Protocol in the forty-plus years since its creation. The decision was a hardheaded calculation that biological weapons were simply not reliable, effective instruments for the projection and use of U.S. military power. The Nixon decision meant that future U.S. biological weapons research would be defensive in nature only.

B. The Biological Weapons Convention

The U.S. unilateral termination of its offensive biological weapons program created the international political conditions necessary to produce the BWC. The BWC was an arms control landmark because it was the first treaty to outlaw an entire class of weapons and to require actual disarmament through destruction of stockpiles. (See Annex 3 for the text of the BWC.) To the prohibition on use in the Geneva Protocol, the BWC added prohibitions against the development, production, stockpiling, acquisition, or retention of biological weapons.

Behind the sweeping, historic prohibitions in the BWC lurked, however, problems. We noted earlier in this chapter difficulties that arise with how the BWC defines a biological weapon. The intent-based prohibition in Article I of the BWC raised the issue whether the BWC would complicate peaceful applications of biological sciences, and Article X attempted to address this concern. It allows states parties to participate fully in the use and exploitation of scientific and technological knowledge for peaceful purposes. This provision then raised questions about how states parties could tell peaceful from nefarious use (see more later). Article X also became a source of friction between developed and developing countries regarding technology transfer, especially in the wake of the developing world's push in the early 1970s for a New International Economic Order.

These problematic first steps in the BWC are followed by others. The BWC requires states parties to take "necessary measures" to ensure that its prohibitions are implemented domestically (Article IV), but the BWC does not define what these measures should substantively entail. Decades after the BWC's adoption, lamentations about the lack of compliance with this central tenet of the BWC have been frequent (Kellman 2006a). Larger compliance questions, however, loomed with respect to the BWC's lack of mechanisms to verify compliance of states parties with the treaty's prohibitions. The dual-use nature of most technologies used to make biological weapons, combined with the intent-based nature of the BWC's prohibitions, created a regime that allowed cheaters maximum technological flexibility and political deniability. In short, states parties that wanted to continue covert biological weapons programs faced little practical risk of discovery under the BWC. Even if a state party was found out, the likelihood of any serious action under the BWC was minimal. In cases of violation, the BWC encourages complaints be submitted to the UN Security Council for its consideration and action (Article VI). The Security Council's moribund state during the Cold War effectively rendered this violation procedure useless.

Even though the BWC was in these, and other ways, a flawed treaty, it nevertheless became the normative center of gravity for international efforts to govern biological weapons. Its pull could be sensed in the abandonment by the United States and other Western democracies of their offensive biological weapons programs, which they had maintained for much of the Cold War. The BWC allowed the cold calculations of military planners about biological weapons' lack of utility and the long-standing moral revulsion at the use of disease as a weapon to converge in ways the Geneva Protocol never accomplished.

The political and military costs of complying with a total ban on biological weapons decreased, while those same costs increased for states not willing to abandon biological weapons. Rational choice theory would predict that, give these cost-benefit assumptions, most states would join and comply with the BWC, which is in fact what has happened. Unfortunately, the BWC's weaknesses provided enough opportunity for a minority of states to defy the sweeping prohibitions and shake the BWC to its foundations.

C. Rise and Fall of the BWC Protocol

By the early 1990s, the BWC was in crisis, reeling in the wake of the revelations about the biological weapons programs of the former Soviet Union and Iraq. As noted earlier, the Soviet program was massive, which not only violated the Soviet Union's obligations as a BWC state party but also beggars rational explanation. Most disturbingly from the BWC perspective, the Soviet Union scaled up its biological weapons program immediately after the BWC was established. Perhaps the Soviet Union saw a military advantage it could gain on the United States following the U.S. unilateral termination of its biological weapons program, or the Soviets did not believe the U.S. renunciation of its offensive program. Whatever the reason, the Soviets created a biological weapons program on a scale no one in the West understood until the Soviet Union broke apart in the early 1990s. Not only did this send shockwaves through the BWC regime, but it also raised the specter of terrorists getting access to the Soviet stockpile as the Soviet Union disintegrated and the new Russia struggled to manage the aftershocks of a superpower's extinction.

The end of the first Gulf War in early 1991 provided the victorious allies with the ability to engage in intrusive inspections of Iraq's programs on nuclear, chemical, and biological weapons. The inspectors were surprised to learn the extent of the Iraqi efforts on biological weapons. Unlike the Soviet Union, Iraq had not been a state party to the BWC, until forced to do so by the UN Security Council after the war (Pearson 2006). But, as with the Soviet Union, most experts agreed that the BWC would not have posed a serious obstacle to Iraq's desire to develop biological weapons. Iraq had created a significant weapons program without intelligence agencies in other countries being aware of its seriousness and extent.

The discoveries of the Soviet and Iraqi biological weapons programs at virtually the same time shook complacency concerning compliance with the BWC and increased calls for BWC states parties to strengthen the BWC by creating a compliance mechanism. The completion in 1992 of the Chemical Weapons Convention (CWC), with its compliance machinery, added momentum to the calls for reforming the BWC through the negotiation of a protocol.

The end of the Cold War, and the successful UN collective security action against Iraq, encouraged many that repairing the BWC's weaknesses was within reach. These hopes proved to be ill founded.

The rise and fall of the BWC Protocol is a complex story (see box), and we highlight only five important features that communicate why this effort failed. First, negotiation of a compliance regime for the BWC proved controversial at virtually every level. Disagreements flared with respect to whether a compliance regime would produce useful verification information given the large number of civilian facilities that would be subject to inspection. Unlike the chemical industry, which generally supported the CWC's compliance machinery, the pharmaceutical and biotechnology industries oscillated between nervous skepticism and opposition to the emerging BWC Protocol. These industries made themselves heard, especially in Washington, D.C., which complicated the politics of the BWC Protocol negotiations.

Second, negotiating the BWC Protocol proved time-consuming and contentious for many reasons, including the normal cut-and-thrust of treaty negotiations and addressing the technical complexities of inspecting diverse facilities that handled biological agents and toxins. The slow progress of the negotiations provided more opportunities for opposition to build and create difficulties for the negotiators. As the years passed, the urgency sensed when the BWC revision process began in 1991 faded and became obscured by other seemingly more pressing issues.

Third, globalization and its impact on science and biotechnology grew as complications during the negotiations. The globalization of the biological sciences meant that the BWC Protocol would have to deal with an exponentially increasing number of entities manipulating microorganisms for academic, industrial, or health-related purposes. Part of this globalization involved the integration into the biological sciences of more powerful genetic engineering techniques and the knowledge provided by faster, more accurate genome sequencing. The science of microbiology and biotechnology underwent a global revolution at the same time arms control negotiators were trying to improve compliance with a thirty-plus-year-old treaty. The rapidly changing global scientific landscape motivated some experts to argue that the effort to achieve verification of BWC compliance had become a fool's errand.

Fourth, the 1990s saw the dramatic increase in security concerns about terrorism generally, but terrorism involving WMD specifically. Fears about terrorist access to the biological weapons stockpile of the former Soviet Union made the BWC Protocol negotiations seem, at times, out of touch with the bio-security threats posed by non-state actors. Terrorists, many observed, did not sign and ratify treaties. The chemical terrorism perpetrated by Aum Shinrikyo in Tokyo in 1995 was, in many ways, a tipping point for the terrorist threat becoming the foremost national security concern in terms of WMD. Dealing effectively with would-be bioterrorists would take more than a BWC Protocol,

---

MAJOR EVENTS IN THE FAILED NEGOTIATION OF THE BWC PROTOCOL

The Third BWC Review Conference in September 1991 launched the process that led to the unsuccessful negotiations on a BWC Protocol on verification. At the Third Review Conference, BWC states parties convened an Ad Hoc Group of Governmental Experts (VEREX) to identify and analyze possible verification measures for the BWC. VEREX worked during 1992 to 1993 and proposed twenty-one potential measures to enhance verification of BWC obligations.

At a special conference in September 1994, BWC states parties agreed to establish an ad hoc group (AHG) to consider appropriate measures, including verification mechanisms, to strengthen the BWC and to be included in a legally binding protocol. The AHG had not completed its work by the Fourth Review Conference in 1996, but the BWC states parties declared their continued support for the AHG and the completion of its work by the Fifth Review Conference in 2001. Between January 1995 and May 2001, the AHG held 23 sessions. The chair of the AHG negotiations issued a Chair's "rolling text" of a BWC Protocol at the seventh session in 1997, and this draft text became the basis for subsequent negotiations.

U.S. opposition to the BWC Protocol increased after President George W. Bush took office in January 2001. The Bush administration rejected the draft BWC Protocol in July 2001, effectively ending the AHG's substantive work. The Bush administration proposed terminating the AHG's mandate at the Fifth Review Conference in December 2001, a proposal so controversial that BWC states parties suspended the Fifth Review Conference for one year. At the reconvened Fifth Review Conference in November 2002, BWC states parties did not revive the BWC Protocol but instead scheduled the "New Process" agenda of annual meetings in 2003, 2004, and 2005 on various issues related to the BWC's objective of preventing proliferation of biological weapons. The Sixth Review Conference, held in November and December 2006, also did not restart the BWC Protocol negotiations.

---

and questions proliferated about exactly how much the Protocol would help in preventing, protecting against, and responding to bioterrorism.

Fifth, the Bush administration, which took office in January 2001, inherited the BWC Protocol negotiations from the Clinton administration and immediately made clear its dislike for the endeavor. In June 2001, the Bush administration announced that it would not support the BWC Protocol because the Protocol could not produce sufficiently useful verification information, did not directly address the terrorist threat, involved intrusive interference with U.S. biodefense programs, and burdened commercial enterprises involved in pharmaceutical and biotechnological pursuits. By the time the Fifth BWC Review Conference opened in November 2001, the BWC Protocol was effectively dead. Not even the anthrax attacks in the United States in October 2001 tempered the Bush administration's opposition to the BWC Protocol.

At the Fifth Review Conference, in one of the more infamous diplomatic episodes in recent years, the Bush administration went for the Protocol's jugular by attempting to terminate the AHG that had negotiated the Protocol since 1995. After pandemonium and profanity erupted in response to the U.S. maneuver, the BWC states parties suspended the Review Conference for one year, an unprecedented move that showed how deep the disagreements on the BWC Protocol between the Bush administration and most other countries had become.

At the reconvened Review Conference in December 2002, the BWC states parties agreed to hold yearly experts' meetings to consider national measures to implement states parties' obligations under Article IV of the BWC, biosecurity measures for protecting pathogens, surveillance and response measures to disease outbreaks, and codes of conduct for scientists. These items became known as the BWC "New Process" agenda. (For more on this agenda, see Chapter 3.) The New Process agenda proceeded as planned, but it did not resurrect the BWC Protocol strategy, as the proceedings and decisions of the Sixth BWC Review Conference at the end of 2006 demonstrated.

After the turmoil of the Fifth Review Conference, the outcome of the Sixth Review Conference was viewed as a positive development for the BWC. The Sixth Review Conference completed an article-by-article review of the BWC, endorsed the results produced during the 2003 to 2005 New Process meetings, decided to establish an Implementation Support Unit, agreed to hold intersessional meetings from 2007 to 2010, revised the confidence-building measures, and supported promotion of efforts to universalize membership in the BWC (BWC Sixth Review Conference Final Report 2006). Compared with the Fifth Review Conference, the Sixth Review Conference was more successful, but whether the substantive outcome of the Conference strengthens the BWC's role in biosecurity is controversial.

The president of the Sixth Review Conference described the Conference's outcome as a historic achievement that demonstrated multilateralism at its best (Meier 2007). Biological weapons experts were less impressed. Pearson (2006) concluded that the Sixth Review Conference only produced very modest progress. Tucker (2007) argued, "The fact that the modest accomplishments of the Sixth Review Conference were hailed as a 'success' suggests how dysfunctional the biological arms control process has become." We examine the outcome of the Sixth Review Conference in detail in Chapter 3.

D. The Norm Against Biological Weapons in the Twenty-First Century

Coming to grips with the problem of biological weapons in the twenty-first century requires assessing the strength of the norm against the use and development of biological weapons fostered by arms control agreements in the twentieth century. The norm's development and travails are sobering because they reveal the existence of a norm that is not entirely driving state behavior concerning biological weapons. Bio-deterrence backed by biological weapons, combined with formidable technical challenges, perhaps better explains the reluctance of states to use biological weapons in armed conflict than does the Geneva Protocol. The prohibition on the development of biological weapons in the BWC owes more to the determinations of many states, most notably the United States, that biological weapons lack sufficient military utility to be worth the effort. The attempt to use the arms control approach to strengthen the norm in international law through the BWC Protocol shattered under the stress created by many factors.

In the wake of the BWC Protocol's death and the controversy about the outcome of the Sixth Review Conference, the norm against biological weapons is, ironically, both stronger and weaker. The interest that most states have in preventing the proliferation of biological weapons is perhaps higher now than ever before, particularly given opportunities state proliferation and scientific developments might give potential bioterrorists. The anthrax attacks also brought home the collateral damage of bioterrorism, giving much of the world of non-state actors, especially corporations, a vested interest in preventing and protecting against the spread and use of biological weapons. No great global debate now rages about the appropriateness of the fundamental substantive objectives of the Geneva Protocol and the BWC.

The weakness emerges in the uncertainty that surrounds future influence of the norm against biological weapons. Three interdependent features cause particular alarm: (1) the increasing powers scientific advances create globally for the manipulation of microbial life, (2) the rise of global terrorism and its potential interest in biological weapons, and (3) the increased willingness of states to exploit the new capabilities of the biological sciences to protect themselves from possible bioterrorism through enhanced biodefense programs. The arms control strategy embedded in the BWC does not address directly the first or second features, but, as Chapter 3 explores, it creates friction with respect to the third.

These interdependent features require a governance response that is more robust and sustainable than the traditional arms control approach. We confront the sad reality that the world is substantially united on the norm against biological weapons but has failed to construct governance strategies to make the norm vibrant in the face of the biosecurity threats of the twenty-first century. In the next chapter, we turn our attention to the challenges of creating governance strategies for preventing, protecting against, and responding to the proliferation and potential use of biological weapons.

3 THE NEW WORLD OF
BIOLOGICAL WEAPONS GOVERNANCE

I. INTRODUCTION

Through the sound and fury in the debate over the problem of biological weapons one item of consensus stands out. Everyone appears to agree that the next phase of governing biological weapons will differ from the traditional arms control approach. This chapter explores emerging features of the new world of biological weapons governance. We argue that four governance trends characterize this new environment: criminalization of biological weapons development and use, regulation of the biological sciences, management of the imperative of biodefense, and public health preparedness and response. We maintain that these trends are not policy fads but represent adjustments to deeper, structural transformations in the policy context affecting biological weapons.

These four trends individually and collectively highlight the four key challenges we identified in Chapter 1 that define biosecurity governance in the twenty-first century. The trends illustrate the normative importance of integrating security and public health, supervising science for biosecurity, embedding biosecurity policy in the rule of law, and globalizing biosecurity governance. This chapter also exposes the complexities and difficulties of achieving these objectives in the emerging political and scientific environment of twenty-first-century biosecurity.

We begin by providing an overview of the four governance trends and how these trends affect the traditional arms control approach embodied in the Biological Weapons Convention (BWC). We then devote sections to each of the four trends to flesh out their significance as well as the difficulties that will make effective governance within each trend a profound test for states and the global community. We highlight how these governance trends relate to the four key challenges facing biosecurity policy. The trends provide more substantive material through which to understand how these challenges shape the future of biosecurity policy.

II. FOUR TRENDS AND A FUNERAL

A. Four Trends in Biological Weapons Governance

The four governance trends this chapter analyzes began to appear in the 1990s as states started to respond to the complex and uncertain developments affecting the threat posed by biological weapons. These trends overlap, thus, with the unsuccessful efforts to strengthen the arms control approach through negotiation of a compliance protocol for the BWC (see Chapter 2). In many respects, the four trends mark recognition that the BWC—even if strengthened with a compliance protocol—would not be adequate to handle the problems biological weapons would present in the future. This recognition involves an important normative and pragmatic shift away from the traditional arms control approach to biological weapons.

The first governance trend involves increasing interest in, and movement toward, using criminal law concepts and approaches to address the threat of biological weapons. The BWC required states parties to implement the BWC's prohibitions through domestic legislation (Article IV), which could include criminal statutes. The intensified focus on criminalizing development and use of biological weapons in the last decade has revealed, however, that compliance with the BWC's domestic implementation requirements has been poor. In a report for the Third BWC Review Conference in 1990, Goldblat and Bernaure (1991) noted that very few states parties had passed legislation to comply with Article IV.

Thirteen years later, Salerno and Estes (2003, 5) observed, "Unfortunately, too few countries have enacted . . . BWC implementation and criminalization measures—leaving the production of biological agents for use as weapons technically illegal, but not punishable in most parts of the world." Salerno and Estes (2003) further noted that responses to the BWC confidence-building measure (CBM) concerning domestic implementation laws and regulations adopted in 1986 have been very poor, even seventeen years after BWC states parties agreed to this CBM. Other research concluded, "A large portion of states parties to the Biological Weapons Convention have no implementing legislation in place as required under Article 4 of the treaty" (VERTIC 2003, 46). Even countries in the thick of Cold War politics showed no sense of urgency in making BWC prohibitions effective in domestic criminal law. For example, the United States only implemented its BWC obligations in this regard in 1989 (Biological Weapons Act 1989), fourteen years after the United States ratified the BWC.

The BWC New Process agenda that followed the troubled Fifth Review Conference included meetings on adopting necessary national measures, including penal legislation, to implement the BWC's prohibitions. The lead-up to the Sixth Review Conference in 2006 continued to see emphasis on the poor quality of domestic implementation of BWC prohibitions. Kellman (2006a, 232) argued that too many states only criminalize use or intent to use biological weapons "but give insufficient attention to preparatory activity that would likely precede commission of a bio-crime."

Poor compliance with Article IV of the BWC has placed strengthening domestic legislation on biosecurity on many agendas. This goal features in ongoing efforts to strengthen the BWC through such initiatives as adoption of model legislation (Harland and Woodward 2006; Interpol 2006c) and the Sixth Review Conference's decision to dedicate an intersessional meeting in 2007 on ways and means to enhance national implementation (BWC Sixth Review Conference Final Report 2006). The current interest in criminalization goes, however, beyond the question of state party compliance with the BWC.

The second governance trend concerns the interest in regulating scientific activities that directly or indirectly affect biosecurity. We explore later, for example, efforts to strengthen regulations concerning access to dangerous pathogens and the security of the facilities in which research on such pathogens is conducted. The BWC's object and purpose encompass actions by states parties to ensure the safety and security of dangerous pathogens and research conducted with them. The BWC was never, however, an engine for the regulation of the biological sciences. This aspect of biosecurity did not historically receive much attention from BWC states parties (Salerno and Estes 2003). Not until 1996, for example, did the United States move to restrict access to dangerous pathogens because of growing fears about bioterrorism (Antiterrorism and Effective Death Penalty Act 1996). This kind of regulatory activity can affect those engaged in peaceful research and thus raises concerns about trade-offs between the control needed for biosecurity and the freedom needed for scientific innovation to benefit human health.

The third governance trend involves biodefense, which has undergone a renaissance. As Chapters 1 and 2 noted, worries about the proliferation of biological weapons, particularly with respect to terrorists, has reinvigorated state interest in biodefense activities. Biodefense programs were important to the United States and other countries after the BWC entered into force. Until the collapse of the Soviet Union, the Cold War remained the defining element of such programs. This collapse, particularly the revelations about the frightening scale and substance of the former Soviet program, threw bio-defense activities into a new global context with more shadowy enemies and fast-moving scientific challenges, all operating on a global scale. In this new environment, biodefense—especially in the United States—began to take on policy importance it never had even during the Cold War. The reinvigoration of biodefense activities affects all of the key challenges of biosecurity policy, particularly the need to embed biosecurity in the rule of law.

The fourth governance trend involves the need governments sensed to engage in public health preparedness and response activities. Preparing for the unthinkable—a biological weapons attack—became thinkable and necessary. During the twentieth century, bio-deterrence contributed to the infrequency of state use of biological weapons. Bio-deterrence underpinned the "no first use" prohibition of the Geneva Protocol and justified the offensive capabilities until countries abandoned their offensive programs. States did not prepare for what would happen if bio-deterrence failed to prevent microbial attack. The BWC addresses assistance to victims of biological weapons use (Article VII), but the BWC contains nothing that amounts to a serious approach to planning for emergency responses to biological weapons use.

The past ten years have seen this policy area explode in significance as an aspect of governing the threat of biological weapons. The U.S. federal government has, for example, allocated more than $32 billion dollars for civilian prevention and defense against biological weapons from fiscal year 2001 through fiscal year 2007 (Center for Arms Control and Non-Proliferation 2007; Lam, Franco, and Schuler 2006). See Figure 3.1. Preparedness and response to intentional releases of biological agents has also become an important consideration for the World Health Organization's efforts to upgrade global surveillance and response capabilities to pathogenic threats (see Chapter 5). This governance trend plays an important role in the integration of security and public health at the heart of biosecurity policy in the early twenty-first century.

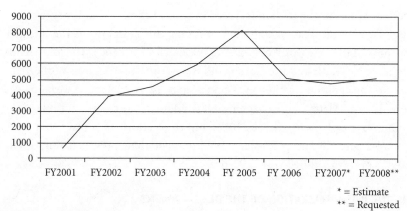

* = Estimate
** = Requested

Figure 3.1 Federal Funding for Bioweapons Prevention and Defense
(Excluding the Department of Defense) (in millions of $U.S.)
SOURCE: Center for Arms Control and Non-Proliferation 2007, 2

B. Funeral for the Traditional Arms Control Approach

Subsequent sections of this chapter analyze each of the four governance trends, but the relationship of these trends to the traditional arms control approach to biological weapons governance is important to consider up front. This approach has been *the* governance strategy for the problem of biological weapons since 1925, but it no longer maintains this status. The issues covered by the four governance trends involve problems that the BWC process either failed to address adequately (implementation of BWC obligations through national law; regulation of pathogen security and dangerous scientific research; biodefense activities) or barely addressed (public health preparedness and response to biological attacks). This chapter's analysis of the four trends highlights how much states and experts on biological weapons are reaching outside the BWC for governance responses to the perceived growing threat. Primary reliance on the BWC's arms control approach for governing the problem of biological weapons is dead. We agree with Littlewood (2005, 240), "The failure of the BWC Protocol negotiations represents the end of approaches designed during the period of the Cold War." We further argue in this chapter that the outcome of the Sixth Review Conference in 2006 confirms the end of the dominance of the arms control approach.

The death of primary reliance on the traditional arms control strategy does not mean the Geneva Protocol and BWC have become ashes and dust. Rather than effective regimes of international governance, these treaties have become icons for the faith in the need to counter the evil that the spread and use of biological weapons represent. Keeping this faith alive is the ultimate purpose of the new world of biological weapons governance. The four trends draw on this faith and thus mesh with the normative objectives of the arms control prohibition on the development and use of biological weapons. As also discussed later in the chapter, states and non-state actors continue to try to improve and strengthen the BWC, but these efforts take place in a more complex and diverse governance environment than prevailed during the BWC's prior thirty-five-year existence.

III. THE CRIMINALIZATION OF THE DEVELOPMENT
AND USE OF BIOLOGICAL WEAPONS

A. From Bio-Deterrence to Criminalization

At one level, the idea that the intentional development and use of biological agents to inflict physical harm, economic damage, and social disruption on civilian populations should be a crime seems obvious. Thus, increasing emphasis on a criminalization approach in biosecurity policy might seem uninteresting. The criminalization of the development and use of biological weapons is, however, more important than first glances suggest. This criminalization is providing a new conceptual foundation for governance of the threat of biological weapons.

To sense the shift toward criminalization, we contrast it with the arms control paradigm on biological weapons. This paradigm focused on states and sought to prevent states from developing and using biological weapons in armed conflict. As Chapter 2 analyzed, the Geneva Protocol's "no first use" prohibition worked, by and large, because states developed biological weapons capabilities and implicitly threatened to use them against states that used biological weapons first. Thinking of the development and use of biological weapons in criminal terms made no sense when bio-deterrence prevailed as the policy ethos. In fact, after World War II, the United States deemed getting information from Japan military personnel involved in the biological weapons activities in China more important than prosecuting those individuals for war crimes.

Policy space for criminalization opened when bio-deterrence lost credibility after the U.S. unilateral termination of its offensive program at the end of the 1960s. A state's acceptance of the BWC eliminated the possibility it could build, stockpile, and threaten to use biological weapons as a military deterrent. Bio-deterrence's illegitimacy strengthened as BWC states parties gradually revoked their reservations to the Geneva Protocol that preserved the right to use biological weapons in a second-strike scenario (Roberts and Guelff 2000).

The BWC's impact still, however, did not produce a strong criminalization trend. The treaty does not require that states parties label a violation of its prohibitions a crime in either domestic or international law. The requirement to "take any necessary measures" to implement the BWC's prohibitions domestically (Article IV) does not expressly mandate that these measures be criminal in nature. Actually, the BWC never uses the terms *crime* or *criminal*, even while condemning the use of biological weapons as "repugnant to the conscience of mankind." The BWC contrasts, thus, with the Chemical Weapons Convention's express obligation on states parties to enact penal legislation (CWC, Article VII). Although states parties have used criminal law in implementing their obligations under Article IV, experts argued before the Sixth Review Conference that states parties should "strengthen the reference to penal legislation" (Pearson, Sims, and Dando 2006, 111).

In addition, the failure of many BWC states parties to implement their BWC obligations as required by Article IV (discussed earlier in this chapter) includes a failure to use criminal law effectively. Indeed, production or transfer of dangerous biological agents is not a criminal act under the domestic law of many nations, including a significant number of BWC states parties (Kellman 2006b). Interpol has, for example, argued,

> In many countries, criminal justice systems are constrained by inadequate legal frameworks governing the detection and repression of bio-weapons. Frequently, no law is violated until the disease or biological agent is actually deployed. Law enforcement officers are therefore unable to begin preliminary investigations into the development of such weapons. Without laws which criminalise activity relating to bio-weapons, there is no basis for legal assistance or co-operation to prevent their production and transport. (Interpol 2006a)

The policy space for criminalization opened, but not filled, by the BWC has only in the last ten years been exploited to support biosecurity. Several factors converged to produce the criminalization trend. Growing fears about bioterrorism connected two bodies of international law previously distinct—the BWC and international law on terrorism. The emergence of international terrorism in the 1970s and 1980s prompted states to adopt many antiterrorism treaties (e.g., Convention for the Suppression of Unlawful Acts against the Safety of Civil Aviation [1971], Convention for the Suppression of Unlawful Acts against the Safety of Maritime Navigation [1988]), and this trend continued into the 1990s (e.g., International Convention for the Suppression of Terrorist Bombings [1997], International Convention for the Suppression of the Financing of Terrorism [1999]).

These treaties were grounded in an international criminal law approach. The treaties required states parties to criminalize in their domestic laws certain defined acts of terrorist violence (e.g., hijacking aircraft), engage in law enforcement cooperation on the defined criminal activities, and prosecute or extradite persons alleged to have committed the specified crimes.

Unlike the antiterrorism treaties, the BWC does not directly speak to terrorist threats. The BWC's "take any necessary measures" requirement targeted state compliance with the treaty's prohibitions and was not directly designed to combat terrorist development and use of biological weapons. Certainly, effective implementation of Article IV would adversely affect bioterrorist activity that might be taking place under a state party's jurisdiction or control. The criminal law approach in the antiterrorism treaties provided, however, an alternative approach that states could apply to bioterrorism.

An example of states connecting bioterrorism with the criminalization model of antiterrorism treaties can be found in the International Convention for the Suppression of Terrorist Bombings (1998). This Convention adopts the classical law enforcement approach of antiterrorism treaties because it criminalized certain acts (in this case, terrorist bombings) and established a "prosecute or extradite" regime for states parties. The Convention specifically included bioterrorist acts in its scope. The Convention defines an "explosive or other lethal device" to mean a "weapon or device that is designed, or has the capability, to cause death, serious bodily injury or substantial material damage through the release, dissemination or impact of toxic chemicals, biological agents or toxins or similar substances or radiological or radioactive material" (Article 1.3(b)). This treaty entered into force in 2001 and currently has 145 states parties.

A second factor in the convergence of approaches to biological weapons and terrorism involves the increasing use of criminal law strategies in international law. After the BWC entered into force, states, international organizations, and nongovernmental organizations demonstrated a growing desire to address serious violations of rules of international law through criminal law.

The war crimes trials after World War II marked the first significant move in international law toward holding individuals, even leaders of states, criminally responsible for their actions. In the decades after these trials, states, international organizations, and nongovernmental organizations continued to develop the idea of "international crimes," or crimes in international law, and to take this idea beyond the laws of war.

Perhaps the best illustration of this criminalization trend involves the prohibition against torture in international human rights law. Torture was not an international legal issue before World War II. After this conflict, torture became absolutely prohibited in treaty law, a *jus cogens* norm in customary international law, and an international crime by the end of the twentieth century. The UN Convention Against Torture (1984) required states parties to criminalize torture in their domestic laws and to prosecute or extradite persons alleged of having committed torture. This treaty's objective was the universal criminalization of torture in domestic and international law.

The human rights context of torture is important for the criminalization story involving biological weapons. The BWC's de-legitimization of bio-deterrence, leavened with the long-standing moral repugnance at the use of disease as a weapon, connected with the criminalization efforts underway in international humanitarian law and international human rights law. This convergence has produced increasing support for criminalizing the development and use of biological weapons in the same manner that crimes against humanity and torture have been universally criminalized. The international criminalization of many terrorist activities also adds weight to the momentum for the criminalization of the development and use of biological weapons.

The most well-known proposal that connects all these dots concerning international law, criminalization, and biological weapons is the Draft Convention on the Prevention and Punishment of the Crime of Developing, Producing, Acquiring, Stockpiling, Retaining, Transferring or Using Biological and Chemical Weapons proposed by Meselson and Robinson (2004). This proposed treaty applies the law enforcement approach found in the antiterrorism treaties to the development and use of biological and chemical weapons. The treaty envisions a regime of universal jurisdiction, like the one that exists for the international crime of torture, for the crimes of developing or using chemical or biological weapons. In proposing this approach, Meselson and Robinson (2004, 58) sought to move beyond adoption of national criminal law to the establishment of a regime that "defines specific acts involving biological or chemical weapons as international crimes, like piracy or aircraft hijacking."

By moving in the criminalization direction, biosecurity policy integrates itself with the international law on terrorism, armed conflict, and human rights. This integration means that use of a biological weapon by a terrorist should be a crime punishable simultaneously under domestic law and international law, a result not produced by the BWC. The criminalization movement makes use of a biological weapon by a state against enemy military forces in armed conflict a war crime. Use of a contagious biological agent, whether by a terrorist or a state, could be considered a crime against humanity—a widespread or systematic attack directed against civilian populations. The criminalization project also seeks to make development of biological weapons a domestic and an international crime.

The reader cannot locate the criminalization of the development and use of biological weapons described earlier in a single treaty or other international legal document because no such document presently exists. The International Convention on the Suppression of Terrorist Bombings (1998) only addresses terrorist use of biological weapons, not the development of such weapons. The Meselson and Robinson proposal for a treaty criminalizing all aspects of biological weapons from development to use has not become the subject of diplomatic negotiations.

The criminalization of the development and use of biological weapons is not complete compared, for example, to how crimes against humanity and torture have been criminalized. The absence of a piece of paper should not divert us, however, from comprehending how biosecurity policy has moved in the criminalization direction. This movement is critical to understanding how governance of the problem of biological weapons is unfolding in the early twenty-first century.

Thinking about use and development of biological weapons as crimes has important purposes. First, it supports the normative objectives of the Geneva Protocol and the BWC, even though neither of those instruments expressly calls for the criminalization of acts that violate their respective prohibitions. Second, criminalization attempts to put all states on notice—including those not party to the BWC—that developing or using biological weapons for hostile purposes subjects the individuals involved to criminal sanctions. Just as with torture, the criminalization approach pierces the fictional personality of the state and targets the individuals directly responsible. The leaders of states who remain interested in, or tempted by, biological weapons no longer enjoy the penumbra of legitimacy conferred by bio-deterrence. Criminalization attempts to raise the stakes of biological weapons development and use in a very personal way.

Third, the criminalization approach provides benefits for addressing the threat that non-state actors might present. Criminalization seeks to move each state to outlaw any person's involvement with biological weapons, to interdict such activities, and to punish persons found guilty of making or using biological weapons. As with other notorious international crimes, the criminalization effort seeks to ensure that states cannot opt out of criminalizing the development and use of biological weapons. They must work to prevent such development and use, and they cannot provide safe haven for those accused of developing or using biological weapons. States must bring those accused to justice or cooperate fully with other states or international organizations that are willing and able to apprehend, prosecute, and punish the perpetrators.

Fourth, the criminalization approach brings law enforcement assets, technologies, cooperative arrangements, and personnel into the larger policy effort of preventing, preparing for, and responding to acts of bioterrorism. As noted more later, the involvement of law enforcement in policy action against biological weapons is a novel feature of the new world of biological weapons governance. Experts consider law enforcement involvement particularly important to the objective of preventing acts of bioterrorism from occurring (Interpol 2006a; Kellman 2001; Kellman 2006a, 2006b).

The criminalization trend raises three issues that deserve more exploration: (1) the implications of engaging law enforcement in biosecurity policy, (2) the potential impact of criminalization on the pursuit of peaceful biological research, and (3) the obstacles to completing universal criminalization of biological weapons development and use. Examination of these three issues reveals the underlying complexities biosecurity policy has to handle.

B. Law Enforcement, Public Health, and Biosecurity

We have stressed how the criminalization of biological weapons reflects not only failure to implement the BWC but also developments in international humanitarian law and international human rights law. These latter comparisons are apt, however, only to a point. Unlike the areas of armed conflict and human rights, which historically have interfaced with law enforcement organizations and personnel, the challenge presented by biological weapons has not been associated with law enforcement. For most of the twentieth century, development of biological weapons by states was legal, and law enforcement agencies did not closely (if at all) monitor state-run biological weapons programs. In addition, few governments were concerned about the threat to security and public health posed by terrorist interest in biological weapons until the last decade of the twentieth century. Past policy approaches on biological weapons did not, thus, groove relationships between the military, law enforcement, and public health. The move toward criminalization forces such relationships to develop.

The growing involvement of Interpol in strengthening law enforcement capabilities against bioterrorism illustrates the bureaucratic and disciplinary convergences that the criminalization approach demands. During the Cold War, Interpol was not engaged in issues relating to biological weapons development or use. Today, Interpol seeks to enhance law enforcement's contribution to preventing, preparing for, and responding to bioterrorism through its Bioterrorism Prevention Program. Interpol launched its formal programs on biological weapons and bioterrorism in 2004, established a unit dedicated to bioterrorism at its headquarters, held a global conference in March 2005, and conducted regional bioterrorism workshops in South Africa (November 2005), Singapore (March 2006), Chile (July 2006), Ukraine (November 2006), and Oman (March 2007). It also began a Biocriminalization Project in September 2006 that seeks to develop a thorough understanding of the legislative frameworks in Interpol member states for prohibiting and preventing bioterrorism, identifying legislative and regulatory gaps, and assisting Interpol member states to improve their legislation and strengthen law enforcement capacity (Interpol 2006b). The Biocriminalization Project also includes draft model legislation to prohibit biocrimes and promote biosafety and biosecurity (Interpol 2006c).

Making development and use of a biological weapon a crime in domestic and international law forces every public and private actor engaging in research and handling of dangerous biological agents to comply with criminal law. As Interpol's bioterrorism efforts indicate, criminalization requires sufficient law enforcement authority, training, and capabilities before this strategy can contribute significantly to biosecurity. Law enforcement agencies may have to investigate alleged violations of criminal prohibitions on the development and use of biological weapons, and these investigations will involve law enforcement officials interfacing with public health experts and scientists. Various "table top" simulations of biological attacks have demonstrated how important cooperation between law enforcement and public health authorities is to effective responses to bioterrorism. Criminalizing the development of biological weapons also brings law enforcement and public health together as a part of biosecurity. The cultures of both law enforcement and public health have had to adjust to this new relationship stimulated by the criminalization paradigm. Efforts to facilitate this adjustment have been made, such as the development of "forensic epidemiology," defined as "the use of epidemiologic methods as part of an ongoing investigation of a health problem for which there is suspicion or evidence regarding possible intentional acts or criminal behavior as factors contributing to the health problem" (Lazzarini, Goodman, and Dammers 2007, 149).

The governance adjustments criminalization requires have perhaps been most challenging for public health. Before the rise of concerns about bioterrorism in the 1990s, public health had rare interactions with law enforcement, usually in the context of needing police help to enforce compulsory isolation orders against uncooperative persons who posed a danger to public health (e.g., people infected with multidrug resistant tuberculosis). In other contexts, such as the transmission of HIV/AIDS, public health experts have not embraced criminal law strategies to prevent or respond to disease events. The preferred approach has been to avoid coercion through criminal law to seek voluntary compliance with public health advice.

The need for public health to develop a more expansive modus operandi with law enforcement forms part of the key biosecurity challenge of integrating public health with security. Public health had to adjust to the security need for law enforcement engagement on preventing the development, transfer, and use of biological weapons. Law enforcement's experience with national security gave it an advantage over public health in connection with the security aspects related to biological weapons. The criminalization approach thrust public health into a policy environment of which it had no prior experience and in which it confronted players with more power and resources. Integration of security and public health with respect to the criminalization trend has required public health to respond to new security and law enforcement demands without subordinating public health's role in biosecurity governance.

C. Criminalization and Scientific Research

The criminalization of the development and use of biological weapons also changes the governance world for civilian scientific research with biological agents. During the twentieth century, the application of ever more powerful and sophisticated scientific techniques, technologies, and knowledge produced unprecedented benefits for humanity's health. This engine of progress operated, by and large, without scientists and policy makers worrying whether research projects would violate criminal law. Certainly, civilian researchers had to comply with rules and regulations violation of which could bring criminal penalties. Criminal law did not, however, intrude deeply into the essence of the scientific enterprise—the search for knowledge. The freedom researchers in the biological sciences enjoyed was virtually unfettered, which contrasted with the heavily securitized and criminalized environment of nuclear research.

The momentum toward criminalization of biological weapons development and use brought criminal law and civilian scientific research face to face. Criminalization forms part of the challenge biosecurity policy faces in supervising the conduct of science to protect security and to advance public health. Criminalization has produced, in this context, a difficult question about preventing the development and use of biological weapons. How can biosecurity policy use criminal law effectively to prevent biological weapons proliferation and use without unnecessarily interfering in the freedom and innovation that makes the biological sciences such an awesome resource for public health?

At the heart of this question is the "dual use" dilemma. Many of the materials, techniques, technologies, and pieces of equipment needed to develop a biological weapon are used around the world daily to conduct peaceful biological research. In this context, use of criminal law has to be finely calibrated to apply to only those activities that threaten biosecurity. The problem is not intent, not in the way intent complicates determining what constitutes a biological weapon under the BWC. Criminal law requires a showing of intent, *mens rea*, before the state can punish individuals for criminal acts. The difficulty is establishing intent before the biological weapon is developed and used in a "dual use" environment where malevolence can lurk undetected. The "dual use" dilemma makes establishment of more objective criteria for application of criminal law attractive. As explored later in this chapter, regulations that condition research access to dangerous pathogens on registration and licensing create "bright line" rules for triggering criminal sanctions.

Other considerations factor into the challenge of supervising science for security and public health with respect to criminalization. Most notably, many countries have well-developed constitutional and statutory requirements that law enforcement authorities must respect when exercising investigatory and coercive public authority under criminal law. Many of these requirements flow from principles attached to the rule of law, especially principles that protect individual rights and liberties from the exercise of state power (see Chapter 6).

Criminalization cannot, and does not, mean that the police or intelligence agencies can conduct surveillance and searches of civilian biological research with nothing more than vague suspicion that something evil might be afoot. The exigencies of biosecurity cannot escape larger governance constructs, such as the rule of law, that apply to the exercise of political power. Protections for individual rights and liberties and the need for procedural due process for those accused of violating criminal law are essential to the rule of law. These protections combine with the "dual use" dilemma to make the criminal law approach to preventing biological weapons proliferation and use difficult.

The tensions evident when the demands of the criminalization strategy interface with the need for scientific freedom and innovation connect to the third trend in governance approaches that we examine later—heightened regulation of the biological sciences. The new regulatory environment does not owe all its features to the criminalization movement, but criminalization—and the problems it causes for biological science research—plays a role in the need for more oversight and control of scientific exploration of microbial life.

D. Globalization and Criminalization: Getting to Universal

The third major issue that the movement toward the criminalization raises is the need for the movement to be universal in scope. If activities related to the preparation or use of biological weapons are not criminalized in most states, then the criminalization strategy suffers geographic gaps. If the criminal law adopted by states varies widely, the lack of harmonization will hinder international law enforcement cooperation on gathering evidence, conducting investigations, sharing evidence, extraditing suspects, and prosecuting criminal defendants. As Meselson and Robinson (2004, 58) argued, "Purely national statutes present daunting problems of harmonizing their various provisions regarding the definition of crimes, rights of the accused, dispute resolution, and judicial assistance, among others." The criminalization approach will be most effective when states throughout the international system have harmonized their criminal laws and policies against the development and use of biological weapons.

Supporting this need for universality is the globalization of the biological sciences that has become a key factor in biosecurity policy. The scale and speed of the global dissemination of knowledge, research, techniques, and technologies in the biological sciences mean that the criminalization strategy has to be universal in scope as well. This dissemination, and its continued acceleration through advances in the biological sciences, has been of particular concern with respect to potential terrorist interest in biological weapons. This reality connects to the challenge of globalizing governance for biosecurity.

One might assume that, given the thirty-plus years of the BWC's existence, the international system of states would be well along the road toward harmonization concerning the criminalization of the development and use of biological weapons. As noted earlier, however, states parties' poor compliance with the BWC requirements on domestic implementation has not produced harmonization with respect to criminal law on biological weapons development and use.

In the wake of the collapse of the BWC Protocol negotiations and the failed Fifth Review Conference in 2001, BWC states parties agreed in 2002 to have experts' meetings from 2003–2005 to discuss BWC-relevant issues. One of these New Process agenda issues was national implementation of BWC obligations. This process revealed a threadbare patchwork of diverse national criminal law approaches to biological weapons. As indicated earlier in this chapter, only a handful of states has made weaponization of pathogens a national crime. Only a handful of states has established regulatory and oversight systems for possession, transfer, acquisition, and research with dangerous biological agents that are critical to a successful criminalization strategy.

The existing threadbare patchwork pattern of criminalization at the national level has many causes. Many states have not moved more strongly in the criminalization direction because they do not perceive that the threat of biological weapons proliferation and use is as serious as other states, such as the United States, claim (VERTIC 2003). Similarly, "Some States Parties might have considered in the past that they do not need to enact specific BTWC implementation legislation since they do not have—or believe that they do not have—relevant materials within their territory" (Assessment of National Implementation of the Biological and Toxin Weapons Convention [BTWC] 2006, 7). Other states may view rogue states rather than terrorists as the real proliferation threat against which criminalization will likely be ineffective in the same way criminalization of torture in international law has not significantly reduced the practice of torture by states. Developing countries may view the momentum toward criminalization as relevant only to countries, such as the United States, that face bioterrorist threats. Developing countries may perceive that naturally occurring infectious diseases, which take a terrible toll in their territories, are a more pressing problem, against which criminalization of biological weapons development and use has little usefulness.

Despite the patchwork, the criminalization agenda has moved forward, helped significantly by UN Security Council actions. In September 2001, the Security Council adopted Resolution 1373, which (among other things) required UN members to ensure that all terrorist acts "are established as serious criminal offenses in domestic laws and regulations and that the punishment duly reflects the seriousness of such terrorist acts" (Security Council 2001, ¶2(e)). As a decision by the Security Council, Resolution 1373 is legally binding on all UN member states (UN Charter 1945, Article 25). Resolution 1373 also established the Counter-Terrorism Committee to monitor UN members' responses to the Resolution. Resolution 1373 connects directly to the obligation in the International Convention for the Suppression of Terrorist Bombings (1998) described earlier, which made use of biological weapons an international crime. The Convention and Security Council Resolution 1373 have moved the criminalization agenda forward at the national and international levels.

In April 2004, the Security Council adopted Resolution 1540, which contained a series of decisions that required UN members to take actions to prevent the proliferation of nuclear, chemical, and biological weapons and their means of delivery by non-state actors. Resolution 1540 stated that the Security Council:

> *Decides also* that all States, in accordance with their national procedures, shall adopt and enforce appropriate effective laws which prohibit any non-State actor to manufacture, acquire, possess, develop, transport, transfer or use nuclear, chemical or biological weapons and their means of delivery, in particular for terrorist purposes, as well as attempts to engage in any of the foregoing activities, participate in them as an accomplice, assist or finance them. (Security Council 2004, ¶2)

This aspect of Resolution 1540 resembles the BWC's obligation for states parties to take any necessary measures to prohibit and prevent the development, stockpiling, transfer, acquisition, or retention of biological weapons. Given the ineffectiveness of this element of the BWC, skepticism may exist about the likely effectiveness of Resolution 1540 contributing to universalizing the criminalization of biological weapons development and use.

Resolution 1540 created a process, however, that brought new scrutiny to how states approached domestic implementation of the obligation to prevent the proliferation of biological weapons to non-state actors. The Security Council established a committee, known as the 1540 Committee, to which UN members were required to submit reports on steps they have taken, or intended to take, to implement Resolution 1540 (Security Council 2004, ¶4). This process produced reports from UN members that, overall, reinforce the need for greater effort to harmonize national efforts to prevent the development, proliferation, and use of biological weapons.

Resolutions 1373 and 1540 are no panacea for the global challenge of the criminalization of biological weapons development and use. The Counter-Terrorism Committee established to oversee Resolution 1373 has experienced difficulties. In extending the 1540 Committee's mandate until April 2008, the Security Council (2006, 1) noted, "Not all States have presented to the 1540 Committee their [required] reports on the steps they have taken or intend to take to implement resolution 1540 (2004)." Resolutions 1373 and 1540 also did not provide any criteria by which to determine whether a UN member complied with the Security Council's mandates to adopt and enforce appropriate and effective laws. UN members may adopt some measures to comply with Resolutions 1373 and 1540, but those measures may fall far short of what the criminalization strategy requires. Other UN members may have adopted "gold standard" criminal provisions but have no realistic chance to enforce them for lack of human and financial resources.

Whether the Security Council will assess UN member compliance with Resolutions 1373 and 1540 and take actions against those members not in compliance also remains unclear. If each UN member is essentially left to determine whether it complies with Resolutions 1373 and 1540 and BWC obligations to adopt and enforce domestic laws relating to biological weapons, then the harmonization required for truly universalizing criminalization of biological weapons development and use will remain difficult, if not impossible, to achieve.

The criminalization of biological weapons development and use as a governance strategy has gained strength in the last ten years, but, as of this writing, it remains incomplete and vulnerable. Even with the BWC, the International Convention on the Suppression of Terrorist Bombings, the growing involvement of Interpol, and Security Council intervention through Resolutions 1373 and 1540, the world has not firmly embedded the crimes of biological weapons development and use into national and international law as other international crimes have been. Whether criminalization makes progress constitutes one of the key governance questions for biosecurity in the next decade.

IV. REGULATION OF THE BIOLOGICAL SCIENCES

The second development that characterizes the new context for governance of biological weapons concerns the move toward heightened regulation of the biological sciences. The momentum for criminalization drives much, but not all aspects, of the trend toward greater regulation of scientific research involving biological agents. The increased interest in, and implementation of, such regulation has ended biology's so-called "age of innocence," when security implications of civilian biological research were rarely a concern.

The trend toward heightened regulation of the biological sciences implicates all four biosecurity challenges identified in Chapter 1. Such regulation clearly implicates the task of supervising the conduct of scientific research for both security and public health purposes. Balancing the needs of security and public health in supervising scientific research affects the biosecurity goal of integrating security and public health. As discussed more later, the challenge of regulating the biological sciences confronts serious governance problems created by globalization. Unilateral or even regional efforts to supervise science for security and public health will produce, at best, only a patchwork regime, which highlights the need for globalized governance mechanisms. The implications of heightened regulation for the principles of scientific innovation, freedom, and expression bring the rule of law into the mix. The central debate today involves calibrating how to regulate the biological sciences appropriately rather than whether policy makers should attempt such regulation at all. The rule of law framework is relevant to sorting out how regulatory approaches can balance competing interests.

A. Balancing Security and Science in the Hot Zone

As noted earlier, criminalization of biological weapons development and use affects research in the biological sciences. The criminalization approach encourages oversight of scientific research involving biological agents. The criminalization strategy and the regulation of the biological sciences are, thus, joined at the governance hip. This reality illuminates the difficulties of integrating security and public health and supervising science to achieve security and public health. Similar difficulties appear within the movement for heightened regulation of the biological sciences. The challenge is to balance security, public health, and scientific exploration such that the regulatory approach produces an outcome that is not too hard for health and science, not too soft for security, but is "just right" for all three governance functions. Finding the "just right" balance proves a delicate yet necessary responsibility for biosecurity.

1. Securing Dangerous Pathogenic Agents and Toxins

The basic approach to increasing regulation of the biological sciences involves identifying what scientific activities are potentially dangerous and then implementing control and oversight mechanisms to ensure that such research does not create or exacerbate biosecurity threats. The U.S. approach to regulating the biological sciences generally illustrates this approach, which essentially involves three prongs. First, the government identifies what agents and toxins create biological weapons concerns. The U.S. government has, for example, identified agents and toxins of concern in its select agent list (see Annex 1).

Second, the government requires persons and facilities conducting research on any select agent to be registered and licensed to engage in such research. The registration and licensing system defines the community of researchers and laboratories the government permits to conduct research on select agents and to transfer, acquire, and retain such agents. Registration allows activities undertaken on select agents within this licensed community to occur with government knowledge, approval, and oversight. Any activity undertaken outside this regulatory system with the identified select agents is presumptively illegal and subjects those involved to possible criminal sanctions.

Third, the government establishes standards for the safety and security of facilities in which research on the select agents occurs, and violation of these standards can lead to criminal penalties. Safety standards ensure that researchers and facilities handle dangerous pathogens appropriately and in ways that do not endanger researchers, the research facility, or outside communities. Researchers and facilities have long been accustomed to biosafety standards because of their importance for occupational safety and public health. Security standards heighten the importance of such biosafety protocols because they seek to make certain that terrorists or criminals do not steal or divert dangerous pathogens from their licensed and regulated uses. Compliance with the safety and security standards forms part of the registration and licensing requirements.

In the abstract, this approach to preventing dangerous pathogens from falling into the wrong hands seems reasonable. Two factors complicate the abstract perspective. First, the select agent regulatory system represented a dramatic change for those engaged in the biological sciences. The registration, licensing, and documentation requirements (not to mention the threat of criminal sanctions) changed the environment for biological research involving select agents (see box).

Second, those engaged in biological research have expressed concerns about the new regulatory system, arguing that the rules unduly restrict and deter peaceful and potentially valuable scientific research. Some scientists have argued that, in the attempt to prevent unintentional or malevolent uses of biological research, "increased government oversight of basic life sciences research would 'kill' the research" (Kahn 2007). For many scientists, regulation is prudent in theory, but the devil is in the details. Scientists complained about some of the new regulatory requirements because they believed that they privileged short-term security fears triggered by the September 11th and anthrax attacks over long-term scientific progress that could yield tremendous benefits for human health. The complexity, scope, and depth of the rules also required institutions, such as universities, to implement costly and time-consuming compliance procedures and administrative mechanisms, taking money and human capital away from scientific exploration.

In addition to these factors, inspections in the United States of government and university facilities working with select agents have found significant problems with security arrangements for such agents. The Office of Inspector General of the Department of Health and Human Services (2004, 2) inspected eleven universities working with select agents and concluded,

> Serious weaknesses compromised the security of select agents at all universities reviewed. Physical security weaknesses at all 11 universities left select agents vulnerable to theft or loss, thus elevating the risk of public exposure. Inadequate inventory and recordkeeping procedures at all 11 universities prevented us from concluding that universities had complied with select agent transfer restrictions. In the area of restricted persons, at least half of the universities had inadequate procedures to identify persons barred from accessing select agents under the USA PATRIOT Act.

Similarly, the Office of Inspector General of the Department of Energy (2005, 2) inspected Department of Energy efforts on research with select agents, including the building of new biosafety level (BSL)-3 laboratories, and concluded that the Department had not developed a coordinated plan for the construction and operation of BSL-3 laboratories, meaning, "There is no assurance that projects are being directed to the laboratory best suited to meet requirements; that resources are being effectively utilized; that security implications are being addressed; and, that capabilities are not being inappropriately duplicated."

Despite these type of failings within countries and the concerns expressed by scientists about the impact of heightened regulation of the biological sciences, states appear to agree that more stringent and harmonized oversight of the safety and security of potentially dangerous pathogenic agents and toxins is warranted. As noted earlier, BWC states parties had not historically paid much attention to this issue, even though the issue falls within the scope of Article IV's requirement to implement the BWC's prohibitions. The safety and security of agents and toxins used in research did, however, feature in the BWC's New Process agenda because one of the intersessional meetings ad-

---

THE PROSECUTION AND CONVICTION OF DR. THOMAS BUTLER

In January 2003, Dr. Thomas Butler, a leading U.S. expert on the plague bacterium, *Yersinia pestis,* reported to Texas Tech University that thirty vials of plague bacteria had been stolen from his laboratory. Dr. Butler had been working on new antibiotic treatments for plague infections. This research, which was funded by pharmaceutical companies, involved fieldwork in Tanzania, where plague is endemic. The U.S. government considered Dr. Butler's work and expertise important for the effort underway to counter bioterrorism. His report on the allegedly stolen vials triggered a bioterrorism "plague scare" that prompted strong responses from the federal government. In April 2003, a grand jury indicted Dr. Butler on fifteen felony charges, including charges that Dr. Butler violated federal law on importing, exporting, and transporting plague bacteria, a select agent under U.S. law, without authorization or proper documentation. Dr. Butler testified that he had not been notified of the new federal regulations on select agents and had transported plague samples as he had always previously done in his research. Dr. Butler was found, however, to have the new regulations in his possession.

Federal prosecutors added more criminal charges in June 2003 related to the research contracts Dr. Butler had with pharmaceutical companies. In December 2003, a federal jury found Dr. Butler guilty on forty-seven of the sixty-nine total charges. Most of the guilty verdicts related to the research contracts, but the jury

---

dressed how to improve national mechanisms to establish and maintain the security and oversight of pathogenic agents and toxins. This objective also received attention in the debates that preceded the Sixth Review Conference (Biosafety and Biosecurity 2006), and BWC states parties agreed to dedicate one of the 2007 to 2010 intersessional meetings to this topic (BWC Sixth Review Conference Final Report 2006). Interpol is also interested in promoting better security for pathogenic agents and toxins (Interpol 2006b, 2006c).

2. Heightened Security for Research in the Biological Sciences

More controversies have emerged with respect to arguments that the government should increase regulation of more than the safety and security of select agents. Many experts believed that the approach informing the select agent approach is backward-looking because it focuses on traditional agents and toxins that state-based military programs explored during the Cold War. With the biological sciences rapidly changing and producing new techniques for manipulating microbial life, future threats could emerge from sophisticated

---

found Dr. Butler guilty of illegally exporting plague bacteria to Tanzania. Dr. Butler served two years in a federal prison in Texas. For full details on Dr. Butler's ordeal, see Mangels (2006a–g).

The arrest, prosecution, and conviction of Dr. Butler caused controversy in the scientific community because many scientists believed the federal government treated Dr. Butler unfairly to send a message to the scientific community about strict compliance with the select agent laws and regulations. The presidents of the National Academy of Sciences and the Institute of Medicine wrote in a letter to Attorney General John Ashcroft, "We are particularly concerned about the impact that Dr. Butler's case may have on other scientists who may be discouraged from embarking upon or continuing crucial bioterrorism-related scientific research—thereby adversely affecting the nation's ability to fully utilize such research capabilities in preparing defenses against possible bioterrorist attacks" (Alberts and Fineberg 2003). The *Wall Street Journal* reported, "Other scientists have cited the Butler case as one reason why they have declined to accept biodefense research work. They criticized the prosecution as overzealous given the raft of complex regulations intended to transform the relaxed atmosphere of university labs into secure biodefense facilities" (Piller 2003).

The missing vials of plague bacteria were never located. Dr. Butler concluded that he must have autoclaved them.

pathogenic manipulation. The Committee on Advances in Technology and the Prevention of Their Application to Next Generation Biowarfare Threats (2006, 160) argued, for example, that the potential for novel threat agents

> does mandate the need to adopt a broader perspective in assessing the threat, focusing not on a narrow list of pathogens, but a much wider spectrum that also includes biologically active chemical agents. The potential threat spectrum is thus exceptionally broad and continuously evolving—in some predictably, in other ways unexpectedly. The viruses, microbes, and toxins listed as "select agents" and on which our biodefense research and development activities are so strongly focused today are just one aspect of this changing landscape of threats. Although some of them may be the most accessible or apparent threat agents to a potential attacker, . . . this situation is likely to change as a result of the increasing globalization and international dispersion of the most cutting-edge aspect of life sciences research.

The expansion of the potential threat spectrum raises hard questions for biosecurity policy. Should governments regulate certain kinds of manipulation of microorganisms? Should regulation include government authority to preclude specific kinds of experiments or publication of certain research? Or, should the scientific community be left to self-regulate to ensure that government interventions do not prevent scientists from exploring the new horizons created by the progress of the biological sciences?

On these questions, a clash of cultures has been evident. The security community's traditional preference is to exercise strong authority vis-à-vis potential threats and keep secret information that may provide an advantage to the enemy. The culture of researchers has historically embraced maximum freedom to innovate and explore and open, transparent dissemination of research findings as critical to the scientific enterprise. The lack of people with training in the biological sciences in the national security arena compounds the culture clash.

The debate about scientific freedom and innovation against the new backdrop of biosecurity has been heated and vigorous. Recommendations from panels and expert groups tend to support open, transparent, and free scientific research and publications, but recommendations often also acknowledge the national security concerns that exist. For example, the Committee on Advances in Technology and the Prevention of Their Application to Next Generation Biowarfare Threats (2006, 162) endorsed "policies and practices that, to the maximum extent possible, promote the free and open exchange of information in the life sciences." The Committee (2006, 162) further recommended, "The results of fundamental research remain unrestricted except in cases where national security requires classification." These statements from an eminent panel of experts capture the balancing act between promoting science and protecting security. As indicated earlier, the normative question today is not whether to engage in this balancing act but how to engage in it effectively.

In many respects, the challenges presented by this biosecurity balancing act resemble challenges found in other policy areas that require calibrating competing interests. For example, governments may think they need to restrict the enjoyment of a civil or political right to maintain social order or national security. The onus to justify the restriction falls on the government, which must satisfy substantive and procedural tests to infringe on the right in question. In other words, the default position is full enjoyment of the right, and the government has to provide legitimate reasons why full enjoyment of the right is not appropriate. A key substantive test is whether the right-restricting measure is the least restrictive measure possible. Procedurally, due process and transparency are critical tests applied to government actions that impinge on individual rights.

These tests are not specific to any particular problem but form a "rule of law" template for the case-by-case analysis that characterizes calibration of human rights and national security. The supervision of the biological sciences for security and public health calls for a similar template for biosecurity. The default position is that research in the biological sciences should proceed unrestricted. Government-imposed constraints on such research must satisfy substantive and procedural criteria to be legitimate biosecurity measures.

Substantively, such constraints must be (1) aimed at preventing a severe and probable biosecurity threat; (2) scientifically valid and effective, in the sense that the measures are based on the most appropriate scientific understanding of the threats posed by the pathogens and research in question; and (3) the least restrictive of scientific research possible to achieve the biosecurity objective sought. Procedurally, biosecurity constraints on scientific research must (1) be transparent so that scientific researchers know in advance the criteria on which the government bases and applies the constraints, (2) provide due process to researchers affected by such constraints (e.g., opportunity to challenge the application of restrictions before a neutral decision maker), and (3) be applied in a nondiscriminatory manner.

The fulcrum for a rule of law approach to potentially dangerous scientific research is the criteria used to vet research experiments. Efforts at identifying scientific work that would raise red flags for biosecurity have been made. The Committee on Research Standards and Practices to Prevent the Destructive Application of Biotechnology identified seven classes of experiments that deserve review and discussion before they are undertaken or, if carried out, before results are published. These are experiments that would:

- Demonstrate how to render vaccine ineffective;
- Confer resistance to therapeutically useful antibiotics or antiviral agents;
- Enhance the virulence of a pathogen or render a nonpathogen virulent;
- Increase transmissibility of a pathogen;
- Alter the host range of a pathogen;
- Enable the evasion of diagnostic/detection modalities;
- Enable the weaponization of a biological agent or toxin (Fink Committee 2004).

A different approach to this problem categorized scientific activities in those of extreme, moderate, and potential concern (Steinbruner, Harris, Gallagher, and Okutani 2005 and 2007) (see box).

Concerns about potential dangers with scientific research have led to the U.S. government's establishment of a National Science Advisory Board for Biosecurity (NSABB) "to provide advice, guidance, and leadership regarding biosecurity oversight of dual use research, defined as biological research with legitimate scientific purpose that may be misused to pose a biologic threat to public health and/or national security" (NSABB Charter 2006, 1). NSABB is charged with recommending strategies for the efficient and effective oversight of federally conducted or supported dual use biological research (NSABB Charter 2006).

Whether applied through mandatory legislation by the government or self-regulation by scientific bodies, the entity applying the substantive oversight criteria would have to establish that restraints would be effective scientifically in preventing the harm perceived and were the least restrictive measures possible to address the potential danger the research posed. The reviewing body would also have to make sure (1) that the substantive criteria were transparent to researchers before restraints were imposed, (2) the researchers affected had

CONTROLLING DANGEROUS PATHOGENS PROJECT

Activities of Extreme Concern (AEC):

- Work with an eradicated agent*
- Work with agent assigned as BSL-4/ABSL-4
- De novo synthesis of above
- Expanding host range of agent to new host (in humans, other animals and plants) or changing the tissue range of a listed agent**
- Construction of antibiotic- or vaccine-resistant listed agent

Activities of Moderate Concern (AMC):

- Increasing virulence of listed agent or related agent
- Insertion of host genes into listed agent or related agent
- Increasing transmissibility or environmental stability of listed agent or related agent
- Powder or aerosol production of listed agent or related agent
- Powder or aerosol dispersal of listed agent or related agent
- De novo synthesis of listed agent or related agent
- Construction of antibiotic- or vaccine-resistant related agent
- Genome transfer, genome replacement, or cellular reconstitution of listed agent or related agent

Activities of Potential Concern (APC):

- Work with listed agent—or exempt avirulent, attenuated, or vaccine strain of a listed agent—not covered by AEC/AMC
- Increasing virulence of non-listed agent
- Increasing transmissibility or environmental stability of a non-listed agent
- Powder or aerosol production of a non-listed agent
- Powder or aerosol dispersal of non-listed agent
- De novo synthesis of non-listed agent
- Genome transfer, genome replacement, or cellular reconstitution of non-listed agent

* This would include, for example, activities with the 1918 influenza virus and chimeric influenza viruses with at least one gene from the 1918 influenza virus.

** This would include, for example, activities with chimeric influenza viruses with at least one gene from a human influenza virus and at least one gene from an avian influenza virus.

SOURCE: Steinbruner, Harris, Gallagher, and Okutani 2005 and 2007

the opportunity to challenge the imposition of restraints, and (3) the review and restraint process operated in a nondiscriminatory manner.

Chapter 6 fleshes out the importance of this kind of rule of law approach to biosecurity generally, but we believe that building such a template to guide supervision of science is critical for effectively integrating security and public health. As the story of Dr. Thomas Butler illustrates, a rule of law template is also critical given the criminalization trend. We do not claim that such a template always produces the "right" policy action or outcome. Calibrating competing interests in different policy areas almost inevitably involves difficult case-by-case decisions, and the template often does not decrease this difficulty, particularly in areas that involve guesswork about what may or may not happen in the future. The template offers, however, a framework for ensuring that calibration of security concerns and scientific innovation, freedom, and dissemination is substantively balanced and procedurally transparent and fair.

Approaching the supervision of science through a rule of law template highlights, however, globalization, a factor that complicates effective calibration of security and science. Globalization's impact on the biological sciences means that the security-science balancing act cannot be confined to a single state or small group of countries but must be global in scope. The challenge of globalizing governance for biosecurity raises its head.

B. Balancing Security and Science in the Globalized Hot Zone

However much the U.S. government might like to bring the culture of security to bear on the biological sciences in the United States, the effort's prospects look shaky because unilateral approaches prove problematical or even quixotic in a globalized world. Regulation of the biological sciences faces the same challenge of globalizing governance as did the criminalization of biological weapons development and use. The challenge may, however, be more difficult with respect to the regulation of the biological sciences than it has proved with respect to criminalization.

The BWC would, again, be a starting point for thinking about a global regime for regulating the biological sciences. As with criminalization, the BWC's obligation for states parties to take any necessary measures to prohibit and prevent the development, production, stockpiling, acquisition, or retention of biological weapons (Article IV) is general and is not a blueprint for the complex security-science balancing challenge. Further, the BWC process did not generate concentrated attention on securing dangerous pathogens and toxins from theft and malevolent diversion within states parties until after the collapse of the BWC Protocol effort (Salerno and Estes 2003).

The Security Council advanced the regulation agenda by mandating in Resolution 1540 that UN members establish domestic controls to prevent the proliferation of weapons of mass destruction (see box). Resolution 1540 highlights not only the criminalization trend but also the security-science regulatory trend. The same problems identified earlier with respect to Resolution 1540 and criminalization (e.g., whether the Security Council will vet UN member compliance with Resolution 1540's mandate) appear again with respect to the regulation of the biological sciences, but perhaps in orders of

---

PARAGRAPH 3 OF UN SECURITY COUNCIL RESOLUTION 1540

"*The Security Council, . . . Acting* under Chapter VII of the Charter of the United Nations, . . .

3. *Decides also* that all States shall take and enforce effective measures to establish domestic controls to prevent the proliferation of nuclear, chemical, or biological weapons and their means of delivery, including by establishing appropriate controls over related materials and to this end shall:

    (a) Develop and maintain appropriate effective measures to account for and secure such items in production, use, storage or transport;

    (b) Develop and maintain appropriate effective physical protection measures;

    (c) Develop and maintain appropriate effective border controls and law enforcement efforts to detect, deter, prevent and combat, including through international cooperation where necessary, the illicit trafficking and brokering in such items in accordance with their national legal authorities and legislation and consistent with international law;

    (d) Establish, develop, review and maintain appropriate effective national export and trans-shipment controls over such items, including appropriate laws and regulations to control export, transit, trans-shipment and re-export and controls on providing funds and services related to such export and trans-shipment such as financing, and transporting that would contribute to proliferation, as well as establishing end-user controls; and establishing and enforcing appropriate criminal or civil penalties for violations of such export control laws and regulations[.]"

---

magnitude greater given the scope of matters implicated by calibrating the needs of security and science.

Another approach outside the BWC context experts have suggested is the negotiation of a biosecurity convention that would attempt to harmonize how states regulate the security of biological agents and toxins within their respective territories. Under one proposal for an international biosecurity agreement, the treaty "should include three basic elements: a legal commitment by the contracting parties; agreed principles for developing progressively higher standards with respect to regulation and licensing of microbial culture collections; and mechanisms for oversight and progressive refinement by each member-state through its national legislative process" (Barletta, Sands, and Tucker 2002). More specifically, this proposal envisioned the treaty would require states parties to:

- Identify pathogens and toxins of potential biowarfare and terrorism concern and to create national registers of culture collections containing these agents, as well as genetically modified and engineered strains containing virulence factors and toxin genes transferred from the registered pathogens or toxins;
- Establish international standards to account for and secure registered pathogens and toxins;
- Pass domestic legislation to impose licensing and import/export controls over registered pathogens and toxins, and to create regulatory agencies to implement the licensing and controls;
- Cooperate with other states parties in implementing the agreed international standards on safety and security and in establishing regulatory authorities;
- To comply with the convention's international safety and security standards within five years;
- To report at regular conferences of the states parties on the operation of their domestic regulatory systems and to respond to other countries' questions regarding compliance;
- Create a small staff in the UN Department of Disarmament Affairs to organize the review conferences and facilitate implementation; and
- To end all commerce and scientific exchanges involving biotechnology with any State that does not join the convention within five years of its entry into force (Barletta, Sands, and Tucker 2002).

As the criminalization trend indicates, many countries will find themselves involved in criminalizing biological weapons development and use, even when they do not believe that biological weapons represent the serious security threat that other countries do. The international dissonance on what threat biological weapons pose is an obstacle to harmonized national approaches to the regulation of the biological sciences. At present, the Security Council has ordered all UN members to strengthen their regulatory frameworks in ways that will affect the biological sciences. Yet, many countries may not view that obligation as a duty to replicate the intensive, expensive, and scaled-up regulatory system the United States has put in place. The U.S. approach may provide incentives for other countries to attract scientific researchers and funding by imposing fewer and less onerous restrictions on the conduct of biological research. U.S. scientists have raised the concern that "stringent mandatory oversight would become so onerous that . . . much of the research would move overseas to countries where such oversight would be considerably weaker or nonexistent" (Kahn 2007). The United States could lose its edge in the biological sciences and achieve little in terms of improving its biosecurity in an environment where the biological sciences are globalized and beyond the control of any single country or small group of like-minded governments.

The globalization challenge to harmonizing national laws on the supervision of science for biosecurity has encouraged approaches that operate outside the traditional box of national legal implementation of obligations contained in arms control treaties. One prominent nontraditional approach is the formulation of "codes of conduct" for persons working in the biological sciences. According to Somerville and Atlas (2005), controversies arose after September 11th "concerning what research should and should not be conducted and what information should and should not be disseminated in the open literature. That dialogue has generated calls for a code or codes of conduct to provide guidance for scientists, publishers, and others facing extremely difficult decisions in the contest of the dual-use dilemma." The role that codes of conduct for scientists could play in addressing the threat of biological weapons use and proliferation has featured in many forums, including the BWC "New Process" agenda, suggesting that it has become part of the discourse on future biosecurity policy (see box). The Sixth Review Conference supports this conclusion because it included in the 2007 to 2010 intersessional meetings the topic, "Oversight, education, awareness raising, and adoption and/or development of codes of conduct with the aim to prevent misuse in the context of

CODE OF ETHICS FOR THE LIFE SCIENCES

"All persons and institutions engaged in any aspect of the life sciences must

1. Work to ensure that their discoveries and knowledge do no harm (i) by refusing to engage in any research that is intended to facilitate or that has a high probability of being used to facilitate bioterrorism or biowarfare; and (ii) by never knowingly or recklessly contributing to development, production, or acquisition of microbial or other biological agents or toxins, whatever their origin or method of production, of types or in quantities that cannot be justified on the basis that they are necessary for prophylactic, protective, therapeutic, or other peaceful purposes.

2. Work for ethical and beneficent advancement, development, and use of scientific knowledge.

3. Call to the attention of the public, or appropriate authorities, activities (including unethical research) that there are reasonable grounds to believe are likely to contribute to bioterrorism or biowarfare.

4. Seek to allow access to biological agents that could be used as biological weapons only to individuals for whom there are reasonable grounds to believe that they will not misuse them.

5. Seek to restrict dissemination of dual-use information and knowledge to those who need to know in cases where there are reasonable grounds to believe that the information or knowledge could be readily misused through bioterrorism or biowarfare.

6. Subject research activities to ethics and safety reviews and monitoring to ensure that (i) legitimate benefits are being sought and that they outweigh the risks and harms; and (ii) involvement of human or animal subjects is ethical and essential for carrying out highly important research.

7. Abide by laws and regulations that apply to the conduct of science unless to do so would be unethical and recognize a responsibility to work through societal institutions to change laws and regulations that conflict with ethics.

8. Recognize, without penalty, all persons' rights of conscientious objection to participation in research that they consider ethically or morally objectionable.

9. Faithfully transmit this code and the ethical principles upon which it is based to all who are or may become engaged in the conduct of science."

SOURCE: Somerville and Atlas 2005. Reprinted with permission from AAAS.

advances in bio-science and bio-technology research with the potential of use for purposes prohibited by the Convention" (BWC Sixth Review Conference Final Report 2006, 22).

The code of conduct approach is interesting from a governance perspective because it constitutes an attempt to respond to challenges globalization presents to harmonization of national laws and policies on the supervision of the biological sciences. As argued earlier with respect to the trends of criminalization and regulation of the biological sciences, the world may not achieve governance harmonization through governmental action alone. The code of conduct strategy seeks to make scientists, in their individual and collective capacities, active participants in biosecurity governance. A vigilant and global community of scientists can support Security Council resolution, treaties, and national laws and supplement these traditional mechanisms with heightened ethical and professional sensibilities about their biosecurity responsibilities.

The code of conduct approach embraces the need for global governance because it directly involves non-state actors governing public and private behavior that may produce biological weapons threats. No proponents of codes of conducts believe that such codes represent a "silver bullet" for the challenge of supervising science for biosecurity. Codes of conduct will not, without formal governmental action, be sufficient. The reverse also appears to be true: Historical experience with national implementation of the BWC indicates that formal governmental action is necessary but not sufficient to reduce the threat biological weapons present.

V. MANAGING THE BIODEFENSE IMPERATIVE

A. Biodefense's New Policy Importance

The third trend that characterizes the new world of biological weapons governance is the rise in policy importance of biodefense activities. Biodefense involves research activities undertaken with biological agents and toxins to understand the threat weaponized pathogens present and to develop protective, defensive countermeasures (e.g., vaccines, antibiotics, protective equipment, sensors). Biodefense is not, of course, a new feature of efforts to address the biological weapons threat. The BWC recognizes, for example, the legitimacy of defensive research (Article I). After the BWC's entry into force, the only legitimate military research on biological agents and toxins permitted was defensive. The policy importance of biodefense has, however, changed in the past ten years, especially in the United States, in light of the

changing nature of biological weapons threats. This change has been controversial and has profound significance for the new world of biological weapons
governance. Many factors have converged to increase the policy profile of
biodefense, but three factors stand out. These factors combine to produce the
"biodefense imperative"—a strong pull for states to re-engage more robustly
with biodefense strategies and activities.

First, the BWC's travails in the 1990s put the spotlight on biodefense activities. The shock caused by the revelations of the former Soviet and Iraqi programs raised interest in more vigorous biodefense activities against potential
"breakout" states. Second, fears about terrorist interest in biological weapons,
exacerbated by the globalization of the biological sciences, again drew policy
makers back toward reinvigorating biodefense. This element was especially
pronounced in the United States, which suffered the anthrax attacks in October
2001 on the heels of the September 11th tragedy. Third, the difficulties of trying
to improve international responses to the new biological weapons threats made
self-help strategies involving biodefense more appealing. The election of an administration in the United States skeptical of, and sometimes hostile to, international regimes that restricted U.S. power helped deepen the attractiveness of
unilateral biodefense initiatives. We examine each factor in more detail later.

The development of new policy significance for biodefense reflects perceived changes in the nature of the threat posed by biological weapons. The
behavior of the former Soviet Union and Iraq, and the potential interest of
terrorists in biological weapons, suggested that the political or military motivations of traditional and nontraditional actors with respect to biological
weapons did not fit the Cold War experience. The perception that technologi-

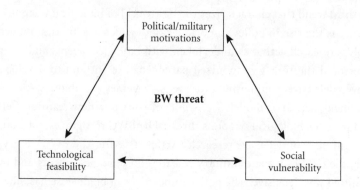

Figure 3.2 Biological Weapons Threat Profile

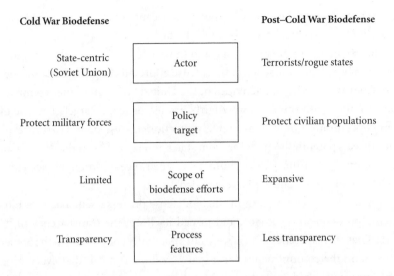

Cold War Biodefense		Post–Cold War Biodefense
State-centric (Soviet Union)	Actor	Terrorists/rogue states
Protect military forces	Policy target	Protect civilian populations
Limited	Scope of biodefense efforts	Expansive
Transparency	Process features	Less transparency

Figure 3.3 Changes in Biodefense from the Cold War to the Post–Cold War Context

cal and scientific advances were making biological weapons easier to contemplate and construct fed into concerns about the motivations of rogue states and terrorist groups.

Finally, the shifts in political/military motivations of state and non-state actors and the technological feasibility of biological weapons also highlighted another concern policy makers developed—the vulnerability of civilian populations to biological attacks. The interdependency of these factors produced a biological weapons profile very different from what prevailed during the Cold War. See Figure 3.2.

This threat profile has, in turn, produced shifts in aspects of policy from the Cold War context, specifically the actors targeted, the scope of policy objectives, the extent of biodefense activities, and certain features of the biodefense enterprise. See Figure 3.3. During the Cold War, biodefense activities were focused against state actors. For the United States, the state-centric focus meant worrying about the Soviet Union. Today, the actors of concern have changed to the point where "rogue states" and terrorists generate the greatest fears rather than geopolitical great power competitors.

Similarly, change is apparent in the objectives of biodefense work. In the Cold War, the primary objective was to protect military forces from biological attack. Protecting the civilian population of the United States was not a strategic goal of the U.S. biodefense program. Policy objectives today involve, however, protecting the civilian population because of awareness of the vulnerability that societies have to biological attacks.

The expanded number of actors, and the concerns about civilian populations, has broadened the scope of biodefense efforts in the post–Cold War period. Cold War biodefense activities in the United States and other countries that complied with the BWC were fairly limited in scope, largely because of their concentration on military force protection against state-based threats. With threats potentially emerging from states and terrorists, and with civilian populations and military forces vulnerable, the range of protective activities biodefense needs to consider has expanded.

A final change can be seen in the biodefense process itself. The U.S. biodefense program worked hard, and prided itself on, the transparency of its work. These transparency efforts were not apparently convincing to the Soviet Union, and the commitment to transparency did not mean that everything done was unclassified. Nevertheless, transparency was an important principle of U.S. biodefense work after renunciation of offensive biological weapons capabilities. The post–Cold War context has raised concerns about the importance of, and commitment to, transparency. As discussed later, pressure developed to move toward less transparency and more secrecy with respect to biodefense work.

The level of transparency of biodefense programs has become one of the hottest controversies in contemporary biosecurity policy, as illustrated by the issues raised during the legislative process that created the Biomedical Advanced Research and Development Authority in the United States. In the Biodefense and Pandemic Vaccine and Drug Development Act (Senate Bill 1873), U.S. senators proposed creating a Biomedical Advanced Research and Development Agency (BARDA) as part of efforts to speed development of new vaccines and drugs for urgent public health threats and the possible use of biological weapons by terrorists. This legislation attempted to fix problems associated with Project BioShield (e.g., the inadequacy of incentives for pharmaceutical companies to invest in research and development of such countermeasures), but aspects of the BARDA proposal generated significant controversy.

Under the proposed legislation, BARDA's mission was to coordinate and oversee activities that support and accelerate the development of countermeasures to disease threats. The bill exempted BARDA from the Freedom of Information Act (FOIA), Federal Advisory Committee Act (FACA), and some

Federal Acquisition Regulations (FAR). The bill's FOIA exemption stated that only the BARDA Director or the Secretary of Health and Human Services could authorize disclosure of information about BARDA activities, and such determination was not subject to judicial review (S. 1873, §3).

The move toward secrecy already detected in military biodefense programs seemed, in the form of the BARDA exemption, to affect civilian research and development on biodefense sponsored by the federal government. Nongovernmental organizations criticized these proposed exemptions, which would allow BARDA to operate without transparency and thus shield it from effective oversight. The Project on Government Oversight (2005) argued that the proposed legislation "makes oversight and accountability of much of America's biodefense efforts nearly impossible."

In December 2006, Congress adopted the Pandemic and All-Hazards Preparedness Act, which established the BARDA. The act did not contain the controversial provisions found in the original legislation, largely as a result of criticisms those provisions provoked. The act applied FOIA to BARDA but created the authority for the government to withhold from disclosure under FOIA "specific technical data or scientific information that is created or obtained during the countermeasure and product advanced research and development carried out under [this Act] that reveals significant and not otherwise publicly known vulnerabilities of existing medical or public health defenses against biological, chemical, nuclear, or radiological threats" (§401). The episode revealed the importance and controversy surrounding transparency in U.S. biodefense activities.

B. Biodefense and the BWC: Back to Bio-Deterrence?

The new context in which biodefense takes place today raises questions concerning the BWC. Some questions relate to the BWC's relevance to concerns about potential bioterrorism (explored later), but many continue to relate to the BWC's traditional focus on states. The continued importance of state-based proliferation of biological weapons finds expression, for example, in President George W. Bush's administration's accusations that the behavior of various countries (China, Cuba, Iran, North Korea, Russia, and Syria) creates BWC compliance concerns.

As noted earlier, revelations about the size, scale, and significance of the former Soviet and Iraqi programs in the early 1990s created a crisis for the BWC. The crisis led to a multilateral process to strengthen the BWC. The shock waves of the crisis also raised deeper questions about whether the BWC could really be an effective regime against state and non-state proliferation of biological weapons in the world dawning after the end of the Cold War. The intensity of these questions increased as technical and political problems bogged down negotiations on the BWC Protocol (see Chapter 2).

With the feasibility of strengthening the BWC in serious contention well before the Bush administration came to power, more traditional incentives concerning possible state-based proliferation of biological weapons emerged. In the period between the Geneva Protocol and the BWC's adoption, states deterred each other from using biological weapons by developing biological weapons capabilities and defenses. A state with bio-deterrence capability could, it was hoped, avoid being surprised by the sudden break out of rival states in the area of biological weapons. With the discovery of the dangerous former Soviet and Iraqi programs, would the United States put all its eggs in the BWC basket (even reinforced by a verification protocol) to prevent future state-based threats? Or would re-invigorating biodefense activities be a more prudent strategy to mitigate vulnerabilities to state-based proliferation of biological weapons, especially in a context where rapidly changing science and technology and the "dual use" problem make verification with BWC prohibitions increasingly difficult?

These questions suggest a rationale for the development of a new kind of bio-deterrence achieved through scaled-up biodefense activities. The new bio-deterrence would not involve stockpiling biological weapons, or even weaponizing biological agents or toxins. The deterrence would arise in keeping a state's knowledge of, and capabilities in, biological weapons at the frontiers of possibilities. The new bio-deterrence would be deterrence based on prowess in cutting-edge biological weapons capabilities rather than actual arsenals.

The BWC was designed to end the old bio-deterrence system by prohibiting states from developing, stockpiling, acquiring, or retaining biological weapons. The new bio-deterrence places great stress on the BWC because states parties can slot their activities into the protective purpose permitted by the BWC. A U.S. biodefense project undertaken in the 1990s, which went under the code name Clear Vision, revealed the stress such biodefense activities create for the BWC. Worried by the efforts of the former Soviet Union and Iraq, the CIA attempted to replicate a biological weapon—a bio-bomblet—the Soviets had allegedly developed to disseminate anthrax (Miller, Engelberg, and Broad 2001). The objective was to see whether the Soviets had, in fact, created a more efficient way of disseminating anthrax. The United States had no intention of creating a stockpile of such munitions. It wanted, however, to understand better where the "learning curve" of adversaries (e.g., Iraq potentially aided by defectors from the Soviet biological weapons program) had taken their potential capabilities.

Debates about Clear Vision's legality under the BWC occurred while the project was underway and after press reports in 2001 revealed its existence. Defenders of Clear Vision argued that the project was legitimate defensive research permitted by the BWC. Critics believed that Clear Vision raised serious questions about U.S. compliance because the United States had developed a weapon designed to use anthrax for hostile purposes in violation of Article I of the BWC.

The essence of the controversy involved the scope of biodefense activities the BWC permits. On one side of the argument stood experts and government officials who argued that, as long as the intent of the research was defensive, then it complied with the BWC. After all, the BWC itself uses intent as a key element in distinguishing legitimate from illegitimate biological research. On the other side of the controversy, people argued that the "defensive intent" thesis was not the proper interpretation of the BWC and was a position the United States would reject if made by countries hostile to the United States suspected of engaging in biological weapons research.

Ambitions to use the broad interpretation of defensive intent created problems for application of the BWC and complicated efforts to bolster the BWC through a verification protocol. Countries, such as the United States, interested in more robust biodefense programs in light of the changed nature of the threat were concerned that a BWC Protocol could unduly interfere with such activities. Moves by the United States to water down or weaken the BWC Protocol to protect reinvigorated biodefense efforts caused friction with the negotiations' objective of tightening the regime to enforce the BWC's prohibitions. The policy pull of increased biodefense activities complicated the BWC Protocol negotiations and ultimately formed part of the Bush administration's reasoning for opposing the Protocol.

The Clear Vision controversy illustrated the pull policy makers in the United States felt toward more aggressive biodefense efforts in the wake of the revelations about the former Soviet and Iraqi programs. Clear Vision demonstrated that this pull was strong in the United States before September 11th and the anthrax attacks. In other words, the dynamics leading to more interest in expanded biodefense activities are deeper than the politics of the Bush administration. September 11th and the anthrax attacks have only increased the willingness of policy makers in the United States to be aggressive on biodefense, as the next section examines.

C. Biodefense and Bioterrorism

The story of the increased importance of biodefense would be incomplete without considering the policy impact of bioterrorism. The intensification of interest in, and expansion of, biodefense activities in the United States from the 1990s onward owes much of its existence to the potential for terrorists to commit biological attacks against the United States. These concerns played no role in the attention biodefense received during the Cold War because bioterrorism was not a threat. We have already analyzed how fears about bioterrorism have shaped the trends of the criminalization of biological weapons development and use and the regulation of the biological sciences, and the specter of bioterrorism also emerges as a key driver in the politics that expanded U.S. biodefense activities in the past decade.

"Forward leaning" biodefense activities with respect to bioterrorism began before September 11th and the anthrax attacks, which illustrates again that this trend is not specific to the Bush administration. The latter half of the 1990s was filled with warnings, reports, analyses, and predictions about the threat of bioterrorism. These concerns presented states with challenges the Cold War biodefense system was not designed to handle. At the same time the U.S. government worried about what exactly the former Soviet and Iraqi biological weapons programs had achieved, experts pondered the nature of the bioterrorist threat. What could terrorists interested in biological weapons accomplish?

During the Clinton administration, the U.S. biodefense program undertook a project code named Bacchus (or BACUS), which tasked personnel to acquire on the open market or otherwise the materials necessary to build a device that could effectively disseminate biological agents or toxins (Miller, Engelberg, and Broad 2001). Part of the project's purpose was to see how easily non-state actors could assemble weapons, equipment, or means of delivery designed to use biological agents or toxins for hostile purposes.

Like Clear Vision, public disclosure by the press of Bacchus' existence caused controversy with respect to its compatibility with U.S. obligations under the BWC. The arguments for and against the activities undertaken in this project mirror those made for and against Clear Vision. The potential threat from bioterrorism encouraged policy makers in the United States to think more expansively about what the BWC permitted under defensive research.

Other developments fed into this shift in biodefense. During the Cold War, biodefense programs did not, by and large, worry about biological attacks perpetrated by non-state actors. Biodefense remained embedded in a state-centric political dynamic. With the rise of the "new terrorism" in the 1990s and its potential convergence with weapons of mass destruction (WMD), the rationality of state-centric politics no longer helped in determining parameters for biodefense. Neither the intent nor the capabilities of most terrorist groups in the WMD area was understood by intelligence agencies of the major powers. Most experts agreed that relying on deterrence would not be prudent in dealing with terrorists interested in biological weapons. Nor did the moral or legal strictures of the Geneva Protocol or the BWC seem reliable bulwarks against non-state actors' interest in microbial malevolence. With the traditional instruments of Cold War biosecurity—deterrence and arms control treaties—inapplicable to the bioterrorist threat, national biodefense activities were an attractive alternative.

Another development contributed to the rise of biodefense concerning the terrorist threat. The progress and global dissemination of the biological sciences were potentially making powerful scientific capabilities more accessible to terrorist groups. As noted earlier, this progress did not mean that making biological weapons had become child's play. Experts were, however, concerned that developments were iteratively lowering—and would continue to lower—the technical barriers that made bioweaponeering difficult for states during the Cold War. These concerns gravitated toward seeing expanded biodefense efforts as a way to figure out what future biological threats from terrorists might emerge.

Another example of a secret U.S. biodefense project, revealed publicly in 2001, helps bring this issue into focus. Project Jefferson involved efforts by the U.S. Department of Defense to genetically engineer vaccine-resistant anthrax (Miller, Engelberg, and Broad 2001). The United States believed this effort was defensive because it allowed the United States to see whether hostile states or terrorist groups could use genetic engineering technologies to defeat existing countermeasures, in this case the anthrax vaccine. The former Soviet biological weapons program attempted to genetically engineer traditional biological weapons agents to make them more potent and dangerous. The terrorist threat combined with the increasing power of biotechnologies raised the possibility that non-state actors might develop similar capabilities. The United States, the argument went, needed to engage in "threat assessment" research to understand the cutting-edge of potential malevolent use of microbes and not just concentrate on how the biological weapons threat presented itself during the Cold War.

Experts worried that the terrorism-biotechnology axis had motivated the United States to proceed down a biodefense path that (1) obliterated traditional understandings of "offensive" and "defensive" biological weapons research, and (2) embraced secrecy rather than the transparency that had prevailed in U.S. biodefense since the early 1970s. Critics raised concerns about the legality and prudence of this approach and argued that the United States was allowing hyped-up fears about bioterrorism, rather than hardheaded threat assessments, to guide biodefense policy. Criticisms also identified the "Pandora's Box" danger—U.S. biodefense research into cutting-edge possibilities could lead to those possibilities becoming capabilities in the wrong hands. The United States would, thus, be creating the very danger it feared.

Other concerns focused on the corrosive effect more aggressive and secretive biodefense research would have on the BWC. Trends in U.S. biodefense policy generated questions about U.S. compliance with the BWC. In addition, the United States had always viewed moves by adversary states toward more expansive but secretive research on biological agents and toxins as danger signs. The United States would never accept a justification by these states that the research was legitimate under the BWC because the intent was defensive. Why should other states worried about U.S. biodefense accept U.S. assurances that the intent was purely defensive?

Defenders of the trends in U.S. biodefense emphasized that the nature of the threat, particularly the potential terrorist use of new biotechnologies, was radically different from what existed during the Cold War. Particularly important to this argument was the appreciation that intelligence information on what capabilities hostile states or terrorists might have in the area of biological weapons was extremely difficult to collect and was getting increasingly so with the global ubiquity of biotechnology knowledge and expertise. The "dual use" dilemma not only rendered arms control notions of verification unworkable but also exacerbated the traditional threat-based approach to defensive strategies that relied on intelligence assessments of an adversary's actual capabilities.

Given this reality, the argument continues, U.S. biodefense activities should incorporate capabilities-based approaches to threat assessment (e.g., what threats could the enemy develop?) to compliment conventional methodologies (e.g., what threat capabilities does the enemy possess?). Capabilities-based approaches, proponents argued, offer U.S. biodefense better ways to think through what countermeasures and other defensive strategies would best protect the country from biological attack.

D. Biodefense and U.S. Hegemony

The moves the United States has made toward more robust biodefense has affected the BWC and multilateral approaches to biosecurity more generally. Those who encourage the current trends in U.S. biodefense interpret the BWC's prohibitions narrowly and the right to engage in protective or defensive research broadly. This interpretation runs counter to BWC proponents, who argue that the BWC's prohibitions need to be applied broadly and its permitted purposes interpreted narrowly. This debate echoes the controversy over the relative breadths of the prohibition on the use of force and the right to use force in self-defense in international law. The Bush administration's doctrine on preemptive self-defense expanded the scope of the right to use force in self-defense and, correspondingly, narrowed the prohibition on the use of force (White House 2002). The international legal arguments about what the BWC requires and allows, and what the rules on the use force are, reflect larger dynamics in international relations that connect to the U.S. status as the global hegemon.

After the Cold War, the United States emerged as the lone superpower politically, economically, and militarily. Constraints the United States faced in its competition with the Soviet Union disappeared, and the United States flexed its hegemonic muscle to reshape the world to better suit its interests and values. This hegemonic power has allowed the United States to move without serious constraints or opposition from other countries toward more vigorous biodefense. The United States perceived that its interests and values were increasingly threatened by the convergence of forces creating the new context for biological weapons proliferation and use. This trend began during President Bill Clinton's administration and continued more strongly under President George W. Bush, so the trend is more deeply rooted in the dynamics of contemporary international relations than in the specific policies of a single administration. In other words, a simple change of presidential administrations in the United States will not take biosecurity policy back to the *status quo ante,* whatever that might be. The biodefense imperative has become a more permanent fixture in the new world of biological weapons governance.

E. The Biodefense Imperative and the Challenges of Biosecurity

The controversies U.S. biodefense actions have caused illustrate the impact the biodefense imperative has on biosecurity policy and governance. Although much of the concern about the increased importance of biodefense relates to the BWC, this development's relevance extends beyond this treaty. For example, the biodefense imperative has implications for criminalization of biological weapons and regulation of the biological sciences. Expanding the range of biodefense activities cordons these activities off from criminal sanction. The biodefense imperative carves out, therefore, a zone in which the thrust of the criminalization movement in biosecurity governance has no application. This impact does not gut the criminalization trend's significance, but it reveals tensions between this trend and the biodefense imperative.

Similar tensions appear between the biodefense imperative and the trend toward regulation of the biological sciences. As noted earlier, transparency will be key to making heightened regulation of the biological sciences work in a way that balances security and science interests. The biodefense imperative has, to date, moved toward secrecy rather than transparency. Secrecy over a more expansive range of scientific research conducted for biodefense may create negative externalities for the effort to scale up regulation of biological research outside biodefense programs. The biodefense imperative complicates, therefore, the need to supervise science for security and public health, which is a key biosecurity challenge for the twenty-first century.

The biodefense imperative also carries the potential to affect adversely the need to integrate security and public health, globalize governance, and embed biosecurity in the rule of law. Expanded biodefense activities could, if not properly controlled and overseen, produce real problems where only imagined threats existed before. This outcome would mean security fears have made matters potentially worse for public health, an outcome that would hardly qualify as integrating security and public health.

The unilateralism of the U.S. biodefense effort also suggests that the biodefense imperative complicates the need to create globalized governance mechanisms for biosecurity. In fact, the logic of the biodefense imperative appears to be that states cannot rely for their security on international and global governance of the threat of biological weapons. The secrecy that emerges with the biodefense imperative raises problems for a rule of law approach to biosecurity because of the importance of transparency and accountability to the rule of law philosophy of governance (see Chapter 6).

As we argued earlier, the biodefense imperative is strong for deep, structural reasons that do not depend on the ideological outlook of a particular U.S. presidential administration. Shaping this imperative into less of a problem for biosecurity governance will be a key policy task in the future. Three critical aspects of this task are (1) moving away from hypothetical capabilities-based threat assessment (e.g., what capabilities could my enemy develop?) toward less speculative threat assessment methodologies; (2) developing more sophisticated intelligence gathering and analysis about trends in the biological sciences that may present biosecurity problems, and (3) crafting greater oversight and transparency for biodefense activities.

VI. RESPONDING TO BIOLOGICAL ATTACK: PUBLIC HEALTH AS A NATIONAL SECURITY ASSET

The fourth trend to characterize the changed nature of policy concerning biological weapons involves the need to prepare for, and respond to, biological weapons attacks. Under the strategy of bio-deterrence, states did not spend time, energy, or funds preparing to respond to the actual use of biological weapons by their enemies. As Chapter 4 explores, national security concerns about biological weapons never translated into public health actions at home or abroad to prepare for biological attacks. The absence of biological warfare between states in the post-World War II period reinforced the lack of policy interest in public health preparedness and response to biological attacks.

The last decade has, however, witnessed growing policy interest in, and action on, preparing societies for responding to biological weapons attacks. Much of this governance trend flows from the worry that neither bio-deterrence nor the BWC has any direct effect on terrorists interested in biological weapons. With bio-deterrence and arms control fragile, governments had to think about the unthinkable—the actual use of biological weapons against their societies. As noted earlier, policy makers in the 1990s began to realize the vulnerability of their societies to such attacks. The shock of the anthrax attacks, and the U.S. government's less than stellar response, reinforced the need to focus on preparing to respond to biological attacks.

This need made a nation's public health system critical for national and homeland security. Integration of public health preparedness into strategies for national and homeland security in the United States represented unprecedented policy moves for both security and public health. This development forms part of the larger biosecurity challenge of integrating security and public health, and Part II of this book looks at the relationship between biosecurity and public health in terms of naturally occurring infectious diseases as well as biological weapons. The policy actions taken to elevate the security importance of public health deserve, however, to be mentioned here because they form part of the new world of biological weapons governance.

The unprecedented nature of making public health a security concern has not meant, however, that improving public health preparedness for biological attacks has been uncontroversial. Controversies have erupted in the United States with respect to specific actions and to the general direction of preparedness and response policy. For example, the Bush administration's plan to vaccinate public health and health care personnel for smallpox as a preparedness measure against a possible smallpox attack failed badly.

On December 13, 2002, President Bush announced a national smallpox vaccination program involving U.S. military personnel and certain civilian workers in health care, public health, and emergency services. The program was "a case study at the intersection of public health and national security, two fields brought together by the threat of bioterrorism" (Committee on Smallpox Vaccination Program Implementation 2005, 1). The program sought to vaccinate 500,000 military personnel and 500,000 specified civilians rapidly. The target for the military was exceeded (with approximately 600,000 military personnel vaccinated), but the program only vaccinated about 39,000 civilians. By the time the program effectively ended in June 2003, it was largely considered a failure.

Difficulties plagued the smallpox vaccination program from its inception. The decision to proceed with the program was controversial from a public health perspective because the main advisory committee on immunization had recommended against smallpox vaccination. Potential civilian vaccinees avoided the program because of fears of the vaccine's well-known potential side effects. Initially, the federal government had no compensation plan in place for those adversely affected by the smallpox vaccine. Experts also faulted poor communication between national security, public health, and affected civilian institutions for the poor civilian response to the program. Failure of the federal government to explain clearly the rationale for the program and its strategy also produced poor results among civilians. The timing of the vaccination program and the launch of the invasion of Iraq in March 2003 raised further skepticism about the motivations behind the program.

The smallpox vaccination program's travails revealed a failure to integrate security and public health effectively. The program privileged security over public health and marginalized input from public health officials in favor of non-transparent national security decisions made by executive branch officials. After thorough review of the program, the Committee on Smallpox Vaccination Program Implementation (2005, 6) concluded, "A policy strategy and mechanism are needed to balance the need for scientific evidence and public health analysis with the imperatives of national security, ensuring in the process that the authoritative voice of the CDC, the nation's public health leader, will be preserved."

Problems also arose with U.S. efforts to increase the availability of medical countermeasures developed for responses to bioterrorist attacks. Proposed in 2003 by President Bush, and enacted into law in 2004 by Congress, the $5.6 billion Project BioShield was intended to increase the number of medical countermeasures available to respond to biological attacks. Project BioShield was the most prominent preparedness and response initiative taken by the federal government, but it has stumbled from problem to controversy since its inception. The pharmaceutical and biotechnology industries have complained that Project BioShield does not provide adequate incentives and protection for companies to invest in developing countermeasures for biological weapons. Public health experts have criticized Project BioShield for focusing too heavily on medical technologies and not sufficiently on basic public health infrastructure improvements. The most significant Project BioShield program—the purchase of 75 million doses of anthrax vaccine—ran into trouble because the manufacturer could not meet the November 2006 contractual deadline for delivery. In April 2006, the Bush administration admitted that Project BioShield had not made sufficient progress, lacked a strategic plan, and required reorganization within the Department of Health and Human Services (Gillis 2006).

The failure of the smallpox vaccination program and the travails of Project BioShield provide some indication of the difficulties public health preparedness and response actions face in light of the biological weapons threat. The question is not whether to make preparedness and response a biosecurity priority but, rather, involves deciding the most effective way to achieve this objective. Chapter 4 examines in more detail the challenge of turning public health into an effective security asset.

VII. THE BWC AMIDST THE FOUR GOVERNANCE TRENDS

Earlier in this chapter we argued that primary reliance on the BWC's arms control approach for governing the problem of biological weapons was dead. The detailed analysis of the four trends that characterize the new world of biological weapons governance revealed how each trend shows state and non-state actors reaching beyond the traditional arms control approach for governance ideas and initiatives. Although much of this new governance world reflects the BWC's weaknesses, the BWC has not vanished and continues to be the object of efforts to improve and strengthen it. Understanding these efforts is important to developing a comprehensive perspective on the new world of biological weapons governance, and this section highlights how experts believe BWC states parties can improve this treaty's contribution to biosecurity.

The lead-up to the BWC's Sixth Review Conference in November and December 2006 revealed both anxiety and optimism about the BWC's future. On the one hand, the collapse of the BWC Protocol negotiations and suspension of the Fifth Review Conference in 2001 continued to cast shadows over thinking about ways to strengthen the BWC. On the other hand, the perceived success of the New Process agenda created some optimism about what states parties could achieve at the Sixth Review Conference. We describe ideas promoted before the Sixth Review Conference, analyze them against the four governance trends explored earlier in this chapter, and then consider what actually transpired at the Sixth Review Conference.

A. Proposals to Strengthen the BWC Made Before the Sixth Review Conference

Verification and investigation. Although support for reviving negotiations on a BWC verification protocol was occasionally voiced after the failure of the BWC Protocol negotiations (UN Secretary-General's High-level Panel 2004), most experts agreed that no serious initiative to revive the protocol idea would emerge at the Sixth Review Conference. The preparatory meeting for the Sixth Review Conference held in Japan in February 2006 revealed consensus (however reluctant) among states parties that revival of a verification or inspection regime as contemplated with the BWC Protocol was not feasible. More broadly, Littlewood (2005, 232) concluded, "When one considers the negotiations on the BWC Protocol together with the developments in international politics from 1991 through the present day the fundamental lesson for the Convention is a simple one: there will be no BWC Protocol."

Instead of focusing on a legally binding protocol, some proposals sought to strengthen the power and capabilities of the UN Security Council to investigate unusual infectious disease outbreaks (UN Secretary-General's High-level Panel 2004; Weapons of Mass Destruction Commission 2006). These proposals built on the role the BWC gives the Security Council in investigating complaints made by states parties about alleged breaches of the Convention (Article VI) by suggesting, among other things, the creation of permanent investigatory capacity within the UN that the Security Council could use to investigate suspicious infectious disease events. (See box for the BWC-specific recommendations of the Weapons of Mass Destruction Commission 2006.)

Enhanced transparency of information. Other recommendations for the Sixth Review Conference concentrated on the need to improve transparency of information important to biosecurity among BWC states parties, particularly information related to biodefense research. These approaches often focused on the need to improve the voluntary confidence-building measures (CBMs) first adopted by BWC states parties in 1986 and revised and expanded in 1991. The CBMs sought to facilitate exchange of certain types of information that would reduce or prevent suspicions or ambiguities concerning states parties' compliance with the BWC. See Table 3.1 for the types of information covered by the CBMs. Interest in upgrading the CBMs was particularly strong given

Table 3.1 Confidence-Building Measures for the BWC

Confidence-Building Measure	Description
CBM A	Part 1: Exchange of data on research centers and laboratories Part 2: Exchange of information on national biological defense research and development programs
CBM B	Exchange of information on outbreaks of infectious diseases and similar occurrences caused by toxin
CBM C	Encouragement of publication of results and promotion of use of knowledge
CBM D	Active promotion of contacts (e.g., planned international conferences, symposia, seminars, and other similar forums for exchange)
CBM E	Declaration of legislation, regulations, and other measures
CBM F	Declaration of past activities in offensive or defensive biological research and development programs
CBM G	Declaration of vaccine production facilities
Declaration Form	"Nothing to declare" or "Nothing new to declare"

SOURCE: Background Information Document on the History and Operation of the Confidence-Building Measures 2006.

the consensus that states parties were unlikely to adopt formal verification, compliance, or investigatory mechanisms at the Sixth Review Conference.

Universalizing membership in the BWC. A frequent pre–Sixth Review Conference recommendation for strengthening the BWC was to increase the number of BWC states parties to achieve universal membership. As of September 2006, the BWC had 155 states parties, with a further 16 states having signed but not ratified the treaty, leaving 24 states that have neither signed nor ratified the BWC (Background Information Document on Status of Universality of the Convention 2006, 1). Universalization proposals drew inspiration from the action plan implemented under the Chemical Weapons Convention (CWC) in 2003 to increase the CWC's membership, which succeeded in adding 33 new states parties to produce, by September 2006, a total of 179 states parties. Some experts believed that a similar concerted effort under the BWC could move the treaty toward universal membership, an effort the Sixth Review Conference could authorize.

RECOMMENDATIONS ON BIOLOGICAL AND TOXIN WEAPONS FROM THE WEAPONS OF MASS DESTRUCTION COMMISSION

"31. All states not yet party to the Biological and Toxin Weapons Convention should adhere to the Convention. The states parties to the Convention should launch a campaign to achieve universal adherence by the time of the Seventh Review Conference, to be held in 2011.

32. To achieve universal adoption of national legislation and regulations to implement the Biological and Toxin Weapons Convention completely and effectively, the states parties should offer technical assistance and promote best-practice models of such legislation. As a part of the confidence-building process and to promote transparency and harmonization, all states parties should make annual biological-weapon-related national declarations and make them public.

33. States parties to the Biological and Toxin Weapons Convention should enhance the investigatory powers of the UN Secretary-General, ensuring that the Secretary-General's office can rely upon a regularly updated roster of experts and advice from the World Health Organization and a specialist unit, modelled on the United Nations Monitoring, Verification and Inspection Commission, to assist in investigating unusual outbreaks of disease and allegations of the use of biological weapons.

34. States parties to the Biological and Toxin Weapons Convention should establish a standing secretariat to handle organizational and administrative matters related to the treaty, such as Review Conferences and expert meetings.

Improving national implementation. Many experts viewed the Sixth Review Conference as an opportunity to adopt new strategies to improve national implementation of BWC obligations. Proposals recognized not only the past problems with national implementation but also the additional attention created by the New Process agenda's meeting on national implementation in 2003, Security Council Resolution 1540, and Interpol's growing interest in biological terrorism and biological crimes. Leading up to the Sixth Review Conference, there was "widespread recognition . . . among BWC members that much more can and must be done to improve national implementation, especially in light of new concerns about bioterrorism" (Center for Arms Control and Non-Proliferation 2006).

Strengthening national measures on safety and security of pathogenic agents and toxins. Related to recommendations for improving national implementation were strategies that focused on ways to strengthen national measures on the safe and secure handling of potentially dangerous biological agents and

---

35. Governments should pursue public health surveillance to ensure effective monitoring of unusual outbreaks of disease and develop practical methods of coordinating international responses to any major event that might involve bioweapons. They should strengthen cooperation between civilian health and security-oriented authorities, nationally, regionally and worldwide, including in the framework of the new International Health Regulations of the World Health Organization. Governments should also review their national biosafety and biosecurity measures to protect health and the environment from the release of biological and toxin materials. They should harmonize national biosecurity standards.

36. At the Sixth Review Conference, in 2006, the states parties to the Biological and Toxin Weapons Convention should reaffirm common understandings reached at previous review conferences and take action on all subjects addressed at Convention meetings since 2003. They should also establish a work programme on additional topics for future meetings. States parties should ensure more frequent reassessment of the implications of scientific and technological developments and reaffirm that all undertakings under Article I of the Biological and Toxin Weapons Convention apply to such developments. The Review Conference should reaffirm that all developments in the life sciences fall within the scope of the Convention and that all developments in the life sciences for hostile purposes are prohibited by the Convention."

SOURCE: Weapons of Mass Destruction Commission 2006, 197–198

toxins. As with national implementing legislation generally, a number of developments converged to highlight the importance of better safety and security regulations for sensitive biological materials, including the New Process agenda's meeting in 2003 on security and oversight of pathogenic microorganisms and toxins, Security Council Resolution 1540, and Interpol's work on biological terrorism and biological crimes. These activities helped reveal that, in this area, "the number of States that have implemented respective legislative and other measures seems surprisingly small" (Biosafety and Biosecurity 2006, 4).

Addressing the challenges of scientific and technological developments. Another set of proposals for strengthening the BWC at the Sixth Review Conference recognized the challenges the rapid developments in science and technology posed for the BWC. One prominent recommendation argued for the establishment of an independent scientific advisory board to advise BWC states parties on developments in the biological sciences that could affect the BWC. According to the Center for Arms Control and Non-Proliferation (2006),

> Such a body could regularly assess and provide advice on the implications of scientific and technological developments for biological weapons control efforts and the BWC. More ambitiously, it could help resolve the tension between the need for members to effectively demonstrate compliance with the norm and the prohibitions of the BWC and their need to maintain legitimate secrecy of some biodefense activities, and address the difficult issue of governance of the life sciences and biotechnology.

Enhancing public health preparedness and response capabilities. The importance of using the BWC process to promote efforts to enhance public health preparedness and response was another recurring theme in discussions about the Sixth Review Conference. The New Process agenda focused on two aspects of this theme, namely (1) strengthening international capabilities for responding to, investigating, and mitigating the consequences of the alleged use of biological weapons or suspicious disease outbreaks, and (2) improving national and international efforts and mechanisms for the surveillance, detection, diagnosis, and combating infectious diseases affecting humans, animals, and plants. Focusing on public health preparedness and response capabilities offered a way for states parties to find common ground on the often contentious Article X of the BWC, which stresses the importance of international cooperation on peaceful uses of science and biotechnology.

Institutionalizing the BWC process. Many experts argued that the Sixth Review Conference should provide the BWC process with more institutional mechanisms and support. Two prominent ideas in this area were (1) convening annual meetings of states parties to address important issues and promote better and more effective common action, and (2) establishing permanent institutional capabilities to facilitate achievement of goals set by BWC states parties (e.g., universalization, improved national implementation, etc.).

The desire for more frequent meetings of BWC states parties reflected a sense that five-year review conferences were not sufficient for states parties to handle the scope and speed of the challenges confronting the BWC in the early twenty-first century. In addition, the generally positive reaction of states parties to the New Process agenda's meetings from 2003 to 2005 stimulated interest in institutionalizing an intersessional strategy. Annual meetings, combined with pursuit of other BWC-enhancing strategies, would create the need for administrative and institutional support dedicated to handling the growing BWC workload. Thus, before the Sixth Review Conference, support grew among states parties and nongovernmental experts for some type of institutional support mechanism for the BWC.

B. Pre-Conference Proposals and Trends in Biological Weapons Governance

Although designed to strengthen the BWC, the various proposals described earlier actually reveal how much the four governance trends described in this chapter affect the context in which the BWC operates. As noted earlier, Security Council Resolution 1540 (2004) advanced the criminalization of biological weapons development and use by focusing on the threat of WMD proliferation by non-state actors. With respect to this threat, Resolution 1540 achieved universal application because, under the UN Charter (Article 25), it is legally binding on all UN members. Universalizing BWC membership would, therefore, merely get the BWC to the point the Security Council already reached under international law with respect to prohibiting and preventing biological weapons development and use by non-state actors.

These observations do not mean that universalizing BWC membership is a bad idea; indeed, even Resolution 1540 called upon states to promote the BWC's universal adoption. The trend toward criminalization of biological weapons development and use supported by Resolution 1540 and other activities outside the BWC (e.g., Interpol's efforts on biological terrorism) indicated, however, that raising the number of BWC states parties was an inadequate response to the pressing challenges facing biosecurity policy. In addition, universalization proposals for the Sixth Review Conference typically did not discuss problems with existing state party behavior, such as weak national implementation and the dismal performance of states parties concerning CBMs. Why would new states parties behave any better than the existing ones? Nor did these proposals address the lack of incentives the BWC process provides for nonparties, virtually all of which are developing or least-developed countries, to join. Indeed, the obligations and scrutiny imposed by Resolution 1540 may reduce a nonparty state's willingness to accept the demands of the BWC.

The proposals related to establishment of an independent scientific advisory board and more attention on safety and security measures related to the conduct of research with biological agents and toxins reflected the governance trend toward heightened supervision of the biological sciences. As noted earlier, the BWC process never really focused on such supervision, but the emphasis on it before the Sixth Review Conference indicated how the BWC process was trying to catch up with biosecurity governance developments happening outside the BWC.

One prominent proposal concerning the need for heightened awareness of developments in the biological sciences came from the UN Secretary-General. In April 2006, the UN Secretary-General (2006a, ¶57) proposed establishing of a forum to bring together diverse public and private stakeholders "into a common programme, built from the bottom up, to ensure that biotechnology's advances are used for the public good and that the benefits are shared equitably around the world." Although the Secretary-General favored strengthening the BWC, he argued that measures beyond the BWC were needed to address threats posed by non-state actors. In his speech to the Sixth Review Conference, the Secretary-General (2006b, 1–2) argued that "developments have transformed the environment in which the Convention operates, and altered ideas about its role and potential," meaning that "we must look at it [the BWC] as part of an interlinked array of tools, designed to deal with an interlinked array of problems."

This argument reinforced the message in Resolution 1540—that the BWC could not adequately address the problem of bioterrorism and must be supplemented by other governance mechanisms. The UN Secretary-General believed the UN was the proper institution to host the proposed forum. The clear and express message was that the BWC was not the best place in which to address the most pressing scientific and technological matters facing biosecurity policy in the early twenty-first century.

Proposals suggesting new mechanisms within the UN to investigate suspicious outbreaks or ways to strengthen the CBM process within the BWC reflected the trend toward more robust biodefense activities, particularly in the United States. Here again, the BWC process was responding to events affecting biosecurity rather than shaping the governance agenda. Increased state interest in more secretive biodefense predictably stimulated calls for more transparency through strengthened CBMs.

Experts saw room for improvement in the CBM process, particularly because (1) most states parties never submitted adequate CBMs (Enhancement of the Confidence-Building Measure (CBM) Process 2006), indicating how little value they placed in this process, and (2) the CBMs failed to adapt to the challenges posed by rapid developments in the biological sciences (Center for Arms Control and Non-Proliferation 2006). Significant strengthening of the CBM process or adoption of other transparency-enhancing strategies at the Sixth Review Conference faced, however, the expected opposition of the United States and other countries interested in more robust biodefense research. The strength of the biodefense imperative as a trend in biosecurity governance would make transparency enhancements within the BWC process difficult to achieve at the Sixth Review Conference.

Finally, proposals that integrated global disease surveillance and other aspects of public health preparedness and response into the BWC process reflected the governance trend that emphasized public health capabilities as essential biosecurity assets. The BWC process did not produce this governance trend, but, starting with the New Process agenda's sessions on aspects of public health preparedness and response, BWC states parties began to consider ways to strengthen and broaden national and international efforts on surveillance, detection, diagnosis, and combating infectious diseases. Recommendations that the Sixth Review Conference continue to integrate public health preparedness and response efforts into the BWC process reflected the process' need to adjust to transformative developments in biosecurity governance.

The proposals concerning institutionalizing the BWC process through intersessional meetings and a dedicated institutional support mechanism clearly attempted to take the BWC out of its traditional modus operandi. As historically structured, the BWC process could not handle the challenges generated by the transformations in biosecurity governance. With trends in biosecurity governance bringing more issues and actors into this policy realm (Secretariat Background Information Document 2006), the BWC process faced competitive pressures to stay relevant and to interface with new initiatives and players. It could not successfully transition into the new world of biological weapons governance without broadening its agenda, increasing the frequency of its deliberations, and connecting itself to other endeavors to improve national and global biosecurity. This reality helps explain the logic of proposals to have intersessional meetings between the Sixth Review Conference in 2006 and the Seventh Review Conference in 2011 and to establish a permanent institutional support mechanism.

C. Outcome of the Sixth Review Conference in 2006

On December 8, 2006, the Sixth Review Conference issued its Final Report, which contained the Conference's Final Declaration and the decisions and recommendations it reached. The main achievements of the Sixth Review Conference were the following:

- Completing an article-by-article review of the BWC, the first time BWC states parties finished this task since the Fourth Review Conference in 1996
- Agreeing to promote universalization of the BWC
- Establishing intersessional meetings from 2007 to 2010 on specific topics of importance to the BWC
- Creating an Implementation Support Unit (ISU) to provide administrative support for the BWC and the CBMs

Although the president of the Sixth Review Conference and some states parties praised the outcome, more objective scrutiny reveals that the Sixth Review Conference did little to strengthen the BWC's contributions to biosecurity. The article-by-article review of the BWC was an important task, but the review produced no material changes in how states parties interpret or apply the BWC. On the positive side, Tucker (2007) highlighted that the states parties' rejected Russia's attempt to introduce an understanding concerning Article I that would have defined more specifically the types and quantities of biological agents and toxins permitted for purposes not prohibited by the BWC. Such an understanding would have broadened the scope of non-prohibited purposes and, according to Tucker (2007), "made the BWC easier to circumvent."

On the negative side, the article-by-article review did nothing to ease controversies created by the obligations in the BWC. Most prominently, the long-standing tension between developed and developing states parties over the relationship between obligations to prevent transfer of agents or technologies that might contribute to the development of biological weapons (Article III) and the obligations to facilitate exchange of information, materials, and technology for peaceful purposes (Article X) seriously strained the negotiations. In fact, this problem prevented the Sixth Review Conference from agreeing to an action plan for improved national implementation. Thus, unresolved problems between states parties about key treaty provisions scuttled ambitions to address one of the most pressing weaknesses of the BWC—national implementation of fundamental BWC obligations. Instead of a detailed action plan, the states parties agree to include the topic of improving national implementation in the new intersessional program scheduled for 2007 to 2010.

The Sixth Review Conference's decision to promote universalization of BWC membership represents agreement to pluck the lowest hanging of the pre–Conference ideas for strengthening the BWC. Universalizing the BWC's membership was noncontroversial but also largely anticlimatic and nonconsequential. The decision was anticlimatic because, as argued earlier, Security Council Resolution 1540 had already universalized legal commitments that overlapped significantly with key BWC obligations. The governance trends toward criminalization, supervision of science, and public health preparedness and response will continue globally with or without universal membership in the BWC.

The decision was non-consequential because it did nothing to change the most serious problems plaguing the treaty, such as noncompliance, failure to implement BWC obligations in national legislation, lack of participation in the CBM process, non-transparency in biodefense activities, the rift among states parties concerning tensions between BWC's nonproliferation obligations and its duties regarding peaceful cooperation in the biological sciences and biotechnologies, and initiatives and activities outside the BWC that increasingly make the Convention marginal to biosecurity policy.

The most significant decision taken at the Sixth Review Governance was establishment of the intersessional meetings from 2007 to 2010. Despite the dismal atmosphere in which they were designed, and the limitations with which they were saddled, the New Agenda process meetings from 2003 to 2005 proved more effective and helpful than many states parties and experts expected. This perception reinforced the belief that five-year review conferences and yearly (but usually inadequate) CBM submissions were not enough for the BWC process to stay connected with the speed and scale of change affecting the governance of biological weapons. Intersessional meetings of states parties, supplemented by input from associated meetings nongovernmental experts, will give the BWC process some limited opportunities to assess issues and challenges more frequently than every five years. The intersessional meetings also provide an opportunity for the BWC process to be a magnet for other international organizations involved in, and initiatives addressing, biosecurity problems.

The topics and dates for the 2007 through 2010 intersessional meetings are listed in Table 3.2. As with the New Process agenda, these topics reinforce three of the four governance trends described earlier in this chapter, and underscore how the BWC has to respond constructively to these trends. The meetings in 2007 on implementation flow directly into the criminalization trend. The 2008 sessions connect with the movement toward heightened supervision of the biological sciences and biotechnologies. The 2009 and 2010 meetings will address issues of public health preparedness and response. The intersessional process will have administrative support from the ISU established by the Sixth Review Conference (see more later).

The intersessional meetings decision is not, however, without drawbacks. First, as with the New Process agenda sessions, states parties cannot take

Table 3.2 BWC Intersessional Meetings, 2007–2010

Year	Topic
2007	• Ways and means to enhance national implementation, including enforcement of national legislation, strengthening of national institutions, and coordination among national law enforcement institutions. • Regional and subregional cooperation on BWC implementation.
2008	• National, regional, and international measures to improve biosafety and biosecurity, including laboratory safety and security of pathogens and toxins. • Oversight, education, awareness raising, and adoption and/or development of codes of conduct with the aim to prevent misuse in the context of advances in bioscience and biotechnology research with the potential of use for purposes prohibited by the Convention.
2009	With a view to enhancing international cooperation, assistance, and exchange in biological sciences and technology for peaceful purposes, promoting capacity building in the fields of disease surveillance, detection, diagnosis, and containment of infectious diseases: (1) for states parties in need of assistance, identifying requirements and requests for capacity enhancement, and (2) from states parties in a position to do so, and international organizations, opportunities for providing assistance related to these fields.
2010	Provision of assistance and coordination with relevant organizations upon request by any state party in the case of alleged use of biological or toxin weapons, including improving national capabilities for disease surveillance, detection and diagnosis, and public health systems.

SOURCE: BWC Sixth Review Conference Final Report 2006, 22

binding decisions during the new intersessional meetings. This approach concerned Tucker (2007) because "the intersessional process will once again be limited to exchanges of information, and any decisions will have to await the Seventh Review Conference in 2011. This pace of work is simply too slow to cope with the urgency of the biological weapons threat."

Second, the topics not selected for intersessional meetings are as revealing as the issues chosen. Matters at the heart of the BWC are not on the intersessional agenda, including strengthening mechanisms to investigate suspected noncompliance, creating ways to verify compliance, improving transparency of biodefense endeavors, enhancing the CBM process, and reconciling tensions between nonproliferation and peaceful cooperation objectives. The list of topics not subject to intersessional scrutiny reflects the impact of the fourth trend we have identified, the biodefense imperative. At the Sixth Review Conference, the United States refused to allow the Conference to address in any serious way ideas or mechanisms that could pose difficulties for its expanded biodefense activities (Pearson 2006; Tucker 2007). Other countries, including Russia and China, also opposed having the intersessional meetings address issues such as stronger CBMs that would focus heightened attention on biodefense research (Meier 2007).

The final affirmative decision of the Sixth Review Conference to highlight is the creation of the ISU. As observed earlier, many pre–Conference proposals favored institutionalizing the BWC process through intersessional meetings and the establishment of a support mechanism or technical secretariat. In addition to the intersessional meetings, the Sixth Review Conference created the ISU, an administrative support mechanism made up of three staff members within the UN Department of Disarmament Affairs in Geneva. The ISU's mandate is limited to providing administrative support to the intersessional meetings, the program on universalizing BWC membership, and the CBM process.

The Sixth Review Conference significantly constrained the ISU's scope of operations not only in the small number of tasks assigned but also in the nature of the tasks. First, as argued earlier, universalization of BWC membership is not a cutting-edge strategy for reviving the BWC's role in the governance of biological weapons. The ISU will be administratively supporting one of the least important issues facing the BWC.

Second, the Sixth Review Conference did nothing to strengthen the CBM process, which was recognized well before the Conference as inadequate and ineffective as a transparency mechanism. In fact, the states parties agreed to make the CBM process less transparent. First, the Sixth Review Conference ordered the ISU to develop electronic CBM forms for use by states parties. Second, the ISU has to develop a password-protected Internet site where completed electronic CBM forms "shall, with the consent of the State party submitting them, be posted on a secure Internet site and made available for the use of States Parties" (BWC Sixth Review Conference Final Report 2006, 23). Presumably, states parties can submit electronic CBMs and refuse to have them posted on the secret Internet site.

Only states parties have access to those electronic CBMs that submitting states parties consent to be put on the Internet site. The ISU may not circulate CBMs to any other person or entity without the express permission of the states parties that submitted the CBMs in question. Nongovernmental organizations interested in tracking CBMs will, in the future, have to rely on information voluntarily made public by states parties or released from the secret Internet site by express permission of the states parties concerned.

For a process that most states parties could not be bothered to use frequently or adequately, the Sixth Review Conference went to some trouble to make this voluntary and marginalized process less helpful for purposes of increasing transparency of information relevant to the BWC. Keep in mind too that the Sixth Review Conference did not change the substantive nature of the CBM process at all. For example, the Conference did not update the CBMs to account for significant changes in science and technology since 1991, when the states parties last revised the CBMs. At the end of the day, the ISU will provide administrative support to an outdated, nonbinding, neglected, and non-transparent mechanism ostensibly designed to increase confidence in state party compliance with the BWC. We can forgive those concerned with biological weapons problems who do not applaud the Sixth Review Conference on this outcome.

D. Concluding Thoughts on the Sixth Review Conference

Before the Sixth Review Conference, Kellman (2006a, 235) asked a question and made a prediction. He asked, "The only question of significance is whether the RevCon will make even a marginal contribution to reducing dangers associated with biological weapons." He predicted,

> At the RevCon, diplomats will no doubt assert that they are doing everything possible to meet this threat. These assertions will be disingenuous half-truths,

deluding all of us about where security may be found and how to get there. The more complete truth is that little will be done in Geneva to ensure security from intentionally inflicted disease[.]

Kellman's question and prediction point a harsh light on what the Sixth Review Conference accomplished. For us, this harsh light supports our argument that continued primary reliance on the BWC's arms control approach as a strategy for governing the problem of biological weapons is dead. Whatever spin one puts on the outcome of the Sixth Review Conference, the impact of the governance trends analyzed in this chapter are clear, and this clarity should help us understand that the BWC's future in biosecurity policy will be different from its troubled past. Just how different remains to be determined.

VIII. CONCLUSION

This chapter argued that the structure and dynamics of governing biological weapons that developed during the twentieth century—the combination of arms control treaties and bio-deterrence—no longer control policy responses to the threats posed by biological weapons. Instead, the last decade has seen four trends develop that now characterize biosecurity policy with respect to biological weapons: criminalization of biological weapons development and use, regulation of the biological sciences, expansion of biodefense activities, and public health preparations for responding to biological attacks. These trends, we believe, will continue to mark governance responses to biological weapons in the next few decades, as our analysis of the Sixth Review Conference illustrates.

In analyzing these four trends in this chapter, we do not claim that they fit together in a cohesive governance approach. The trends share some features, such as each trend's assumption that the BWC, in its current form, is not sufficient to achieve biosecurity with respect to the diversity of threats biological weapons pose today. Each trend represents a different policy move to shore up aspects of biosecurity that the BWC simply cannot deliver in its present condition.

In addition, the trends affect and influence each other, but not always in ways that produce policy synergies. We noted how criminalization of biological weapons development and use requires heightened regulation of activities involving biological agents and toxins, and this requirement joins these two trends at the hip. The criminalization/regulation joint venture places new pressures on, and creates new difficulties for, peaceful research and development activities involving the biological sciences.

The biodefense imperative sits uneasily, however, with the criminalization, regulation, and public health preparedness trends. Criminalization seeks more clarity with respect to what constitutes legitimate and illegitimate activities involving biological agents and toxins. The expansion of biodefense activities in the United States seeks to enlarge the space for what is defensive research, which blurs the line criminalization would like to draw more starkly. The reinvigorated biodefense activities both feed and weaken the trend toward regulating activities in the biological sciences. On the one hand, biodefense strengthens the desire to regulate and control research to ensure that dangerous pathogens and scientific techniques are properly secure and will not fall into the wrong hands. On the other hand, the biodefense imperative is keen on increasing secrecy in biodefense activities, which undermines the transparency and oversight a regulatory framework provides. Scaled-up biodefense research and development may also pose problems for public health preparedness if such research and development hampers efforts to improve public health infrastructures (see Chapter 5).

More generally, the four trends of the new world of biological weapons governance highlight the four major policy challenges affecting biosecurity. The criminalization trend directly connects to the biosecurity tasks of supervising science for security purposes, globalizing biosecurity governance, and embedding biosecurity in the rule of law. Criminalization's need for strengthened regulation puts supervision of the biological sciences in a new policy environment, and balancing the interests and rights of scientific researchers with the government's interest in security makes the criminalization/regulation joint venture a rule of law priority. The outcome of how science is supervised for security purposes could also affect, perhaps adversely, public health, which connects criminalization and regulation to the challenge of finding the best way to integrate security with public health. We also noted how both the criminalization and regulation trends confronted difficulties created by globalization, which shines the spotlight on not only the need to but also the difficulties of globalizing governance for biosecurity.

Biodefense affects all four challenges of biosecurity policy as well. Experts have asked whether increased biodefense activities provide an appropriate way to integrate security and public health needs. The biodefense interest in exploring the frontiers of biological weapons capabilities raises concerns about how such dangerous science will be properly supervised and controlled. The unilateralism in U.S. expanded biodefense efforts challenges those who argue that only by globalizing biosecurity through multilateral institutions can the United States and other states be more secure. Historically, the type of strong national security justifications used to defend the biodefense imperative have caused rule of law controversies, and allegations of violations of domestic and international law, combined with increasing levels of secrecy, ensure that the challenge of how to embed biosecurity in the rule of law remains firmly on the agenda.

How the four trends analyzed in this chapter play out among themselves, and how the trends affect resolution of the fundamental challenges of biosecurity policy, remains to be seen. The new world of biological weapons governance is still in its formative stages. The criminalization, regulation, biodefense, and preparedness trends all accept the evils that biological weapons proliferation and use represent and reveal intent to overcome these evils. Whether they mesh together to keep this faith alive in this new world is by no means certain. Sometimes the path to hell is paved with good intentions.

BIOSECURITY AND PUBLIC HEALTH   Part II

4 THE SECURITIZATION OF PUBLIC HEALTH

I. INTRODUCTION

Our definition of biosecurity—society's collective responsibility to safeguard the population from dangers presented by pathogenic microbes—asserts something that, conceptually and historically, is radical. This definition maintains that the policy worlds of public health and security are interdependent, and the definition connects to our arguments that integrating security and public health is central to biosecurity governance. But, as one of us previously observed, "In the not too distant past, attempts to connect public health and national security would have raised eyebrows and perhaps condescending sympathy from experts in both fields" (Fidler 2003a, 787). The emergence of biosecurity reveals that the days when public health and security never intersected as governance tasks have ended.

The convergence of security and public health has produced the "securitization of public health" (Kelle 2005a, 2005b). Securitization means that the theory and practice of public health are increasingly considered in security terms. Linking public health to different concepts of security became ubiquitous in the past decade, whether discourse focused on homeland, national, collective, global, or human security. These linkages revealed a widespread belief that securitizing public health was a productive strategy to achieve greater protection from pathogenic threats (Fidler 2007a). A critical aspect of the securitization process involved elevating public health as political priority in domestic governance, foreign policy, and international diplomacy.

The securitization phenomenon represents one of the most important policy shifts creating the new governance challenge of biosecurity. Part I of this book examined the transformation of governance approaches to biological weapons, and we identified public health preparedness and response as a key characteristic of the new world of biological weapons governance. As elaborated more later, the preparedness and response trend constitutes part of the securitization of public health. The securitization development extends, however, beyond the problem of biological weapons to include naturally occurring infectious diseases. The Pandemic and All-Hazards Preparedness Act adopted by the U.S. Congress in December 2006 provides a sense of the impact of the securitization idea. In this law, Congress mandated, for the first time in U.S. history, that the federal government prepare a National Health Security Strategy to guide improvement of the country's public health emergency preparedness and response capabilities. This and many other developments convince us that the securitization of public health deserves detailed consideration as a leading feature of biosecurity governance in the early twenty-first century. This chapter explores this unprecedented convergence of security and public health policy.

As analyzed later, two dangers have driven security and public health together—the threats posed by biological weapons and by naturally occurring infectious diseases. These threats, individually and collectively, have forced policy makers to understand the security significance of public health. This process affects public health in profound ways. The securitization of public health is not, however, simply a story of security transforming public health. The securitization process involves a feedback loop from public health to security. Understanding the security significance of public health has encouraged changes in how policy makers think about security. The characterization of naturally occurring infectious disease threats, such as pandemic influenza or HIV/AIDS, as security problems best illustrates this feedback. The securitization of public health means that neither security nor public health policy will ever be the same again.

The two-way dynamic resonates with a key message for policy makers: the need to improve public health infrastructures nationally and globally. The securitization of public health is, thus, normatively critical for effectively integrating security and public health in biosecurity governance.

The unprecedented nature of the securitization of public health has, however, raised controversy and opposition from traditionalists in both security and public health. Security skeptics often want security policy to remain narrowly focused on threats of physical violence from enemy states or terrorists. This approach excludes naturally occurring infectious diseases as a security threat. Public health traditionalists worry that securitization is a one-way street dominated by security considerations that will corrode public health's humanitarian mission of improving population and individual health.

The convergence of these previously unconnected policy pursuits has, therefore, not been smooth, and many questions remain unanswered. Addressing the security-public health relationship forms, however, part of the agenda of biosecurity now and in the years to come. The forces that produced the securitization of public health will continue to create challenges that require better, more effective integration of security and public health policies, particularly through scaled-up improvements of public health capabilities and resources.

We begin our analysis of the securitization of public health with an overview of public health because this policy area is often misunderstood by those not familiar with it. We analyze misperceptions about public health and focus on its key functions—surveillance and intervention. Next we explore the gap that existed historically between the policy worlds of security and public health. This background is needed to comprehend how revolutionary the linkage of public health and security is. This chapter examines the governance revolution that occurred when the policy worlds of security and public health collided. Finally, we consider the securitization of public health in light of the key challenges facing biosecurity policy. These considerations set up Chapter 5's analysis of the new world of public health governance.

II. OVERVIEW OF PUBLIC HEALTH

Understanding the new politics created by the securitization of public health requires grasping what "public health" means and what it entails. Our experiences working on public health issues make us aware that many people do not know what public health means conceptually or involves practically. Misunderstandings about public health largely relate to the neglect of, and complacency about, public health prevalent in most countries for the past few decades. This section describes, therefore, basic features of public health. We do not pretend that this overview captures all important features about public health, which has always been, and is increasingly becoming more, complex. This background is important for our later analysis of how the policy convergence between public health and security is unfolding.

A. Misperceptions About Public Health

As Garrett (2000) noted, many Americans think of public health as health care for poor people. Similarly, the perception that international health activities are merely humanitarian endeavors conceives of these activities as health for poor people in foreign countries. This perception is wrong at national and international levels for two reasons. First, public health focuses on population health rather than on the health needs of only part of a society. Public health activities serve rich and poor alike. The idea that public health is health care for poor people arises from a lost sense among the more affluent that public health directly affects their lives. In essence, public health's success in many countries has made it invisible to those who directly benefit from it. More visible is the health care system, through which physicians deliver medical care to individual patients.

Second, public health is not the same as medical professionals providing health care. Some of public health's most important functions, such as disease surveillance, do not involve health care services. In fact, delivery of health care often comes at the end of public health activities through interventions to prevent or contain a threat to population health. Delivery of health care without awareness of public health can itself be dangerous. For example, the public health problem of antimicrobial resistance develops partly because physicians prescribe antibiotics to individuals infected with viruses, against which antibiotics have no effect. The antibiotics provide the individual with no health benefit and stimulate development of drug-resistant bacteria, which complicate and make more expensive health care for those infected with resistant microbes.

Misperceptions about public health obscure not only its utility in human societies but also its relationship to social fairness, equity, and justice. Public health's population focus forces policy makers to look, literally, at the "big picture." Disease and health trends provide markers for how well governance systems fare in protecting their populations. Public health operates, in many ways, as a sentinel system for political, economic, and social problems that raise questions of equity, fairness, and justice. In short, public health is critical to realizing conceptions of the good society.

B. Public Health Infrastructure

Public health practitioners often refer to the "public health infrastructure" when discussing the systems they operate. This infrastructure contains the governance capabilities essential to protecting and promoting population health. For these objectives to be met, public health capabilities have to be robust in terms of detecting threats to population health and intervening to prevent, contain, or eliminate the threats. At its most basic, the public health infrastructure requires capabilities to conduct surveillance to identify disease threats and to mount interventions against them.

Public health infrastructure involves many components from both the public and private sectors. Private actors are important to achieving public health, and are increasingly so in a globalizing world. But, public health has historically been, and continues to be, predominantly a governmental and intergovernmental responsibility. Public health infrastructure has to be grounded, therefore, in public entities because private, non-state actors do not have sufficient incentives or resources to protect population health nationally or internationally. The convergence of security and public health accentuates the role of public bodies because both security and public health are quintessential "public goods."

Public goods are goods or services the use of which (1) is open to all (non-exclusive use), and (2) by one person does not prevent another person from also using the service or function simultaneously or later (non-rival use) (Kaul et al 2003a). Examples used to illustrate the public good concept are lighthouses for ships and traffic lights for cars. Security and public health have long been considered non-exclusive and non-rival in their respective usages, at least theoretically. One citizen cannot privatize the security provided by national defense policies; such security remains open to all and non-rival in the protection it affords the citizenry. Similarly, one person or a small group of people cannot appropriate or exhaust the health protection afforded by widespread immunization of the population against childhood diseases.

The public health infrastructure is made up of capabilities for surveillance and for interventions. Surveillance capabilities allow public authorities to know what health threats are affecting what parts of which populations. Intervention capabilities let public authorities act to prevent, protect, or contain disease threats to population health. As explored later, surveillance and intervention capabilities within a public health infrastructure are interdependent. To produce the public good of biosecurity, both capabilities are critical.

C. Surveillance and Intervention Capabilities

Without question, the most important public health function is surveillance. As defined by the Centers for Disease Control and Prevention (2001b,

2), "Public health surveillance is the ongoing, systematic collection, analysis, interpretation, and dissemination of data regarding a health-related event for use in public health action to reduce morbidity and mortality and to improve health." Preventing, containing, or eliminating disease threats are impossible if public authorities cannot recognize and act against threats in a timely manner. See Figure 4.1.

With threats identified, reported, and analyzed, public health officials can, if necessary, intervene against them. Public health involves three basic types of interventions. See Figure 4.2. First, interventions can prevent disease threats from affecting populations. The objective of these interventions is to prevent disease harms, such as pathogenic microbes, from reaching the population. An example of a prevention intervention is the treatment of water supplies to ensure that pathogens or other contaminants do not cause death and illness in a population. Eradication campaigns are also prevention interventions because successful eradication of a disease means that no one comes into contact with it. Thus, smallpox's global eradication in the late 1970s has prevented millions of people from being exposed to the smallpox virus and represents one of the most significant public health interventions in human history.

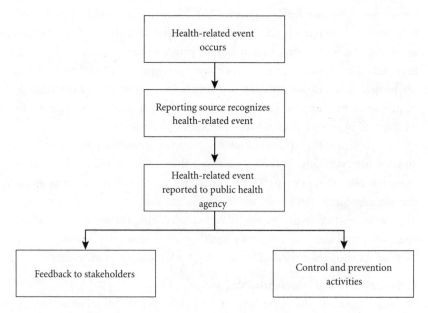

Figure 4.1 Steps in Public Health Surveillance System
SOURCE: CDC 2001B

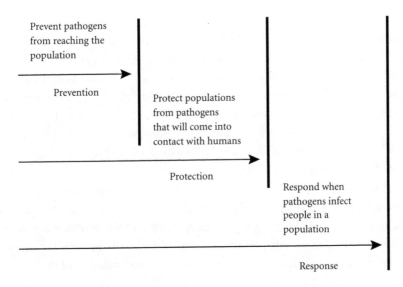

Figure 4.2 Three Intervention Strategies Concerning Pathogenic Microbes

Second, interventions can seek to protect people from pathogenic microbes with which they might come into contact. Protection interventions include something as simple as hand washing or as sophisticated as a vaccine. Hand washing is a tried-and-tested intervention that reduces the likelihood that a pathogen in the environment will infect the hand washer. For example, public health experts emphasize hand hygiene as a protection measure against pandemic influenza. Vaccination also represents a protection intervention because the vaccine affords the recipient protection against a pathogen (e.g., influenza virus) circulating in the community. Protection interventions in the context of HIV/AIDS include behavior change interventions, such as the promotion of abstinence and "safe sex." The premise of protection interventions is that people will come into contact with germs, but protection interventions "harden the target" against incoming microbes.

Third, response interventions occur when a pathogenic microbe infects a population, causing illness. Such interventions seek to contain infection by breaking the chain of transmission and to mitigate the infection's impact on victims and the population at large. Response interventions can involve complex technologies, such as antimicrobial drugs, or low-tech techniques, such as quarantine and isolation. Response interventions attempt to bring infection under control to provide the opportunity to undertake prevention and protection interventions in the future. Public health's goal is to try to make sure response interventions are needed as infrequently as possible.

These basic types of interventions are not mutually exclusive but may be used at different points in addressing a public health threat. Concerning severe acute respiratory syndrome (SARS), public health authorities first relied on response interventions (e.g., isolation, quarantine, clinical treatment of the infected). Subsequently, prevention interventions, such as prohibiting sales of animals suspected of hosting the SARS virus, helped keep the virus away from human populations. Finally, the search for a SARS vaccine represents an effort to develop a protection intervention. A different pattern emerged with HIV/AIDS, where, until the development of antiretroviral treatments, the emphasis was on behavior change concerning sexual practices, essentially a protection intervention. Prevention interventions were not feasible in the absence of a vaccine, and response interventions were limited until the advent of antiretroviral drugs.

Even this description of surveillance and intervention suggests that their effective application requires a significant commitment of trained personnel, economic resources, and sustained political understanding of the societal importance of public health. Together, such personnel, resources, and commitment constitute the infrastructure critical to public health. Further, the infrastructure's components are interdependent. Weak surveillance will undermine the effectiveness of any type of intervention. Likewise, inadequate intervention capacities will squander the benefits of information provided by a surveillance system. Weak or waning political support for public health will have a debilitating effect on the quality and sustainability of surveillance and intervention capabilities.

III. DISTANT STRANGERS: PUBLIC HEALTH AND SECURITY IN NATIONAL AND INTERNATIONAL POLITICS

The coming together of public health and security in the last decade challenged traditional conceptualizations of these previously distant policy pursuits. To appreciate how radical the securitization of public health is, some background on their traditional places in national and international politics proves helpful. We explore both theoretical and policy reasons why security and public health were, until the last decade, distant strangers in national and international politics.

A. Theories Apart: Security and Public Health
   in Foreign Policy and International Relations

One way to explain the difference between the importance accorded security and the neglect of public health is to explore how the study of foreign policy and international relations has viewed these policy areas. Students of foreign policy and international relations have long considered a state's security to fall within the realm of "high politics"—that category of state interests that constitutes the most important and vital aspect of national and international politics. National and international security have been prominent in efforts to understand domestic and international politics, both theoretically and historically.

By contrast, the study of foreign policy and international relations has largely ignored public health (Kickbusch 2003; Lee and Zwi 2003). To the extent that public health factored into analysis of international politics and foreign policy, it appeared as part of "low politics"—those aspects of world affairs not central to the struggle for power, security, and survival among states. The conventional perception has been that international health cooperation entails technical, humanitarian, and nonpolitical activities. The gap between public health and national and international security has, historically and conceptually, been enormous.

Brief consideration of international relations theories sharpens this point. The question of security has been at the heart of realism, which has been the dominant theory of international relations. Realism describes international relations as perpetual competition by states for power and survival (Holsti 1995). The condition of anarchy in which states exist forces each state to be responsible for its own security and survival. States achieve these objectives by acquiring and maintaining material power, especially military power. Realism defines security, therefore, as national security—the security of the state. Threats to national security are exogenous and come from rival states that likewise seek power and security in anarchy. Realism posits that international cooperation represents the temporary and expedient convergence of state interests. Cooperative arrangements break down when the national interests of states change, so self-help is the only reliable strategy for a state's security.

Under realism, the pursuit of national security involves power politics among states, creating the "security dilemma"—one state will perceive another state's effort to achieve national security as constituting a threat, necessitating a response, which the other state views as a threat, and so on. Under this dynamic, states only achieve national security by maintaining military power and other forms of material power (e.g., economic and technological capabilities) and preserving a balance of power among competing states. The great powers maintain international security through maintenance of a balance of power.

The realist approach left its imprint in traditional definitions of security threats—violence perpetrated or threatened by military forces of rival states. Such violence could include the use of biological weapons, as the practice of bio-deterrence in the twentieth century illustrated, but the traditional conception of security did not include threats to a state's interests, such as naturally occurring infectious diseases, that did not emanate from the military power of other states.

The centrality of security to realism contrasts with the paucity of attention international relations theory has paid to public health (Fidler 1997, 2003b). The theoretical approach sometimes associated with public health—functionalism—approaches international relations from a perspective fundamentally at odds with realism (Haas 1964). Functionalism maintained that inter-state cooperation on technical, nonpolitical issues could, over time, transform international relations and end the dangerous, violent competition for power historically witnessed in international politics. From a growing web of technically focused cooperative endeavors, states would over time learn to ground their relations on more peaceful and productive bases than military force and the balance of power.

Under functionalism, cooperation on public health and other similar technical, nonpolitical endeavors in the "low politics" would slowly transform the nature of anarchy among states. Functionalism aimed for a deeper, more sustainable form of security that would emerge from bottom-up, technical cooperation. For functionalism, public health held no particular significance as an issue; it was merely one area in which functional cooperation among states was needed and could develop. Theoretically, public health's separation from traditional notions of security was essential to functionalism's conception of international relations and its vision for a new world order. To connect public health with concepts of competition for power among states would taint the role public health could play in functionalist politics.

The contrast between realism and functionalism provides a glimpse of the gap that existed in the study of foreign policy and international relations between security and public health. The only connection between them appeared in functionalism's rejection of realism's conception of security and its willingness to include public health in the competent, bottom-up construction of a web of functional cooperation among states. Realism's dominance in international relations theory through the Cold War meant, however, that functionalism's openness to public health remained, like functionalism itself, marginalized and neglected.

B. Policy Worlds Apart: Security and Public Health in the Twentieth Century

The gap between security and public health seen in the study of foreign policy and international relations was replicated in the policy world for most of the twentieth century. Security policies dealing with biological weapons did not incorporate public health in their strategies, and public health approaches to naturally occurring infectious diseases did not frame these threats in security terms. The policy worlds of security and public health had essentially no relationship at all.

1. Security Threats from Biological Weapons

The threat or use of biological weapons represented the most obvious area in which connections between public health and security might have developed historically. How states addressed the threat of biological weapons reflected, however, no serious linkages with public health. As discussed in Part I of the book, states used bio-deterrence and arms control agreements to deal with the threat of biological weapons. States did not supplement these strategies by drawing on public health principles should bio-deterrence and arms control fail to prevent the use of biological weapons. Neither the Geneva Protocol nor the Biological Weapons Convention (BWC) contains provisions informed by public health principles on responding to outbreaks of infectious diseases. The most the BWC included was the undertaking of each state party to provide or support assistance to any BWC state party "exposed to a danger a result of violation of the Convention" (Article VII).

If public health factored at all in biological arms control, it was as a source of friction. Prohibitions on biological weapons development did not apply to peaceful research on, and uses of, biological agents because such activities were necessary for health purposes, such as basic research on pathogens and applied research on, and development of, drugs and vaccines. Chapter 2 explored the difficulties the dual use nature of research and development in the biological sciences creates for biological arms control.

Similarly, national and international public health operated without any connection to national and international security concerns about biological weapons. States never applied the international legal instruments for infectious disease control developed in the late nineteenth and first half of the twentieth centuries—the international sanitary conventions, which were eventually replaced after World War II by the World Health Organization's International Health Regulations (IHR) (IHR 1969; International Sanitary Regulations [ISR] 1951)—in ways supportive of security concerns about biological weapons. The balancing act attempted in the international legal regime on infectious disease control was between public health and state and commercial interests in trade and travel. Nor did governments design or apply national and international public health systems and resources with the threat of biological weapons in mind.

A connection between public health and biological weapons existed briefly in the immediate aftermath of World War II because the United States feared possible Soviet use of biological weapons (Fee and Brown 2001). This fear helped stimulate development of U.S. federal public health capabilities, such as the Epidemiological Intelligence Service. This convergence of public health and national security proved short lived as the two policy areas subsequently developed along different tracks with no interdependence nationally or internationally.

The separate development of security and public health as policy spheres was not irrational or illogical but reflected the nature of the threats posed by biological weapons. The prospect that a state would use biological weapons against the troops or civilian populations of another state was remote. Japan used biological weapons against Chinese troops and civilians before and during World War II, but no state subsequently used biological weapons in armed conflict. Although many countries developed biological weapons programs after World War II, these programs did not trigger serious fears that use of such weapons was imminent or even likely. In addition, states realized that developing and using biological weapons effectively was scientifically and technically difficult, even for countries with sophisticated scientific talent and resources.

The U.S. decision to abandon unilaterally its offensive biological weapons program in the late 1960s (see Chapter 2) reinforced the separation of security and public health. Although the Soviet Union accelerated its offensive program after the United States terminated its offensive efforts, the U.S. move, combined with the BWC's adoption, took the biological-weapons edge off Cold War international politics. Incentives for public health preparations, especially for civilian populations, to address possible biological weapons attacks were, thus, minimal if not nonexistent.

2. Naturally Occurring Infectious Diseases and the Gap between Security and Public Health

In terms of naturally occurring infectious diseases, many factors contribute to explaining why states never considered such diseases security threats. First, most of the twentieth century witnessed progress by developed countries in reducing illness and death caused by infectious diseases. During World War II, Winslow (1943, 377) noted how the United States had achieved an "astounding reduction in the major epidemic diseases," progress that was likely to continue with the introduction of antimicrobial drugs. The U.S. Surgeon General declared in the late 1960s that infectious diseases had been conquered (Berkelman and Hughes 1993), creating the opportunity for public health to move more aggressively against chronic diseases, such as cancer and cardiovascular ailments. These public health trends produced no basis on which to connect naturally occurring infectious diseases and concepts of security within developed countries.

Second, traditional concerns about external military threats and the geopolitical balance of power dominated security thinking in the latter half of the twentieth century. The idea that naturally occurring infectious diseases could threaten national security, as traditionally defined, would have only made sense if outbreaks could adversely affect a country's military power and preparedness vis-à-vis a rival state. The only infectious disease outbreak in the first eighty years of the twentieth century that might have qualified as a national security threat was the 1918 to 1919 influenza pandemic. Despite the impact of this influenza pandemic on military preparations and operations during World War I (Barry 2004), this calamity did not produce efforts to broaden the concept of national security beyond its traditional military and geopolitical focus to accommodate the threat of naturally occurring infectious diseases.

Third, public health activities at the international level underwent significant changes in the post–World War II period. From the mid-nineteenth century until World War II, ensuring that national public health measures, such as quarantine, did not unnecessarily restrict the international trade of powerful nations dominated international health cooperation (Goodman 1971). This balancing act was not concerned with improving health conditions inside countries, be they developed or developing. After World War II, the theory and practice of international health changed dramatically.

This change can be sensed in the principles contained in the preamble of the Constitution of the World Health Organization (WHO)(1946) (see box).

PREAMBLE OF THE WHO CONSTITUTION

"The States parties to this Constitution declare, in conformity with the Charter of the United Nations, that the following principles are basic to the happiness, harmonious relations and security of all peoples:

Health is a state of complete physical, mental and social wellbeing and not merely the absence of disease or infirmity.

The enjoyment of the highest attainable standard of health is one of the fundamental rights of every human being without distinction of race, religion, political belief, economic or social condition.

The health of all peoples is fundamental to the attainment of peace and security and is dependent upon the fullest co-operation of individuals and States.

The achievement of any State in the promotion and protection of health is of value to all.

Unequal development in different countries in the promotion of health and control of disease, especially communicable disease, is a common danger.

Healthy development of the child is of basic importance; the ability to live harmoniously in a changing total environment is essential to such development.

The extension to all peoples of the benefits of medical, psychological and related knowledge is essential to the fullest attainment of health.

Informed opinion and active co-operation on the part of the public are of the utmost importance in the improvement of the health of the people.

Governments have a responsibility for the health of their peoples which can be fulfilled only by the provision of adequate health and social measures.

Accepting these principles, and for the purpose of co-operation among themselves and with others to promote and protect the health of all peoples, the Contracting Parties agree to the present Constitution and hereby establish the World Health Organization as a specialized agency within the terms of Article 57 of the Charter of the United Nations."

SOURCE: WHO 1946

The WHO Constitution's preamble stated, for example, that the enjoyment of the highest attainable standard of health is a fundamental human right. This principle shifts the focus of international health activities from the trade interests of the great powers to the health conditions inside states that affect individuals. The WHO Constitution's preamble also contains a concept of security that bears little resemblance to the traditional definition. The preamble interprets security to include health: "The health of all peoples is fundamental to the attainment of peace and security[.]" Security in this perspective is not military security embedded within a balance of power but is more like what experts later in the century called "human security."

Although the WHO Constitution contained a concept of security that incorporated public health, the concept had little impact on how states and foreign policy makers conceived of security. The Cold War struggle kept traditional interpretations of security dominant. In its policies and activities, however, WHO pursued the vision set out in its Constitution's preamble by turning its attention to improving health conditions in developing countries and regions. This direction in international health fed perceptions in foreign policy that public health was "mere humanitarianism," a form of "low politics" peripheral to the real game of international politics.

Here, we see evidence of the gap between realism's focus on military power and security and functionalism's embrace of public health as a technical, nonpolitical but potentially transformational endeavor. With the Cold War hardening acceptance of traditional concepts of security, and with WHO shifting international health away from the trade interests of powerful countries toward efforts aimed at helping those most in need, public health and security continued to go their separate ways.

IV. POLICY WORLDS COLLIDE: A REVOLUTION IN THE RELATIONSHIP BETWEEN SECURITY AND PUBLIC HEALTH

The policy worlds of security and public health collided in the past ten years. Developments in the areas of biological weapons and naturally occurring infectious diseases dramatically changed these worlds and their relationships with each other. These distant strangers were thrust together under tremendous pressure with no historical experiences or precedents on which to draw. Just as the governance of biological weapons had to adjust after the Cold War ended, the collision between the worlds of public health and security produced an unprecedented context in which public health and security became dependent on each other.

A. Changes in the Biological Weapons Threat

Chapter 3 argued that one of the trends that characterizes the new world of biological weapons governance involves action directed at responding to biological attacks. During the past decade, policy interest in preparing societies for responding to biological weapons use has significantly increased. The Cold War complacency about the use of biological weapons by states evaporated with the perceived threat of bioterrorism arising against the background of rapidly advancing scientific capabilities and profound societal vulnerability to biological attacks.

In short, within the last decade, the perceived increased threat of biological attack transformed public health from a nonfactor in security discourse into a critical asset in achieving national, homeland, and international security against biological weapons. This transformation accorded public health's surveillance and intervention capabilities security significance never previously seen. Recognition of this transformation occurred within individual states and collectively in the United Nations.

The embrace of public health as a critical asset for national and homeland security is best illustrated through U.S. policy responses to bioterrorism. Experts recognized the significance of public health surveillance and intervention to security responses to the perceived rising threat of bioterrorism in the latter half of the 1990s, well before the September 11th and anthrax attacks. Initially, the role of the public health infrastructure to security was obscured by a more general concern about improving capabilities to respond to terrorism involving weapons of mass destruction (WMD)—nuclear, radiological, chemical, or biological weapons. Public health initially was lumped with traditional emergency first responders, such as the police, firefighters, and emergency medical personnel. The unique nature of public health's role in responding to bioterrorism emerged through more effective engagement of public health experts in questions of national and homeland security.

Policy makers working to clarify public health's response role in addressing biological attacks had to confront the reality that public health infrastructure in the United States was woefully unprepared for the tasks it would be expected to undertake as part of national and homeland security efforts. Moves to shore up surveillance and intervention capabilities began before September 11th and the anthrax attacks, but accelerated and expanded after those tragedies helped expose weaknesses and vulnerabilities in U.S. public health.

This unprecedented incorporation of public health capabilities into national and homeland security policy is recorded in historic documents issued by President George W. Bush's administration. The *National Security Strategy of the United States*, issued in September 2002, includes consequence management in response to the use of WMD as a strategic plank of the Bush administration's comprehensive strategy against the WMD threat (White House 2002). For biological weapons, the core of consequence management is public health. The Bush administration's *National Strategy for Homeland Security*, issued in July 2002, also stressed the critical role the nation's public health system played in preparing for responses to biological attacks (Office of Homeland Security 2002).

Recognition of public health's importance to responses to bioterrorism was not confined to the United States. Two reports on the future of the United Nations captured the phenomenon of public health and security concerns converging in the face of bioterrorism. In December 2004, the UN Secretary-General's High-level Panel on Threats, Challenges and Change (2004, ¶143) argued that better public health defenses were key to addressing the threat to possible bioterrorist attacks, but it warned, "At present, international aid for infectious disease monitoring, detection and response is lacking, security planning and spending are poorly coordinated with health-care policies and budgets, and there is insufficient understanding that an inevitable, new biological future makes active bio-defence the most viable option against the likelihood of attack." Echoing these arguments, the UN Secretary-General (2005, 23) argued in March 2005 in his UN reform strategy, "The threat of biological terrorism differs from that of nuclear terrorism. There will soon be thousands of laboratories around the world capable of producing designer bugs with awesome lethal potential. Our best defence against this danger lies in strengthening public health. . . ."

Evidence of the international recognition of the need to connect public health and security also appeared in WHO's adoption of the new IHR in May 2005 (IHR 2005). As indicated earlier, the old IHR continued the approach crafted in the international sanitary conventions adopted in the late nineteenth and first half of the twentieth centuries. These regimes attempted to balance the need for an international system of surveillance with the need to make sure public health interventions did not unnecessarily restrict international trade and travel. The old IHR were never concerned about security issues related to biological weapons.

The negotiation and adoption of the IHR 2005 did, however, grapple with the integration of public health and security concerns with respect to potential biological attacks. Although negotiations were difficult and controversial on this issue, the IHR 2005 applies to public health events that may involve the intentional use of biological agents or that may stem from illicit activities involving biological agents (Fidler 2005c). Overriding concerns about mixing public health and security in the IHR 2005 was the realization that appropriate public health surveillance and intervention responses are needed to disease events whatever their source or origin.

The IHR 2005 highlights the critical security role the core public health functions of surveillance and intervention play. The security contribution the IHR 2005 makes to addressing the threat of biological weapons and bioterrorism is one reason the United States strongly supported the IHR 2005. Further, the proposals to strengthen the BWC through enhancing global disease surveillance and assistance in cases of biological attack mentioned in Chapter 3 follow the new surveillance and intervention paths already blazed by the IHR 2005. Regardless what happens with the BWC, the IHR 2005 now forms part of the international mechanisms that address the threat of biological weapons, and the IHR 2005 is a remarkable example of the shift in thinking not only about the governance of biological weapons but also about the relationship between security and public health.

B. The Resurgence of Naturally Occurring Infectious Diseases

The relationship between security and public health also changed under the influence of the development of a global crisis in emerging and reemerging infectious diseases. After decades of complacency about infectious diseases, developed and developing states realized that complex factors were driving a resurgence of naturally occurring infectious diseases (see box). The sense of safety individuals and populations had developed concerning infectious diseases eroded. In connection with the HIV/AIDS pandemic, states in the developing world faced microbial-related destruction of their populations, economies, development prospects, and military power and preparedness. Developed states too began to worry about their direct and indirect vulnerabilities to resurgent infectious diseases, worries compounded by the global health crises created by HIV/AIDS pandemic, SARS, antimicrobial resistance, and avian influenza.

Concerns about the resurgence of infectious disease stimulated efforts to connect this threat with different concepts of security. These efforts were unprecedented. Apart from some rhetoric about health and security in the pre-

FACTORS IN INFECTIOUS DISEASE EMERGENCE

Microbial adaptation and change

Human susceptibility to infection

Climate and weather

Changing ecosystems

Economic development and land use

Human demographics and behavior

Technology and industry

International travel and commerce

Breakdown of public health measures

Poverty and social inequality

War and famine

Lack of political will

Intent to harm

SOURCE: Institute of Medicine Committee on Microbial Threats to Health in the 21st Century 2003

amble of the WHO Constitution (noted earlier), neither the security nor the public health community attempted to frame its mission as intertwined with the other. The last ten years have, however, produced an explosion of attempts to connect public health and security as a response to the threat of emerging and reemerging infectious diseases.

We noted earlier that traditional definitions of security had no tolerance for thinking about nonviolent, nonmilitary threats as security problems. The last decade has seen, however, many experts inside and outside of government arguing that resurgent infectious diseases, and especially HIV/AIDS and the threat of pandemic influenza, constitute threats to national security. Many arguments attempted to show that epidemic and pandemic infectious diseases could, if not addressed effectively, attack, undermine, and weaken the material sources of a country's power in the international system (Price-Smith 2002).

Infectious diseases could directly hurt national security by reducing military strength and preparedness, harming economic performance and stability, eroding governance capacities, and undermining a population's confidence and trust in the political leadership and system. Infectious diseases could indirectly harm national security by causing political and economic damage in countries in which a state had vital security, foreign policy, and trade interests. These direct and indirect arguments tried to demonstrate that states had to think more broadly about their material power and threats to it than they had done during the Cold War. The arguments embraced the traditionalist focus on a state's interest in power but widened the national security lens to consider threats to power not emanating from the military forces of rival states. These arguments appear to have won the day in the Bush administration because the *National Security Strategy* issued in 2002 and 2006 both prominently characterize naturally occurring infectious disease epidemics, such as HIV/AIDS and pandemic influenza, as threats to U.S. national security (White House 2002, 2006a).

More radically, the resurgence of infectious disease encouraged some experts to include public health in efforts to transform what security means. Challenges to the traditional definition of security as concerned only with violent threats to state power and survival began during the last decade of the Cold War. One well-known early attempt to redefine security came from Ullman (1983), who proposed that security be defined to include events that degrade the quality of life of a state's inhabitants or that narrow the policy choices of a government or non-state actors within a country. Ullman (1983, 133) included "decimating epidemics" as a security concern in his broadened concept of security.

Reconceptualization of security continued through the 1980s and early 1990s, with efforts to connect environmental degradation and security being prominent (Myers 1989; Deudney 1990; Homer Dixon 1999). The effort reached an apogee of sorts with the promulgation of the concept of "human security" by the United Nations Development Programme (UNDP). The UNDP (1994, 22) criticized traditional concepts of security for being too fixated on the security of states from external military violence and for not focusing more on "the legitimate concerns of ordinary people who sought security in their daily lives." Thus, the UNDP (1994) asserted that attention should turn toward achieving human security, which would protect people from (1) chronic threats, such as hunger, disease, and repression, and (2) sudden and harmful disruptions in the patterns of daily life. The space the human security concept opened for connecting public health and security was significant, and subsequent high-profile efforts applied the human security idea to advocate for more national and international attention on public health (Chen 2004; Helsinki Process 2005).

We even have attempts to blend the traditional national security outlook with the more radical human security approach, with the resulting concept also emphasizing the security importance of public health. In its December 2004 report, the UN Secretary-General's High-level Panel on Threats, Challenges and Change (2004) advocated for what it called "comprehensive collective security," which recognized the continued relevance of traditional national security concerns and endorsed the broadening of the concept of security to include concerns raised by the human security strategy. In explaining comprehensive collective security, the High-level Panel (2004, ¶19) turned to public health and argued "the security of the most affluent State can be held hostage to the ability of the poorest State to contain an emerging disease." Identifying security's need for public health infrastructure, the High-level Panel (2004, ¶47) argued that the "emergence of new infectious diseases, a resurgence of older diseases and a spread of resistance to a growing number of mainstay antibiotic drugs... signify a dramatic decay in local and global public health capacity." The panel recommended major improvements to national and global public health infrastructure as part of achieving comprehensive collective security.

So concerned was the High-level Panel with the infectious disease threat that it recommended a mechanism for cooperation between the UN Security Council and WHO in establishing effective response measures in extreme cases of a threat posed by a new, emerging infectious disease or the intentional release of an infectious agent (UN High-level Panel 2004, ¶70). Under such a mechanism, the High-level Panel (2004, ¶144) argued that the Security Council "should be prepared to support the work of WHO investigators or to deploy experts reporting directly to the Council" and "should be prepared to mandate greater compliance" by states during investigations of an overwhelming natural outbreak of an infectious disease.

This call for Security Council intervention in the handling of infectious disease outbreaks was radical but not entirely without precedent. In 2000, the Security Council held meetings on the threat to international peace and security posed by the HIV/AIDS pandemic—the first time in this organization's history it addressed a naturally occurring infectious disease as a security threat (UN Security Council 2000). The High-level Panel was taking the HIV/AIDS precedent one step farther by integrating public health more firmly into the mandate of the UN body primarily responsible for maintaining international peace and security.

The UN Secretary-General picked up the arguments made by the High-level Panel in his March 2005 report on UN reform. The Secretary-General (2005, ¶63) identified infectious disease surveillance and monitoring as priorities for global action, arguing, "The overall international response to evolving pandemics has been shockingly slow and remains shamefully under-resourced." The Secretary-General (2005, ¶105) further promised to use his powers under the UN Charter "to call to the attention of the Security Council any overwhelming outbreak of infectious disease that threatens international peace and security." In this statement, the Secretary-General directly connected public health and security as part of his vision for UN reform.

Another attempt to connect security and public health appeared in WHO's efforts to strengthen "global health security." WHO used global health security as a framing concept for its activities on improving global disease surveillance and response in the face of emerging and reemerging infectious diseases (WHO 2001). The global health security strategy involved many elements, including creating a global "network of networks" to harness new information technologies for surveillance purposes and revising the IHR (WHO 2002). For WHO, global health security encompasses threats posed by the use of biological weapons and by naturally occurring infectious diseases. This approach also underscored the need to strengthen public health infrastructure nationally and internationally for security purposes.

C. Biosecurity and the Securitization of Public Health

The diverse efforts made to connect security and public health in the last ten years demonstrate that the collision of these policy worlds has affected how both security and public health are conceptualized and pursued. The process of securitizing public health has made strengthening national and international public health infrastructures a critical biosecurity priority. Achieving this priority means melding the former "high politics" of security with the "low politics" of public health into a new type of politics without historical precedent.

In different ways, each attempt described earlier to connect security and public health represents a reconceptualization of security and public health as policy endeavors. Each security-public health linkage broadens the meaning of security beyond the traditional concern with military violence perpetrated by rival states. As worries about bioterrorism illustrate, threats might arise from non-state actors using nontraditional means of violence. Further, the realization that naturally occurring infectious diseases can damage a country's material power, international interests, and domestic way of life has provided the basis for broadening what security means. Security traditionalists particularly dislike this latter expansion because they prefer security policy to remain focused on deterring and defending against intentional violent threats against a state's power and interests.

The securitization process has forced public health out of the realm of neglected humanitarianism into the harsh and unforgiving context of national and international politics related to security. Many public health practitioners, particularly those involved in global health, who are accustomed to approaching public health through human rights and humanitarian principles, have found the securitization process difficult to accept normatively and handle practically. Public health advocates sometimes worry that the securitization process could corrupt or corrode the enterprise they know and cherish.

The new politics generated by the securitization of public health tends to emphasize the dual use nature of improvements to public health infrastructures. In other words, such improvements support both defense against biological weapons and naturally occurring infectious diseases. The UN Secretary-General (2005, ¶93) emphasized this point when he argued that recommendations for improving public health capabilities "have a double merit: they would both help to address the scourge of naturally occurring infectious disease and contribute to our safety against manmade outbreaks." Strengthening public health infrastructure offers the prospect of producing more biosecurity bang for the bug, so to speak. The extent to which this "double merit" exists, and is being produced by current biosecurity policies, is one of the central questions facing the governance world created by the securitization of public health. Chapter 5 examines this question in detail.

V. PUBLIC HEALTH SECURITIZATION AND THE CHALLENGES OF BIOSECURITY POLICY

Despite misgivings from both security and public health traditionalists, the securitization of public health reveals the attractiveness and power of integrating security and public health as policy pursuits. This integration is, of course, one of the four main challenges that characterizes contemporary biosecurity politics. Although public health securitization reflects the collision of the policy worlds of security and public health, this process has not yet produced an integration that is stable and sustainable. The diversity of different ways to integrate security and public health described earlier—national security, comprehensive collective security, human security, and global health security—does not suggest deep consensus exists about how security and public health policy should integrate. Securitization's inclusion of naturally occurring infectious diseases makes the integration challenge more serious, and raises questions about whether biological weapons or naturally occurring epidemics should receive biosecurity priority.

The securitization of public health also stimulates the challenge of supervising science for security and public health. The securitization process heightens the need to supervise science in two ways. First, securitization includes the threat of biological weapons, which underscores the security interest in regulating aspects of the biological sciences discussed in Chapter 3. As the "first responder" to any biological attack, public health's interest in making sure the principles of scientific innovation, freedom, and open dissemination of research are not intentionally abused or recklessly applied has increased. Public health now is itself a guardian of security. In short, the challenge of supervising science is not simply a matter of pitting security against public health. The reality is more complicated and difficult.

The appeals to improving public health infrastructures found in all the concepts of security demonstrate that the securitization of public health also involves the challenge of globalizing governance for biosecurity. As the reports on UN reform emphasized, strengthening public health's contribution to individual, national, and international security requires not only more cooperation among states but also the construction of globalized governance mechanisms involving input from non-state actors. The proposals to involve the UN Security Council more directly in outbreaks of epidemic disease are more indicators that the securitization of public health has forced governance to go in new directions previously unthinkable. The difficulty of constructing globalized health governance parallels the dilemmas of globalizing governance in connection with the criminalization of biological weapons development and use and the regulation of the biological sciences explored in Part I of the book.

Finally, the securitization of public health also draws attention to the challenge of embedding biosecurity governance in the rule of law. The securitization process stimulates rule of law issues that exist with respect to security and public health. Arguing that certain public health measures are required for security purposes raises tensions that often exist between claims of security exigencies and the demands of the rule of law, especially in situations of urgency and danger. Securitization of public health heightens the importance of appropriately balancing public health actions with individual rights and liberties, but, by adding security imperatives to the mix, it also complicates the process through which such balance is achieved.

Questions of justice also appear. Is securitization contributing to or undermining the pursuit of justice within and among states? Does viewing public health threats through the lens of security make states more nationalistic or enlightened in their biosecurity policies? In short, the securitization of public health increases the political stress the rule of law experiences in the life and death situations societies face in the realm of biosecurity. We return to these issues in Chapter 6.

VI. CONCLUSION

Debates about whether the securitization of public health is a positive or negative development continue. The collision of the policy worlds of security and public health has, we believe, made the securitization of public health a permanent fixture of the biosecurity governance landscape. Thus, this securitization is akin to the landmark changes that have reshaped governance of biological weapons. The context in which security and public health were distant strangers has vanished, just as has the willingness of states to rely on the traditional arms control approach of the BWC to address the problem of biological weapons.

As this chapter communicates, the securitization of public health represents a policy earthquake, the aftershocks of which are still being felt. Biosecurity policy has to grapple with the post-earthquake reality that securitization has happened and is not going to fade away like some superficial post–Cold War fad hyped by policy wonks and ivory tower academics. The securitization of public health means that biosecurity policy now confronts the task of understanding and managing a new world of public health governance. The next chapter explores this new world and the challenges it presents.

5 THE NEW WORLD OF PUBLIC HEALTH GOVERNANCE

I. INTRODUCTION

The analysis of the securitization of public health in Chapter 4 repeatedly returned to the need to strengthen the public health infrastructure. The effectiveness of the public health infrastructure has traditionally been the responsibility of public health governance. The securitization of public health has transformed the world of public health governance through the collision of the policy worlds of security and public health. As we did for the new world of biological weapons governance, we need to focus attention on the challenges public health governance faces with respect to the rise of biosecurity. This chapter undertakes this task.

The repeated policy emphasis on strengthening public health infrastructures to address the threats of both biological weapons and naturally occurring infectious diseases has made producing synergy between these two aspects of biosecurity a prominent issue. The synergy idea promotes adoption of policies that, to the maximum extent possible, advance simultaneously defense against biological weapons and naturally occurring infectious diseases. As discussed later, literature on biosecurity frequently features the "synergy thesis"—the argument that improvements in biodefense will also contribute to preventing, containing, or responding to naturally occurring epidemics or pandemics, and vice versa. Chyba (2002, 132) expressed the synergy thesis when he argued, "Fortunately, many of the steps that are needed to prepare for bioterrorism will also improve recognition of and responses to natural disease outbreaks. Spending on biological defenses therefore represents a win-win situation in which society benefits even if no further bioterrorist attacks take place."

The synergy thesis is important for the new world of public health governance for practical and normative reasons. On the practical side, the objective of creating synergistic effects for national security concerns about biological weapons is part of what has transformed the public health enterprise in the past ten years. This objective did not feature in public health governance during the Cold War for the reasons explained in Chapter 4. Instead, public health experts debated other governance questions, such as the pros and cons of a biomedical versus social determinants approach to public health, or of disease-specific programs versus sector-wide health system reforms.

Normatively, the synergy thesis is significant because it represents, conceptually, the balance between security and public health that is critical to their successful integration. The synergy thesis accepts the normative significance of thinking about public health in terms of security. The stronger synergy is between policies on biological weapons and infectious diseases the more robust and sustainable biosecurity governance will be.

This chapter critically analyzes the synergy thesis as the central question of the new world of public health governance. We argue that, all too often, the synergy thesis is trotted out, used loosely to justify policies and proposals, and never subjected to the scrutiny it deserves as a critical element of biosecurity policy in the twenty-first century. We put the synergy thesis under the microscope with respect to the two key functions of public health, surveillance and intervention. We attempt to ascertain where the synergy thesis has substantial or only superficial merit. We conclude that the synergy thesis presents serious problems for biosecurity policy, especially with respect to intervention strategies.

These problems with the synergy thesis highlight two "fault lines" in biosecurity governance. These fault lines represent policy tensions between (1) efforts against biological weapons versus naturally occurring infectious diseases, and (2) a focus on national needs rather than international problems. The fault lines indicate that the synergy thesis is vulnerable to policies that emphasize defense against biological weapons at the expense of improvements to public health infrastructure. We raise concerns that these fault lines appear prominently in U.S. biosecurity policies, indicating that such policies are not producing synergies that improve public health infrastructure. We posit that U.S. policy may be creating a "biodefense industrial complex" that undermines the nation's ability to achieve robust and sustainable biosecurity.

II. BIOSECURITY AND PRIORITIZATION
IN PUBLIC HEALTH GOVERNANCE

Before considering the synergy thesis in detail, one effect of the securitization of public health on public health governance should be briefly noted. The importance of public health in biosecurity policy generated by the need for strengthened public health infrastructure creates new governance challenges. Acknowledging convergence of security and public health is easier than devising approaches to ensure that public health adequately addresses both kinds of biosecurity threats. Just as states, international organizations, and nonstate actors have engaged in efforts to construct new governance strategies for the biological weapons problem, similar efforts are required with respect to calibrating the convergence of security and public health.

The new world of public health governance has far-reaching implications for biosecurity and public health governance beyond this particular concern. This chapter focuses on governance challenges that arise within the new policy space of biosecurity, but the reader should be aware that this new governance world affects other aspects of the public health endeavor. The securitization of public health has significant consequences for public health governance in the area of priority setting. The process of securitization has, in essence, been a process of prioritization. This dynamic helps explain why so many different ways to connect public health to security appeared in the last decade—many bits of the public health endeavor wanted to jump on the securitization bandwagon.

Such bandwagoning stimulated cynicism about the sincerity of some efforts to connect public health and security. Playing the "security card" looked to some skeptics like a desperate, perhaps even Faustian, attempt to get public health more political attention and economic resources. Ironically, the deeper this cynicism is the stronger is the argument that the securitization of public health has produced a new governance context. The cynicism acknowledges that coldly calculating appeals to security considerations can help improve public health. Both the rhetoric and practice of public health governance now have to sort out security issues, arguments, and priorities.

As Chapter 1 noted, the emergence of biosecurity as a policy arena does not mean that all public health issues become security problems. Such an approach would simply conflate security and governance in terms of public health. Biosecurity policy is concerned with infectious disease threats that have the potential to disrupt the normal functioning of societies. The biosecurity approach privileges infectious over non-communicable diseases as a governance matter. Biosecurity has, thus, a narrower governance scope than WHO's concept of global health security, which includes threats to human health that may arise from emergencies involving chemical, nuclear, or radiological substances or agents. Many public health experts worry that biosecurity's privileging of a narrow range of infectious disease threats deepens the historic neglect of non-communicable diseases, which are emerging as a global health menace.

Thus, laments are heard that increased funding for biosecurity reduces political, human, and financial capital available for non-communicable diseases. An example of these concerns is found in reactions to President George W. Bush's proposed budget for fiscal 2007. In February 2006, the *Washington Post* reported, "President Bush has requested billions more to prepare for potential disasters such as a biological attack or an influenza pandemic, but his proposed budget for next year would zero out popular health projects that supporters say target more mundane, but certain, killers" (Connolly 2006, A03). This quote illustrates the tension between giving priority to biosecurity (e.g., billions to protect the country against biological weapons and pandemics through Project BioShield) over health problems that involve non-communicable diseases (e.g., obesity epidemics).

Whether blame for budgetary cuts to non-communicable disease programs should be laid at the feet of biosecurity is questionable because complex factors make up a government's decisions to appropriate resources. The more general point is, however, important. Biosecurity's privileged status may create negative externalities for efforts against non-communicable diseases. Biosecurity helps magnify the priority infectious diseases receive in other areas of public health governance, such as development. The health-related UN Millennium Development Goals only target infectious diseases and do not identify non-communicable diseases as a development problem despite the growing toll non-communicable diseases create in developing countries (Yach, Leeder, Bell and Kistmasamy 2005).

Most non-communicable disease experts realize that they cannot play the "security card" because the nature of these diseases does not lend itself to notions of security, however broadly defined. Biosecurity's rise, and its effects on public health governance, makes the task of those engaged in non-communicable diseases more difficult. This difficulty is not going to subside, requiring strategies on non-communicable diseases for adapting to the new world of public health governance created by the securitization of public health.

III. BIOSECURITY, PUBLIC HEALTH GOVERNANCE,
AND THE SYNERGY THESIS

The emergence of biosecurity as a policy concern has, without question, focused increased attention on public health surveillance and intervention capabilities at national and international levels. Perhaps no other development in the history of public health has created the awareness that now exists about public health infrastructure around the world. Recall, for example, the UN Secretary-General's identification of infectious disease surveillance as a global priority in reforming the UN mentioned in Chapter 4.

Addressing the threats posed by biological weapons and resurgent infectious diseases requires robust public health surveillance and intervention capacities nationally and globally. Framing both threats as security challenges makes these public health governance functions more important politically than they had previously been. As Chapter 4 emphasized, security officials and public health experts reached the same conclusions about the condition of national and international public health—significant improvements would be required for biosecurity to be achieved. The UN Secretary-General (2004, viii) again captured this consensus when he emphasized, "We need to pay much closer attention to biological security."

As mentioned earlier, a prominent feature of thinking about public health and security converging in biosecurity policy is the synergy thesis. This thesis posits that improvements made to public health benefit efforts against both biological weapons and infectious diseases. When an outbreak occurs, the first line of defense is the public health system, whether the outbreak was intentionally caused or naturally occurring. Thus, strengthening public health through biosecurity policy would achieve the dual purpose of defending against biological weapons and protecting societies from resurgent infectious diseases. The UN Secretary-General (2005, ¶93) appealed to the synergy thesis when he argued that strengthening public health has "double merit" because it serves as a defense against bioterrorism and naturally occurring infectious diseases. Appeals to the synergy thesis often imply that biosecurity policy does not have to choose between security and public health, or between defense against biological weapons and protection from naturally occurring infectious diseases. Synergy arguments sometimes inform advocacy for governments to adopt an "all hazards" approach to biosecurity. This approach "would offer political as well as security benefits" because "natural outbreaks are inevitable but bioterrorist attacks are not," which means that "preparedness measures that cover all infectious disease threats would not only be far more cost-effective but politically more sustainable, particularly if a major bioterrorist event does not occur for many years, if ever" (Grotto and Tucker 2006, 21). The synergy thesis constitutes, thus, a major characteristic of the new world of public health governance.

Understanding the synergy thesis is, therefore, critical to evaluating biosecurity policies. Too often experts appeal to the synergy thesis without examining how robust the thesis is or whether the thesis contains tensions that affect policy formation and implementation. As subsequent sections of this chapter argue, the synergy thesis has merit but not as much as frequent uses of it suggest.

Close examination of surveillance and intervention reveal a more mixed situation that general references to the synergy thesis cannot explain. This situation means that biosecurity policy is more complex and difficult than most applications of the synergy thesis reveal. The reality of biosecurity policy is that governments and international organizations have to make hard choices about where to invest scarce resources because synergy is not inevitably the goal or the product of biosecurity initiatives.

Generally speaking, the synergy thesis proves more robust in connection with surveillance than with interventions. The synergy thesis does not, however, capture tensions or frictions that exist between policies designed to deal with biological weapons and those needed to address resurgent infectious diseases. The synergy thesis has become biosecurity's equivalent of the "harmony of interests" doctrine familiar to international relations experts (Carr 1939). This doctrine described how states, especially powerful countries, would often assert that a harmony existed between their interests and the interests of other countries and the international community. The reality of international politics usually reveals not a harmony but a divergence of interests. Similarly, the reality of biosecurity suggests that the manner in which the synergy thesis is often used is insufficient to understand the challenges created by coupling security and public health to respond to threats from biological weapons and infectious diseases.

One way to explore these tensions involves consideration of two fault lines running through the new world of public health governance—fault lines between (1) biological weapons and naturally occurring infectious diseases, and (2) a national and an international focus on biosecurity. These fault lines represent points where security and public health come together in the new world of public health governance but not necessarily in an integrated and stable fashion. As discussed later, the two policy "plates"—biological weapons and naturally occurring infectious diseases—push against each other, creating pressures that reveal problems for biosecurity. These problems suggest that the collision of security and public health has not produced a partnership of equals in the new world of public health governance.

IV. BIOSECURITY AND SURVEILLANCE

A. Recognition of Surveillance's Important Biosecurity Function

As Chapter 4 emphasized, experts recognize the importance of surveillance to defend against biological weapons and resurgent infectious diseases. Real world crises, including the HIV/AIDS pandemic, the global crisis in emerging and reemerging infectious diseases, the problem of antimicrobial resistance, the anthrax attacks, the spread of West Nile Virus in North America, the global severe acute respiratory syndrome (SARS) outbreak, polio's breakout from west Africa across the Middle East and into Asia, and avian influenza's international spread, have hammered home the critical role surveillance plays in all biosecurity contexts. Surveillance that picks up pathogenic threats earlier, faster, and more accurately increases the prospects that interventions can be effective. This principle holds whether the pathogen is intentionally released or naturally occurring.

With security and public health stressing surveillance, this endeavor has received more attention and resources than ever before. Confronted with the dangers of bioterrorism and resurgent infectious diseases, the United States has made efforts to strengthen surveillance within its territory during the past ten years, and especially after the anthrax attacks. In 2004, for example, the Bush administration launched the National Biosurveillance Initiative to strengthen U.S. capacities for surveillance and early warning of bioterrorist attacks and infectious disease outbreaks (Department of Homeland Security 2004). This initiative established the National Biosurveillance Integration System in 2005 to combine and evaluate information collected from human, animal, plant, food, and environmental monitoring systems at local, tribal, state, and federal governmental levels, as well as from private-sector surveillance. Supporting enhanced biosurveillance is the BioSense program, which collects health information from hospitals and healthcare facilities in major metropolitan areas to identify trends and developments that improve local, state, and federal capabilities for real-time biosurveillance, situational awareness, and public health preparedness and response (Centers for Disease Control and Prevention [CDC] 2006b). In 2003, the Bush administration also created Project BioWatch, a $100 million dollar effort to place pathogen sensors in thirty cities to detect possible biological attacks in the United States to enhance early warning capabilities of local, state, and federal authorities (Shea and Lister 2003; White House 2003).

The various efforts to improve surveillance all recognize that international cooperation on surveillance plays a critical role in a government's attempts to achieve biosecurity. Regional activities to strengthen surveillance have taken place, for example, in the Asia-Pacific region (APEC 2006) and in the European Union through creation in 2004 of the European Centers for Disease Prevention and Control (ECDC), which "will work in partnership with national health protection bodies across Europe to strengthen and develop continent-wide disease surveillance and early warning systems" (ECDC 2006).

Improving surveillance globally has also been a key theme of most bodies and experts making recommendations about how to manage the threats of biological weapons and resurgent infectious diseases. For its part, WHO began improving global surveillance in the latter half of the 1990s with the Global Outbreak Alert and Response Network (GOARN). For WHO (2006a), GOARN's capabilities bolster defenses against bioterrorism and naturally occurring infectious diseases and are central to its strategy of achieving global health security. The UN Secretary-General (2005, ¶¶ 63, 93) called for UN member states to increase financial and other support for GOARN as part of the UN's new vision of comprehensive collective security.

WHO member states moved toward improving global surveillance by adopting the new International Health Regulations (IHR) in May 2005 (IHR 2005). For many reasons, the IHR 2005 constitutes a major development in the use of international law for public health (Fidler 2005c; Fidler and Gostin 2006) and contains significant provisions relating to surveillance. The IHR 2005 requires WHO member states to notify WHO of any disease event that may constitute a public health emergency of international concern (Article 6). This requirement differs radically from what had prevailed in the previous international legal regimes supporting international disease surveillance. The international sanitary conventions of the late nineteenth and early twentieth centuries, and the old IHR, only required states parties to report outbreaks of a small number of infectious diseases the spread of which was associated with international trade and travel. The limited scope of the surveillance in these treaties reflected their main purpose—to ensure that public health measures did not unnecessarily restrict world trade and travel.

The IHR 2005's provisions on surveillance reflect a more ambitious strategy designed to match the global threats posed by pathogenic microbes and other possible international public health emergencies (Baker and Fidler 2006). The IHR 2005 contains a "decision instrument" in Annex 2 that guides states parties through the process of determining whether they must report a disease event to WHO. See Figure 5.1. This approach is unlike anything seen previously in the international legal regimes establishing surveillance obligations. Its scope is as broad as the potential threats that might emerge from either the malevolent use of pathogens or the mysteries of the microbial world.

The IHR 2005 goes even farther in terms of recognizing the need to strengthen surveillance. The new regulations require states parties to develop and maintain core national surveillance capabilities within five years of the entry into force of the IHR 2005 in June 2007 (i.e., by 2012) (Article 5 and Annex 1). Again, no previous treaty connected with international disease surveillance ever mandated anything on this scale. The IHR 2005's mandate represents the recognition by WHO member states that national and global disease surveillance capabilities are interdependent, and that significant improvements at the national level around the world are needed.

The IHR 2005 contains yet another radical element that supports the strengthening of global disease surveillance. Under the IHR 2005, WHO can collect, analyze, and use surveillance information supplied by non-state actors (Article 9). The old IHR limited WHO to information supplied only by governments of the states parties. This limitation crippled WHO's surveillance capabilities because states parties often refused to provide information about outbreaks of diseases in their territories subject to the IHR. The IHR 2005 allow WHO to receive and gather surveillance information from governments and nongovernmental entities, which permits WHO to harness the globalization of nongovernmental organizations (NGOs), the media, and new information technologies, such as the Internet and e-mail, in building rapidly a more accurate picture of disease events around the world.

These remarkable changes in the international law on disease surveillance reflect recognition by WHO member states that biosecurity requires radical changes in surveillance. Each obligation concerning surveillance in the IHR 2005 imposes serious responsibilities that significantly affect sovereignty. Sovereignty-sensitive states have even agreed to allow WHO to construct and

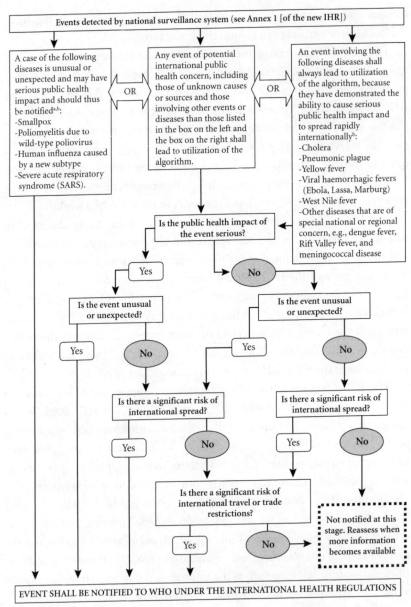

Events detected by national surveillance system (see Annex 1 [of the new IHR])

A case of the following diseases is unusual or unexpected and may have serious public health impact and should thus be notified[a,b]:
-Smallpox
-Poliomyelitis due to wild-type poliovirus
-Human influenza caused by a new subtype
-Severe acute respiratory syndrome (SARS).

OR

Any event of potential international public health concern, including those of unknown causes or sources and those involving other events or diseases than those listed in the box on the left and the box on the right shall lead to utilization of the algorithm.

OR

An event involving the following diseases shall always lead to utilization of the algorithm, because they have demonstrated the ability to cause serious public health impact and to spread rapidly internationally[b]:
-Cholera
-Pneumonic plague
-Yellow fever
-Viral haemorrhagic fevers (Ebola, Lassa, Marburg)
-West Nile fever
-Other diseases that are of special national or regional concern, e.g., dengue fever, Rift Valley fever, and meningococcal disease

Is the public health impact of the event serious?

Yes

No

Is the event unusual or unexpected?

Is the event unusual or unexpected?

Yes

No

Yes

No

Is there a significant risk of international spread?

Is there a significant risk of international spread?

Yes

No

Yes

No

Is there a significant risk of international travel or trade restrictions?

Yes

No

Not notified at this stage. Reassess when more information becomes available

EVENT SHALL BE NOTIFIED TO WHO UNDER THE INTERNATIONAL HEALTH REGULATIONS

[a] As per WHO case definitions.
[b] The disease list shall be used only for purposes of these Regulations.

Figure 5.1 The Decision Instrument of the New International Health Regulations
SOURCE: IHR 2005, Annex 2

operate global health governance for surveillance by building non-state actors directly into surveillance capabilities. For these reasons, the IHR 2005 provides one of the best windows through which to appreciate the new world of public health governance being shaped nationally and globally by biosecurity policy.

B. Surveillance and the Fault Lines of Biosecurity Policy

As noted earlier, two fault lines run through the new world of public health governance in connection with the synergy thesis: tension between (1) policies for biological weapons and for naturally occurring infectious diseases, and (2) national needs versus international requirements. Both fault lines appear in the need for improved surveillance and thus are cause for concern.

Generally, surveillance lessens the potential for the fault line between biological weapons and naturally occurring infectious diseases to damage the prospects for biosecurity. Improving the scope, speed, comprehensiveness, and technological capabilities of national and global surveillance is a "dual purpose" or "all hazards" objective of biosecurity policy. Synergy between security and public health interests on surveillance tends, generally, to be strong.

The most frequent criticism made concerning surveillance is that, despite recognition of its importance and realization of some progress, national and global surveillance capabilities still fall short of what biosecurity requires. Reports on U.S. preparedness for health emergencies have noted the inadequacy of U.S. surveillance capabilities despite infusion of resources from the federal government (Trust for America's Health 2003, 2004, 2005, 2006). The Global Pathogen Surveillance Act passed by the U.S. Senate in December 2005 stated, "The United States lacks an effective and real-time system to detect, identify, contain, and respond to global threats and also lacks an effective mechanism to disseminate information to the national response community if such threats arise" (§2(a)(2)).

The global spread of HIV/AIDS, the SARS outbreak, growing problems with malaria and tuberculosis, the spread of polio from West Africa to Asia, the development of antimicrobial resistance, the emergence of avian influenza, and the possibility of pandemic influenza have illustrated the weaknesses of surveillance in many countries. These domestic weaknesses fracture the architecture of global surveillance. Weaknesses exist because public health has, in the words of the UN Secretary-General (2005, ¶63), been "shamefully underresourced." The lack of resources is particularly acute for many developing countries because, as the U.S. Senate noted, these countries "often are unable to devote the necessary resources to build and maintain public health infrastructures" (Global Pathogen Surveillance Act 2005, §2(a)(9)).

These issues bring biosecurity's fault line between a national and international focus into play. Again, the robustness of the synergy thesis means that surveillance improvements nationally benefit surveillance capabilities internationally. The main reason for this situation is humanity's division into approximately 200 sovereign states. International surveillance is built, in large part, on national surveillance capabilities.

This reality is why the IHR 2005 requires all states parties to develop and maintain core national surveillance capabilities. Despite widespread acceptance of the need to strengthen global public health surveillance, the objective remains fraught with difficulties (Calain 2007a). One serious problem is the "surveillance gap" between developed and developing countries, a gap widened and deepened by biosecurity's rise. Within the new world of public health governance, developed states seek to improve surveillance within their jurisdictions. Developing countries largely have to rely on much smaller amounts of international financial and technical assistance. In addition, donor assistance for surveillance improvements in developing countries can exacerbate the surveillance gap through strategies that contribute to the fragmentation of national health capabilities and priorities in developing countries (Calain 2007b). The surveillance gap represents the widening gulf between the ability of developed and developing countries to conduct surveillance when biosecurity needs the gap to narrow, especially with respect to naturally occurring infectious diseases.

This gap forms part of perennial public health disparities between rich and poor countries, especially disparities concerning infectious disease morbidity and mortality. Most developing countries need improved surveillance for public health purposes rather than security against biological attacks, and these countries need significant financial and other forms of assistance to improve national surveillance. The gap between global surveillance needs and the resources available to improve such surveillance is enormous.

Unfortunately, no strategy currently exists that addresses how development and maintenance of core national surveillance capabilities required by the IHR 2005 will be financially supported. Fear in developed countries that avian influenza's spread across Asia and into other regions of the world will trigger an influenza pandemic is, as of this writing, producing increased aid for strengthening national surveillance. But, with each new country and region in which avian influenza has appeared, the scale of the inadequacy of national and global surveillance capabilities has been made more painfully clear. The sums being made available by the United States and other developed countries appear inadequate given both avian influenza's march out of Southeast Asia into Europe, the Middle East, South Asia, and Africa and the potential for pandemic influenza.

The inadequacy of national and global surveillance systems and the shortage of resources to improve them raise questions about surveillance and early warning initiatives that do not build dual-purpose or all-hazards capabilities for both biological weapons and infectious diseases. The U.S. BioWatch program is a case in point. BioWatch was designed to detect possible biological attacks in U.S. cities earlier than general surveillance systems, thus giving response and recovery activities more time to be effective.

Leaving aside concerns about the implementation of BioWatch (EPA Office of Inspector General 2005), BioWatch's sensors do not contribute to overall public health surveillance because they seek to detect low probability releases of biological weapons agents, and, "[u]nfortunately, BioWatch is not accurate enough to provide a cost-effective way of strengthening the nation's surveillance capacity" (Grotto and Tucker 2006, 26). Security concerns about biological weapons have produced an early warning program offering little benefit to either defense against biological weapons or public health's task of addressing resurgent infectious diseases nationally and internationally. Biosecurity policy might more appropriately target the millions spent on BioWatch on problems plaguing infectious disease surveillance in the United States and internationally. Public health authorities and health care providers badly need more rapid, accurate, and affordable diagnostic technologies that allow them to identify infections regardless of the source. Given the avian influenza threat, Garrett (2006) has, for example, argued, "Wealthy nations and biomedical companies should work hard on developing a rapid, simple method of diagnosing flu infections in people."

The BioWatch initiative helps illustrate how biosecurity policy in the United States often emphasizes narrowly conceived national security interests focused on biological weapons over more broadly framed global needs connected to infectious disease problems. The failed national smallpox vaccination program exhibited the same emphasis (see Chapter 3). BioWatch sensors in U.S. cities sniffing the air for biological weapons agents will not help any country, including the United States, detect emergence or reemergence of virulent pathogens. The surveillance gap reinforces warnings about biosecurity policy disproportionately focusing on national fear of biological weapons at the expense of broad-based global improvements in surveillance of infectious disease events of whatever origin.

V. BIOSECURITY AND INTERVENTION STRATEGIES

As Chapter 4 analyzed, the second function of public health governance involves interventions to prevent, protect against, or respond to disease threats. Without intervention capabilities, governments would waste information provided by surveillance to the detriment of population health. Biosecurity literature recognizes the interdependence of surveillance and intervention. Intervention strategies have received significant attention, and, as with surveillance, experts often stress potential synergies created by developing intervention capabilities for responding to a biological attack or a naturally infectious disease outbreak.

For example, emergency response plans developed for a bioterrorist attack using smallpox may prove beneficial in the event of pandemic influenza, and vice versa. Intervention capabilities developed to deliver smallpox vaccines could also benefit distribution of a pandemic influenza vaccine. Similarly, antivirals stockpiled for a biological attack may be used to address an unforeseen epidemic triggered by the emergence of a new virus. Training and planning for using isolation and quarantine to contain a contagious pathogen are useful regardless of the source of the pathogen. Emergency response centers, procedures, and personnel crafted and trained to prepare for biological attacks have been useful in coordinating actions against naturally occurring infectious diseases.

The fault lines of biosecurity policy are, however, more prominent with intervention than surveillance. Part of this prominence reflects the diversity of intervention strategies. As Figure 4.2 depicted, prevention, protection, and response interventions are distinct, and, within each category, multiple approaches exist. Such complexity means that some interventions relevant to infectious diseases may have little relevance for defense against biological weapons, and vice versa. Despite its preference for abstinence as an HIV/AIDS intervention, the Bush administration does not stress abstinence in its approach to biological weapons because this intervention makes no sense in defending against biological attack. Similarly, focusing on developing new pharmaceutical countermeasures against biological weapons agents, which was the main purpose of Project BioShield, may produce little of value for public health's broader fight with resurgent infectious diseases.

Similarly, the complexity of intervention highlights tensions that may arise between national and international approaches. Compared with surveillance, interventions prove more difficult to advance through globalized governance. Is a developed country's national vaccine, antiviral, or antibiotic stockpile to be shared with developing countries in the event of an international disease emergency? Despite attempts to create global intervention capabilities, such as the global stockpile of antivirals controlled by WHO for use in case of an influenza pandemic, intervention strategies remain more firmly tied to national governmental capabilities and needs, which, as with surveillance, creates uneven intervention capacities between developed and developing states. The uneven quality of intervention capabilities around the world weakens biosecurity policy both nationally and globally.

Planning for pandemic influenza illustrates the problems unequal intervention capabilities present for biosecurity. National and international plans for preparedness and response for pandemic influenza recommend stockpiles of antivirals to facilitate interventions to control, and perhaps contain, influenza outbreaks (WHO 2006e). Developed countries have acted to build national stockpiles, but many developing countries, especially in regions considered high-risk for pandemic influenza (e.g., Asia), face obstacles in stockpiling antivirals.

First, developing countries often do not have resources to devote to purchasing antivirals for a stockpile. Second, the stockpiling activities of developed countries (and even non-state actors) drive up the price of the main antiviral for pandemic influenza, Tamiflu, which makes developing country stockpiling even more difficult. Third, moves to increase Tamiflu supply for developing countries through generic production has re-ignited controversies related to the World Trade Organization's Agreement on Trade-Related Aspects of Intellectual Property Rights (TRIPS) about patent rights of pharmaceutical companies (e.g., Roche in the case of Tamiflu) and developing-country access to essential medicines.

Thus, many developing countries cannot without great difficulty create a key intervention capability for pandemic influenza recommended by public health experts. WHO intends to use its stockpile of three million courses of

Tamiflu (donated by Roche) in developing countries affected early by influenza of pandemic potential (WHO 2005). Developed countries can also deploy parts of their stockpiles to developing countries, as the United States did in May 2006 by pre-positioning supplies of Tamiflu in Asia (U.S. Federal News 2006). These actions by WHO and the United States respond to, but certainly do not alleviate, the disparity between developed and developing countries in stockpiling Tamiflu for pandemic influenza.

This section examines prevention, protection, and response interventions against the backdrop of the synergy thesis and the two fault lines of biosecurity policy. The analysis reveals problems with the synergy thesis in the area of intervention and highlights points at which the fault lines create difficulties and hard choices for efforts to address biological weapons and resurgent infectious diseases.

A. Prevention Interventions: Synergies in Tension

Comparing prevention interventions for biological weapons and infectious diseases illustrates the difficulty of creating robust, dual-purpose interventions to biosecurity threats. The synergy thesis relies on overlaps between policies on biological weapons and infectious diseases because these overlaps represent capabilities that can be used against either type of biosecurity threat. The deepest synergies appear when the approach to a pathogenic threat remains the same regardless of the origin of the microbe in question. Creating deep synergies in the area of prevention interventions proves difficult for many reasons.

For example, one strategy used to prevent pathogens from infecting populations has been disease eradication through vaccination, as happened with smallpox and as WHO is attempting with polio. Eradication is not, however, relevant for preventing biological weapons from being developed and used. In fact, disease eradication creates biological weapon opportunities. Smallpox's eradication has made smallpox a potentially fearsome weapon because of the vulnerability of unvaccinated populations. A similar dynamic may unfold if polio eradication is successful, creating the need for keeping poliovirus stocks secure from theft and misuse against populations not vaccinated in the wake of eradication.

The prevention objective concerning biological weapons is to prevent biological agents and toxins from being obtained, developed, and used by states or terrorist organizations. As Chapter 3 explored, this objective requires regulating and controlling the storage and transfer of dangerous pathogens; the safety and security of laboratories; vetting the backgrounds of scientists and technicians who work with, or in facilities housing, biological weapons agents; and overseeing scientific research done on dangerous pathogens or with techniques that could produce dangerous microbial life forms. Many of these tasks are familiar to national biodefense programs but not to civilian scientific research, which has not been subject to extensive regulation for security purposes until concerns about bioterrorism arose in the latter half of the 1990s.

Ensuring pathogen, laboratory, scientist, and research security with respect to dangerous pathogens delivers benefits for public health because it helps prevent intentional or accidental releases of potentially harmful germs. Biosecurity policy can create synergy through such prevention interventions for both defense against biological weapons and protection against infectious diseases.

The interests of the two components of biosecurity in these prevention interventions are not, however, a mirror image. For prevention of biological weapons proliferation and use, the prevention interventions mentioned earlier are perceived as critical. The policy incentive is to move toward ever-tighter regulation to reduce as much as possible the potential for abuse of the biological sciences and their research facilities by malevolent actors.

From a public health perspective, the synergy in such prevention interventions comes at a price, which brings the fault line between biological weapons and infectious diseases into view. Increasing pathogen, laboratory, scientist, and research security creates a regulatory and oversight system that requires significant human and economic resources to sustain. For public health, these resources represent an opportunity cost because the money and human capital spent on these prevention interventions cannot be used to address other problems in need of funds and personnel, such as improving surveillance or strengthening other types of intervention capabilities. Public health's incentive with regard to regulation of the biological sciences as a prevention intervention is to minimize the burdens such regulation imposes on the public health mission of protecting and promoting population health. The different incentives that appear on the biological weapons and infectious disease sides of biosecurity policy with respect to these prevention interventions highlight the difficulties raised by integrating security and public health and supervising science for biosecurity.

Further, other policies designed to address biological weapons could increase these prevention intervention costs for public health. These policies include expanding research into dangerous pathogens to develop countermeasures (e.g., drugs and vaccines) against biological weapons agents or to understand how states or terrorists might use new scientific techniques and technologies to create novel biological weapons. The United States has expanded research into dangerous pathogens considered likely or possible biological weapons agents, through initiatives such as Project BioShield and the National Biodefense Analysis and Countermeasures Center (NBACC).

NBACC has been particularly controversial. The U.S. Department of Homeland Security created NBACC to "provide the nation with essential biocontainment laboratory space for biological threat characterization and bioforensic research" (Department of Homeland Security 2005). NBACC's research into the infectious properties of infectious agents, countermeasure effectiveness, decontamination procedures, and bioforensics is designed to support policy makers' development of policies, programs, and technologies. NBACC houses the National Bioforensic Analysis Center (NBFAC), which will analyze materials recovered after a biological attack, and the Biological Threat Characterization Center (BTCC), which will perform studies and experiments to enhance understanding about current and future biological threats to guide development of appropriate countermeasures.

NBACC's mission caused significant controversy when arms control experts raised concerns about NBACC/BTCC plans to engage in activities, such as threat assessment analysis that involves modifying pathogens and experimenting with genetically altered microbes, activities considered by many countries and experts as potentially prohibited by the Biological Weapons Convention (BWC). In addition, some proposed NBACC/BTCC activities involve research considered increasingly dangerous for biosecurity and that need extra supervision and oversight. The Bush administration defended its approach to novel threat characterization research by arguing that its intent was purely defensive, and thus allowed by the BWC, and that its strategy responded to the changed nature of the biological weapons threat in the early twenty-first century.

NBACC and other policy initiatives have prompted critics to argue that expanded U.S. biodefense research (1) is not justified by the low probability of biological weapons attacks, (2) makes it more likely that dangerous pathogens may fall into the wrong hands or cause public health problems through failures in laboratory safety and security, (3) drains funding from other areas of scientific and public health research, (4) potentially violates U.S. obligations under the BWC, and (5) encourages other countries to pursue research that threatens to undermine the BWC (Cohen, Gould, and Sidel 2004; Grotto and Tucker 2006; Leitenberg 2005; Leitenberg, Leonard, and Spretzel 2004; Wheelis and Dando 2003). These arguments express the fear that U.S. policy subordinates public health to biodefense and, thus, fails to integrate security and public health in appropriate and sustainable ways.

Moreover, intensifying research into dangerous pathogens or ways pathogenic virulence can be enhanced through genetic engineering highlights the ambiguous line between "defensive" and "offensive" research with respect to biological weapons. As indicated earlier, concerns have been raised that some post–Cold War U.S. biodefense research may violate, or be perceived to be violating, the BWC. The United States justifies its biodefense research activities as necessary to anticipate how states or terrorists may work with, manipulate, or bioengineer pathogens to overcome established U.S. defenses and countermeasures.

The U.S. position narrowly interprets the BWC's prohibitions on the development of biological weapons and broadly construes the permitted purpose of protective research. Following the U.S. lead, other countries could adopt this approach, expand their national biodefense programs, and claim their intent is purely defensive, all of which would threaten to marginalize the BWC in biosecurity governance. This controversy reveals the biosecurity fault line between national and international interests and connects to the policy challenge of globalizing governance for biosecurity.

In other contexts, prevention interventions related to biological weapons do not overlap with prevention strategies for naturally occurring infectious diseases, and vice versa. These situations provide no opportunities for creating synergies through biosecurity policy. For example, the United States has initiated the Proliferation Security Initiative (PSI), which aims to interdict transfers and shipments of weapons of mass destruction (WMD), WMD-related material, and WMD delivery systems, including biological weapons. The United States, countries that have joined the PSI effort, the UN Secretary-General, and the Security Council believe that PSI constitutes an important effort in preventing WMD proliferation and use. PSI objectives are mainly pursued through law enforcement and military resources and assets. This program creates no dual-purpose capabilities that would assist public health authorities to prevent infectious diseases from harming population health. Similarly, public health prevention interventions aimed at increasing access to clean water in developing countries provide no synergies for preventing state or terrorist development, acquisition, or use of biological weapons.

This overview reveals the complexity and difficulty of achieving synergies between prevention objectives for biological weapons and naturally occurring infectious diseases. The synergies that exist with respect to regulating the biological sciences contain internal tensions that make them potentially unstable. As such, the synergies require constant attention and sensitivity to the need to recalibrate the balance between preventing biological attacks and fighting naturally occurring infectious diseases.

B. Protection Interventions: No Synergies

The category of protection interventions does not produce synergies between the biological weapons and public health components of biosecurity policy. Public health uses many protection interventions (e.g., vaccines, education, behavior modification techniques) because it assumes that people will come into contact with pathogenic microbes. Public health protection campaigns educating people to protect themselves through vaccination, "safe sex," proper food preparation, or hand hygiene operate on the basis that microbes circulate in the community, posing risks to human health.

The policy world focused on biological weapons does not assume that military or civilian populations are regularly exposed to biological agents or toxins against which they have to protect themselves. Exposure of military or civilian populations to intentionally released biological agents or toxins would trigger post-attack response interventions rather than pre-exposure protection interventions. Protection interventions concerning biological weapons would, instead, involve vaccinating in advance military or civilian personnel who might be exposed intentionally to pathogens during biological attacks.

Protection interventions made by public health, such as vaccination for seasonal influenza, produce no obviously exploitable synergies for biosecurity with respect to defending against biological weapons. Similarly, military vaccination of troops against smallpox and anthrax to protect them against battlefield use of these pathogens has no dual-purpose potential for protecting populations against naturally occurring infectious diseases. Protection interventions for biological weapons and public health proceed, generally speaking, as distinct rather than converging tasks in biosecurity policy.

Two examples illustrate the lack of synergies in the area of protection interventions. First, the U.S. military has required active duty military personnel to be vaccinated against anthrax because states frequently weaponized *Bacillus anthracis* in the past. Controversies developed, however, with respect to the safety and efficacy of the anthrax vaccine and its potential adverse health side effects. These problems created opposition to mandatory anthrax vaccinations inside and outside the U.S. military. The controversy ended up in U.S. federal courts, which declared mandatory anthrax vaccination illegal absent informed consent or a presidential waiver until the U.S. Food and Drug Administration could declare the anthrax vaccine safe and effective (*Doe v. Rumsfeld* 2004).

Second, the attempt in the United States to vaccinate public health and health care personnel for smallpox in 2003 reveals the extent to which protection interventions for biological weapons do not produce broader public health benefits, and may actually generate public health harms. The strategy to vaccinate individuals who would represent the "troops in the trenches" in case of a smallpox attack was to protect such essential personnel in advance of the crisis. This rationale is essentially the same reason the military wanted to vaccinate active duty troops for anthrax. As Chapter 3 described, the smallpox vaccination campaign failed to achieve anything close to the original goal for civilians. An overwhelming proportion of people targeted for vaccination decided not to be immunized because the health risks associated with smallpox vaccination were greater than the likelihood of a smallpox attack.

A similar fate probably awaits vaccines and drugs developed in the future as countermeasures to biological weapons agents, which means that such technologies will function as response interventions rather than interventions that governments could use in advance to protect populations from microbial threats. The federal government's purchase of millions of doses of anthrax vaccines and hundreds of thousands of doses of antitoxin for botulinum toxin under Project BioShield are resources for response rather than protection interventions.

C. Response Interventions: Potential for Deeper But Still Problematic Synergies

Deeper synergies for biosecurity policy are possible with respect to response interventions. Security and public health experts acknowledge that addressing intentionally caused or naturally occurring outbreaks requires similar interventions to control the epidemic, break any chain of transmission, treat the infected, and move society toward recovery. Such interventions include distribution and administration of antibiotics or vaccines, surge capacity in health care facilities to provide clinical treatment to the ill, and quarantine and isolation of persons infected with or exposed to contagious pathogens.

Synergies in response interventions can potentially be deeper than synergies in prevention interventions because public health principles and epidemiology determine the most appropriate way to respond to outbreaks, regardless of the source of the pathogen. Quarantining family members and contacts of a person exposed to anthrax is not appropriate because anthrax is not contagious. This epidemiological conclusion is valid whether a bioterrorist or sheep exposed the person to anthrax. This situation echoes the epidemiologically strong synergy biosecurity policy can develop with surveillance.

The IHR 2005 proves interesting with respect to the synergy potential in response interventions. The prior international sanitary conventions and the old IHR never required states parties to develop public health response capabilities except at certain points of potential disease entry and exit (e.g., seaports and airports). This approach was consistent with the treaties' objective of balancing trade and health interests. Radically, the IHR 2005 requires states parties to develop and maintain core public health response capabilities by 2012 (Article 13 and Annex 1). WHO designed these core capabilities to facilitate effective response interventions regardless of the outbreak's origin or source. In other words, such designed core response capabilities can be effective against biological attack or naturally occurring infectious diseases, and thus can create deep synergy for biosecurity policy nationally and internationally.

The potential for deep synergy in response interventions is not, however, comforting for two reasons. First, policy on neither biological weapons nor naturally occurring infectious diseases prefers to rely on response interventions. The need for such interventions means that efforts to prevent and protect populations from microbial harm did not succeed. The attention response interventions have received in the last decade demonstrates, however, that policy makers are aware that governments can no longer assume that effective response capabilities are not needed in the face of potential biological attacks and emerging and reemerging infectious diseases. The IHR 2005's mandate on national core response capacities stands as evidence of WHO member states' acknowledgment that microbes will penetrate defenses and create demand for timely and adequate response interventions.

Second, deep synergies only develop if response interventions are designed to be appropriate for dealing with both biological weapons and naturally occurring infectious diseases. Unfortunately, the fault lines of biosecurity policy appear strongly in the area of response interventions. Pressures exist to privilege responses to biological weapons over dual-purpose response capacities and to prioritize national over international response capabilities. The task of generating synergy in response interventions faces, therefore, difficult choices and potentially contentious political contexts.

Decisions in the United States about response interventions illustrate these tensions. The U.S. government has committed billions of dollars to the development and stockpiling of drugs and vaccines to bolster responses to biological attacks. These initiatives include a strategic stockpile of medicines for treating victims of bioterrorist attacks, a stockpile of smallpox vaccine large enough to cover every U.S. citizen, and Project BioShield's effort to encourage the development and acquisition of new vaccine and drug countermeasures against biological weapons agents.

With the exception of general antiviral treatments and medical supplies (e.g., masks, gloves) in the strategic stockpile, none of these initiatives provide dual-purpose capabilities for the United States in the event of pandemic influenza, which many public health specialists consider more likely than a bioterrorist attack. Much like BioWatch's irrelevance for surveillance of naturally occurring infectious diseases, intervention capabilities narrowly tailored for responses to specific types of biological attack do not generate much, if any, synergy for response capabilities needed in the face of infectious diseases. Claims that what is good for biodefense is good for public health should, therefore, be critically scrutinized.

These observations about the biological weapons/infectious disease fault line do not mean that every biosecurity decision related to response interventions must create deep synergy. The main point is that synergy is not necessarily or naturally the result of decisions made to bolster response intervention capabilities, which is often the impression given in the bioterrorism literature. Biosecurity policy confronts the task of ensuring that decisions made in the realm of response interventions do not neglect or marginalize either side of the biosecurity project. The best strategy available to achieve this objective is to develop and maintain, as much as possible, response interventions that produce deep synergy.

The national/international fault line also appears in the area of response interventions. Although improved national capabilities to respond to severe infectious disease outbreaks contribute to international outbreak response strategies, policies that focus almost exclusively on national interests do not significantly help efforts to increase response intervention capacities globally. Nationalistic biosecurity policies run the risk of increasing the "response gap" that exists between developed and developing countries on preparedness to manage severe infectious disease outbreaks.

The controversy triggered by Indonesia's decision to withhold samples of the avian influenza A (H5N1) virus from WHO illustrates the reality of the national/international fault line in connection with developing vaccines for pandemic influenza. In early February 2007, international media reported that Indonesia had stopped sharing with WHO avian influenza samples collected in its territory and had entered into negotiations with a pharmaceutical company for the development of vaccines against avian influenza (Aglionby and Jack 2007a, 1). Indonesia was angry that pharmaceutical companies in the developed world had used samples Indonesia provided to WHO for vaccine development, without compensation for Indonesia or any arrangement that would provide Indonesia affordable access to the vaccines developed.

According to the *Financial Times*, "Indonesia blamed the World Health Organization . . . for the government's decision to stop sharing samples of the H5N1 bird flu virus, claiming that the United Nations agency passed them on to pharmaceutical companies to make vaccines that Jakarta had to buy at high prices" (Aglionby and Jack 2007b, 9). Indonesia was particularly upset that an Australian pharmaceutical company developed an avian influenza vaccine from a sample provided to WHO by Indonesia (Reuters 2007). Indonesia intended its agreement with the pharmaceutical company to provide it with intellectual property rights over the samples and access to any vaccines developed from them.

Indonesia's actions sent shock waves through the global health community, which had been trying to construct multilateral strategies for fighting avian influenza and preparing for pandemic influenza. Indonesia's decisions threatened critical aspects of the public health approaches being built to address avian and pandemic influenza. Public health authorities require access to samples of viral or bacterial strains that cause communicable diseases to undertake surveillance and develop intervention strategies.

Analyzing pathogen samples allows public health officials to understand what disease-causing organisms are circulating within populations. Such samples are very important for conducting surveillance on changes in pathogen strains, such as the development of drug-resistant strains. Surveillance information allows public health to update diagnostic reagents and to develop interventions (e.g., vaccines, antibiotics) to address the characteristics of the viral or bacterial strain in question.

Thus, without samples, public health authorities cannot conduct effective surveillance or make scientifically informed recommendations on vaccines, and pharmaceutical companies could not develop vaccines needed to reduce influenza-related morbidity and mortality. Current fears about the potential for avian influenza to mutate into virulent strains capable of sustained human-to-human transmission highlight the urgency of having access to samples of avian influenza strains. The importance of such samples explains why public health officials reacted with such alarm to Indonesia's decisions.

Many experts criticized Indonesia for jeopardizing global public health cooperation, but support for Indonesia's position was also voiced, especially with respect to Indonesia's highlighting of the inequitable manner in which the current global strategies operate for many developing countries, which share information and samples but receive insufficient help from developed countries.

Thailand raised similar issues at WHO's Executive Board meeting in January 2007, and its representative argued, "We are sending our virus [samples] to the rich countries to produce antivirals and vaccines. And when the pandemic occurs, they survive and we die. . . . We are not opposed to the sharing of information and virus [samples], but on the condition that every country will have equal opportunity to get access to vaccine and antivirals if such a pandemic occurs" (Branswell 2007, A05).

Reflecting the alarm felt in global public health, WHO met with the Indonesian government to find a way to restart sample sharing and to address Indonesia's concerns about inequitable access to avian and pandemic influenza vaccines. On February 16, 2007, the Indonesian Ministry of Health and WHO issued a joint statement under which Indonesia agreed that "the responsible, free and rapid sharing of influenza viruses with WHO, including H5N1, is necessary for global public health security" and agreed to "resume sharing viruses for this purpose" (WHO 2007a).

For its part, WHO supported Indonesia's decision to discuss contractual arrangements with pharmaceutical companies for vaccine production and agreed to work with Indonesia and other countries "to assess and develop potential mechanisms, including Material Transfer Agreements, that could promote equitable distribution and availability of pandemic influenza vaccines developed and produced from these viruses" (WHO 2007a). Indonesia and WHO also agreed to convene a meeting in the Asia and Pacific region "to identify mechanisms for equitable access to influenza vaccine and production" (WHO 2007a).

News reports indicated, however, a lack of agreement between WHO and Indonesia about when Indonesia would begin sharing samples again. The WHO representative expressed his hope that Indonesia would start sample sharing again within a week or two after the joint statement (Aglionby 2007). The Indonesia Health Minister indicated, however, that sharing would only begin again once the new mechanism for equitable access to influenza vaccine and production was in place (Aglionby 2007).

Indonesia's decision to stop sharing samples with WHO flowed from its concern that it and other developing countries were not treated equitably after they shared samples with WHO. Vaccine development based on the samples occurs mainly by pharmaceutical companies in developed countries, which patent their vaccines, making them more expensive for developing countries to obtain. In addition, given that influenza vaccine manufacturing capabilities are mainly found in developed countries, developing countries fear that they will have little to no access to vaccines if a pandemic strain emerges. Thus, developing-country participation in sharing viral samples to support global surveillance produces a process that renders access to vaccine interventions inequitable.

In a context permeated by concerns about pandemic influenza, such inequitable access reduces incentives for developing countries to participate fully in sample sharing for surveillance purposes. Instead, Indonesia's negotiations for a commercial arrangement with a pharmaceutical company reveal a desire to exploit the potential of the samples more directly for the benefit of Indonesia and perhaps other developing countries.

The global health crisis created by Indonesia's withholding of the avian influenza samples was not resolved until the World Health Assembly (WHA) meeting in May 2007. At this meeting, and only after agreement in last-minute negotiations, the WHA adopted a resolution on sharing influenza viruses and promoting access to vaccines in connection with pandemic preparedness (WHO 2007c). The WHA resolution sets out a series of actions to achieve both "the timely sharing of viruses and specimens" in the WHO

Global Influenza Surveillance Network and ensuring and promoting "trans-parent, fair and equitable sharing of the benefits arising from the generation of information, diagnostics, medicines, vaccines and other technologies" (WHO 2007c). Through the resolution, WHO member states requested that the WHO director-general undertake activities designed to achieve fair and equitable sharing of benefits derived from influenza surveillance activities, especially access to vaccines (WHO 2007c). The resolution attempts to build a multilateral process to address the lack of fair and equitable access in developing countries to the pharmacological benefits derived from the sharing of influenza virus samples, and, in this respect, the resolution contains a new vision for global influenza governance.

The Indonesian episode helps emphasize that, for much of the developing world, naturally occurring infectious disease, such as avian or pandemic influenza, rather than biological weapons, is the greatest concern with respect to response preparedness. Regarding response interventions, the biological weapons/infectious disease and national/international fault lines generate serious tensions that must be managed in light of the divergent interests that exist between developed and developing countries. Unfortunately, effective management of these fault lines is becoming more difficult because developed states are struggling to improve their own response capabilities in the face of growing biosecurity threats.

Training exercises, such as the bioterrorism-focused "Top Officials" (TOPOFF) exercises in the United States and elsewhere, and real-world outbreaks, such as anthrax, SARS, and avian influenza, have demonstrated that even public health and health care systems in developed countries are unprepared for the response challenges severe infectious disease outbreaks create. Analyses of U.S. preparedness for responding to bioterrorism have concluded that the United States is not prepared for a serious biological attack, despite the billions that have been spent to improve preparedness and response capabilities (Trust for America's Health 2003, 2004, 2005, 2006).

The failure of the local, state, and federal governments to respond effectively to Hurricane Katrina in 2005 raised more doubts about the response preparedness of governments for serious shocks to populations in the United States. Criticisms that the federal government, and especially the Department of Homeland Security, had neglected disaster relief by focusing too much on the terrorist threat also emerged from the debacle in New Orleans. Congressional findings in early 2006 were also scathing with respect to the preparedness and response of the federal government (Select Bipartisan Committee to Investigate the Preparation for and Response to Hurricane Katrina 2006).

The nightmare of Hurricane Katrina was followed by acknowledgments by the federal government that the United States was not prepared for pandemic influenza. A flurry of U.S. pandemic influenza preparedness initiatives then took place in 2005 and 2006 that sought to improve response preparedness in the United States (White House 2005 and 2006b). In December 2005 and June 2006, Congress appropriated $6.1 billion for pandemic influenza preparedness, and the United States has pledged $334 million for international cooperation (U.S. Department of Health and Human Services 2006a), which represents approximately 5 percent of the total congressional appropriations. Figure 5.2 shows how the U.S. Department of Health and Human Services allocated the $3.3 billion it received in a December 2005 appropriations statute. Of this amount, the department will spend only a small fraction ($125 million, or 4 percent) on international activities (U.S. Department of Health and Human Services 2006b).

Given the lack of adequate response intervention capabilities within the United States for biological attacks or serious infectious disease outbreaks, the preoccupation of U.S. leaders with improving the domestic situation is understandable. This internal focus subordinates, however, the needs of other

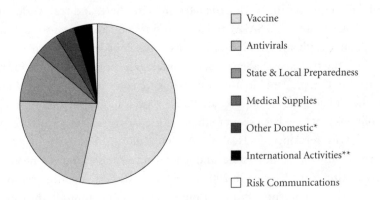

□ Vaccine

▨ Antivirals

▨ State & Local Preparedness

▨ Medical Supplies

■ Other Domestic*

■ International Activities**

□ Risk Communications

* Other Domestic includes Surveillance, Quarantine, Lab Capacity, Rapid Test
** International Activities includes International Preparedness, Surveillance, and Response

Figure 5.2 Pandemic Influenza Plan Funding: Breakdown of the U.S. Department of Health and Human Services' $3.3 Billion Allocation of Pandemic Preparedness Appropriations
SOURCE: U.S. Department of Health and Human Services 2006b, 2

countries and international organizations to domestic priorities. The same lack of financial resources that threatens the IHR 2005's mandate on core national surveillance capacities also undermines the similar obligation on core national response capacities. Again, no strategy exists about how to assist financially developing countries in complying with their response obligations in the IHR 2005.

Developed states have pledged some money to help improve public health infrastructures in developing countries in the fight against avian influenza and the possibility of pandemic influenza. The list of developing countries and regions that need funding has only increased as avian influenza has appeared in Europe, the Middle East, South Asia, and Africa, as of this writing. The pledges that once sounded impressive now appear diminished by the emerging scale of what biosecurity improvements the developing world requires. The enormity of the task, and the difficulty of improving public health infrastructure in developing countries, may ironically encourage developed states to concentrate their resources on their own protection. These self-help dynamics familiar from *realpolitik* may increasingly characterize *microbialpolitik* in the early part of the twenty-first century.

D. Biosecurity and Growth in Global Health Resources

Some readers might protest that we have not mentioned the significant increases in global health funding that have occurred in the last decade. The evidence is undeniable—developed states, international financial organizations (e.g., the World Bank), public-private partnerships (e.g., Global Fund to Fight AIDS, Tuberculosis, and Malaria [Global Fund]) and non-state actors (e.g., the Bill and Melinda Gates Foundation) have increased the scale of financial resources dedicated to global health problems (Cohen 2006; Garrett 2007). New, innovative financing mechanisms are also moving forward, including the International Finance Facility for Immunization (IFFIm), UNITAID, and (Product)[Red] (see box).

This influx of money contributes to biosecurity because the resources target serious infectious disease problems in the developing world, such as HIV/AIDS. Further, much of the new funding pays for scaling up protection interventions (e.g., IFFIm's objective of increasing rates of childhood vaccination) and response interventions (e.g., UNITAID's financing of antiretroviral treatments for persons living with HIV). Such new global health spending perhaps lessens the tension along the fault lines of biosecurity analyzed in this chapter because it concentrates on international assistance with respect to naturally occurring infectious diseases.

How much the increase in global health resources lessens the pressures building in biosecurity's fault lines remains, however, an open question. Although welcomed and praised, the expansion in global health spending witnessed during the last few years has generated controversy about the effectiveness and sustainability of the funding increases.

A number of common threads appear in these debates. One argument, most prominently made by Sachs (2005, 2007) is that, despite the recent surge in funding, global health requires more resources to help the developing world escape the debilitating effects of poverty, disease resurgence, and decades of neglect of public health and health care systems. The Global Fund's chronic shortage of resources illustrates why pleas for more resources continue in the global health arena.

Although not opposed to greater aid for global health, other experts argue that the increased levels of funding may be doing damage to long-term prospects for improving public health in developing countries and globally. For example, Garrett (2007, 14) asserted, "Because the efforts this money is paying for are largely uncoordinated and directed mostly at specific high-profile diseases—rather than at public health in general—there is a grave danger that the current age of generosity could not only fall short of expectations but actually make things worse on the ground." To avoid this fate, Garrett (2007, 38) argues that, in addition to more funding, state and non-state actors have to collaborate to transform "the structures of global health provision" and construct "not only effective local health infrastructures but also local industries, franchises, and other profit centers that can sustain and thrive from increased health-related spending."

The controversy extends into how key elements of the current influx of money for global health operate. The staggering sums made available for global health by the Bill and Melinda Gates Foundation have raised concerns among public health specialists worried about the disproportionate power this non-state actor wields in global health. On the ground, well-funded NGOs can distort and damage local public health and health care systems by taking doctors, nurses, and specialists out of communities to service better-paying NGO and donor-sponsored disease programs.

Most of the new money made available by donor governments remains subject to demands, conditions, and preferences of such governments. This

INNOVATIVE GLOBAL HEALTH FINANCING MECHANISMS

International Finance Facility for Immunization (IFFIm)

IFFIm raises funds by issuing bonds to private investors. Governments participating in IFFIm (currently Brazil, France, Italy, Norway, South Africa, Spain, Sweden, and the United Kingdom) have committed to paying the principal and interest on the bonds when they mature. IFFIm channels the money it raises through the GAVI Alliance (formerly the Global Alliance for Vaccines and Immunization), which uses the funds to deliver immunization and other health services in developing countries. By spending funds as they are raised, IFFIm can "frontload" health services by, for example, immunizing more children against childhood diseases. IFFIm anticipates that raising US$ 4 billion "is expected to help prevent five million child deaths between 2006 and 2015, and more than five million future adult deaths by protecting more than 500 million children in campaigns against measles, tetanus, and yellow fever." IFFIm's first bond issuance occurred in November 2006, when it successfully issued US$1 billon in five-year bonds earning 5 percent annual interest to investors in North America, Europe, the Middle East, and Asia.

UNITAID

UNITAID is an international drug-purchase facility that raises money to buy drugs for HIV/AIDS, tuberculosis, and malaria in developing countries. UNITAID raises funds through an "international air-ticket solidarity levy," a tax charged on the purchase of airline tickets. France has already mandated the payment of the tax, and UNITAID anticipates that the French levy will collect €200 million annually for UNITAID. Four other countries (Chile, Côte d'Ivoire, Gabon, and Mauritius) have also agreed to mandate payment of the levy. Nineteen other countries have agreed to allow air travelers to make voluntary contributions. Norway has agreed to contribute a portion of the tax it collects on airline tax on carbon dioxide emissions. UNITAID hopes its strategy will produce sustainable revenue streams for purchasing HIV/AIDS, tuberculosis, and malaria drugs.

(Product)[Red]

Under this mechanism, companies (e.g., Apple, Motorola, Gap) designate certain products as (Red) products, and the companies contribute a percentage of (Red) product sales to the Global Fund. (Product)[Red] was launched in the fall of 2006, and, in January 2007, (Product)[Red] estimated that it had raised approximately US$21 million for the Global Fund.

SOURCES: IFFIm 2007; UNITAID 2007; (Product)[Red] 2007

problem replays the traditional international health concern about donor-controlled, vertically oriented health programs dominating aid expenditures at the expense of horizontal, systemwide public health infrastructure improvements. In addition, the "strings" that come attached to public aid may not correlate with the specific needs or contexts that prevail in recipient nations. The most prominent example raised to illustrate this problem is President Bush's Emergency Plan for AIDS Relief (PEPFAR). PEPFAR's contributions to making prevention and treatment programs available to tens of thousands of people in the fifteen target developing countries are recognized in global health circles. PEPFAR's impact is, however, clouded by controversies about conditions the United States places on use of PEPFAR funds. The United States requires that 33 percent of PEPFAR funds be spent on abstinence-until-marriage efforts (U.S. Leadership Against HIV/AIDS, Tuberculosis, and Malaria Act 2003). Many recipient governments, experts, and NGOs question or oppose the emphasis on abstinence, as well as other conditions PEPFAR imposes (Center for Public Integrity 2006; General Accounting Office 2006; Human Rights Watch 2005; Lancet 2006).

From the perspective of biosecurity, most worrying is the view that all the new cash is not contributing to the construction of sustainable public health infrastructures in the developing world—a point on which experts appear to agree. As the IHR 2005's requirements for states parties to develop and maintain core national surveillance and response capabilities indicate, biosecurity is best achieved when public health infrastructures are strong and resilient. Despite the new money for global health, the resources are not contributing much to creating or strengthening the kind of surveillance and intervention capabilities biosecurity requires. Public health infrastructures are so weak in some developing countries that they have difficulty absorbing new funds donors have made available. The continued emigration of trained public health, medical, and health care personnel from developing to developed countries exacerbates public health infrastructure problems in developing states (WHO 2006b; Garrett 2007).

The unprecedented increases in financial resources that governments, international organizations, and non-state actors have made available for global health in the past decade play an important role in global biosecurity efforts. These new resources have not, however, revolutionized the processes for building sustainable public health surveillance and intervention capabilities in developing countries. This task is as daunting as ever, and in some respects more so. The importance of improving public health infrastructures remains a constant refrain in global health literature, but, to date, "never have so many advocated for a solution so consistently to so little effect" (Lee and Fidler 2007, 230).

VI. EMERGENCE OF A BIODEFENSE INDUSTRIAL COMPLEX IN THE UNITED STATES

Chapter 3 noted that the position of the United States as the preeminent power in international politics affects the new world of biological weapons governance. U.S. hegemony has given the U.S. response to the biodefense imperative global significance, especially with respect to the BWC's future. U.S. power also gives its policies on biodefense significance in the new world of public health governance.

Effective management of the fault lines of biosecurity policy may be made more difficult if current trends in U.S. public health governance are not reassessed. The momentum in U.S. biosecurity policy that disproportionately privileges biological weapons over naturally occurring infectious diseases and national over international interests may groove governance in ways that deepen these fault lines and make policy recalibration more difficult. A "biodefense industrial complex" may emerge in which government bureaucracies, academic institutions, and private-sector enterprises develop entrenched interests in the continuation and expansion of present policy directions.

The dramatic increase in U.S. government attention on, and appropriations for, the threat of biological weapons has already produced a biodefense industry that encompasses federal and state governments, universities, and for-profit and nonprofit entities. Calls for even more spending on national defense against biological weapons, such as former Senator Bill Frist's support in January 2005 for an initiative on U.S. biodefense "that even dwarfs the Manhattan Project" (Hirschler 2005), indicate that biodefense may continue to be a growth industry for governmental and nongovernmental actors and interests for years to come.

The resources spent on U.S. biodefense create bureaucratic turf (e.g., Department of Homeland Security), academic institutional commitments (e.g., universities seeking to build biosafety level (BSL) 3 and 4 laboratories to do biodefense work), and potential profits for pharmaceutical and high technology companies (e.g., economic incentives created by BioShield and BioWatch).

All this encourages people invested in biodefense to argue that continued, and even more, funding is required to protect the United States from biological attack.

The biodefense industrial complex may develop as these interests seek to influence government decisions about the amount and kind of spending required to protect the United States from bioterrorism. Reynolds (2005) highlighted this phenomenon by pointing out that the United States now spends "nearly $2 billion for each known victim of bioterrorism. Yet taxpayers are still assaulted by periodic hysteria-fanning studies from opportunistic institutes claiming, 'The United States remains woefully unprepared to protect the public against terrorists wielding biological agents.'"

Those involved in public health have increasingly voiced concerns about U.S. biodefense policy and the dynamics it creates. For example, in March 2005, 758 microbiologists wrote an open letter to the U.S. National Institutes of Health (NIH) arguing, "The diversion of research funds from projects of high public-health importance to projects of high biodefense but low public-health importance represents a misdirection of NIH priorities and a crisis for NIH-supported microbiological research" (Open Letter to Elias Zerhouni 2005).

Similarly, experts criticized a highly publicized smallpox outbreak exercise, called Atlantic Storm, conducted in January 2005, because they believed that the exercise involved implausible assumptions predicated on worst-case scenario analysis that overstated the threat for political purposes (Ruppe 2005). Both episodes demonstrate that the biosecurity fault lines analyzed are real and threaten to become more entrenched as U.S. biodefense policy funds bureaucracies, institutions, and companies dependent on the present policy trajectory. Thus, a biodefense industrial complex may be emerging that could make needed reforms in U.S. public health governance more difficult.

Worries that U.S. biodefense efforts increase both the public health and security threats from pathogenic microbes compound concerns about the development of a biodefense industrial complex. Critics of U.S. biodefense activities point to disturbing mishaps that suggest the federal government's expansion of biodefense activities creates clear and present public health dangers. These mishaps potentially include the anthrax attacks in 2001. Investigations following the attacks indicated that the anthrax used originated in U.S. biodefense facilities. If accurate, the attacks revealed problems with pathogen safety and security at government biodefense facilities. Later research suggested that the anthrax was perhaps not military grade and was a more common anthrax strain prepared with less sophistication than initially thought (Lengel and Warrick 2006). If correct, the later research forces the anthrax investigation to expand its search for suspects beyond scientists with involvement with U.S. biodefense facilities. Unfortunately, the investigation has made little progress, much to the frustration of members of Congress, who have expressed anger at the FBI's handling of the case and unwillingness to brief Congress on the investigation (Stein 2006). Even with the uncertainty surrounding the source of the anthrax, the episode creates doubts about the prudence of ramping up the scale and intensity of biodefense work inside and outside the federal government.

Other episodes have raised questions about current U.S. biodefense policy. In 2004 and 2005, a number of events raised alarm bells. First, a private military biodefense contractor, Southern Research Institute, accidentally sent live anthrax from its laboratory in Maryland to a hospital in California (Bioterrorism Week 2004). Second, mice infected with bubonic plague went missing from the Public Health Research Institute in New Jersey, prompting U.S. biodefense critic Richard Ebright to comment, "This is astonishing. We're greatly expanding access to biowarfare agents without ensuring that those resources are secure" (MacPherson and Sherman 2005, 1).

Third, laboratory-contracted cases of tularemia at Boston University but not reported to public health authorities in a timely manner as required by law drew more attention to the potential problems of expanding work on dangerous pathogens without appropriate safety, security, training, and accident-response systems (Lawler 2005). Boston University's plans to expand its involvement in biodefense research proceeded, and, "Incredibly, despite the carelessness reflected by this accident, the university received a major NIH grant to build a Biosafety Level 4 (BSL-4) laboratory for work with the most dangerous and incurable pathogens" (Grotto and Tucker 2006, 43).

A similar failure to report cases of staff infected with bacteria on the U.S. select agent list occurred in early 2006 at Texas A&M University, which did not report the infections to the CDC until April 2007 (*Nature* 2007). After investigation, the CDC suspended select agent research at five Texas A&M laboratories in June 2007, prompting an editorial in *Nature* to raise questions about the troubling manner in which the United States has expanded biodefense research (*Nature* 2007).

Fourth, in April 2005, WHO and the U.S. government scrambled to ensure immediate destruction of proficiency testing samples that contained the dangerous 1957–58 strain of pandemic influenza (H2N2) distributed by the College of American Pathologists to 3,747 laboratories in eighteen countries (Garrett 2005b). This virus strain is fully transmissible among humans and could have spread globally if it had infected persons handling the samples. This episode generated more worries about the inadequacy of biosafety and biosecurity procedures in the United States and elsewhere concerning dangerous pathogens. Laboratory accidents leading to infections involving the SARS virus in China, Singapore, and Taiwan demonstrated the potential global scope of inadequate biosafety capabilities (Normile 2004).

In light of the developments producing the biodefense industrial complex, these incidents create serious public health and security worries about the direction of U.S. biodefense policy. Public health experts feared that not only was the focus on bioterrorism diverting resources and attention away from naturally occurring infectious diseases, but it also threatened to create more dangers at home and abroad by expanding access to and work on dangerous pathogens in a context of inadequate biosecurity procedures, training, and capabilities.

In short, the biodefense imperative was accelerating policy faster than the supervision of science for biosecurity purposes could handle, threatening the overall integration of security and public health that biosecurity requires. The continuation of this dynamic could produce an earthquake for public health governance at the fault lines of biosecurity policy, sending damaging shock waves through the realms of both security and public health in the United States and around the world.

VII. CONCLUSION

The securitization of public health has produced a new world of public health governance that this chapter explored. The convergence of security concerns about biological weapons and public health worries about naturally occurring infectious diseases has generated a new environment in which the primary public health governance functions of surveillance and interventions operate. This convergence and the new environment constitute the medium in which the biosecurity challenge of integrating security and public health reveals its necessity, complexities, and difficulties.

Literature that considers the interface between protecting public health and defending against biological weapons often emphasizes the synergy thesis: Improvements made to the public health infrastructure create benefits for policies aimed at reducing the threats of both biological weapons and naturally occurring infectious diseases. The synergy thesis offers potential "win-win" options that promise to reduce the difficulty of integrating security and public health. The synergy thesis also raises the possibility that building dual-purpose surveillance and intervention capabilities could contribute to effective supervision of science and globalizing governance for biosecurity. Given the importance of the synergy thesis for this new world of public health governance, this chapter examined how persuasive the thesis is.

Our examination looked conceptually at how much synergy biosecurity policy could produce in the areas of surveillance and intervention, and we considered the extent to which the potential that is available is, in fact, being harvested. As a general matter, the chapter exposed that the synergy thesis is not what its routine invocation suggests. The synergy thesis proves more robust with respect to surveillance than to interventions. Improvements to surveillance tend to reduce stress in the biosecurity fault line between biological weapons and naturally occurring infectious diseases and thus ease the challenge of integrating security and public health policies. Virtually universal consensus exists on the synergistic potential of efforts to strengthen surveillance for pathogenic threats.

The major problem with respect to surveillance is the lack of sufficient progress on improving surveillance nationally and globally. To be sure, progress has been made, and we emphasized the unprecedented surveillance system established in the IHR 2005 as one indication of progress on surveillance. The potential for strengthening surveillance capabilities nationally and globally has not, however, been realized. The "surveillance gap" between developed and developing countries persists, and the international spread of avian influenza has revealed both the surveillance progress that has been made and the improvements that are still needed before biosecurity is realistically within reach. These problems reveal the depth of the challenge of globalizing governance for biosecurity.

With respect to interventions, this chapter revealed a much more complicated and difficult situation with the synergy thesis than exists with respect to surveillance. In terms of prevention interventions, potential for synergies with respect to some biosecurity initiatives concerning the regulation of the biological sciences (e.g., pathogen security and laboratory safety) exists. But tension accompanied these synergies because the security interest in tighter, stricter regulations causes friction with public health's interest in more scientific freedom, innovation, and dissemination of research. These uneasy synergies highlight the challenge of supervising science for biosecurity.

We found no potential synergies with respect to protection interventions. In public health, these interventions rely on certain assumptions about population exposure to circulating pathogens. The world of defending against biological weapons does not, and largely cannot, make similar assumptions. Protection interventions for public health and biological weapons advance, therefore, as independent rather than reinforcing activities. In addition, protection interventions against biological weapons (e.g., the vaccination programs for anthrax and smallpox) may raise public health problems for the goal of integrating security and public health.

Deeper synergies are possible in terms of response interventions, and much attention has been given to the dual-purpose benefits that strengthened preparedness and response capabilities can produce. The potential for deep synergies is, however, weakened because the fault lines of biosecurity policy appear strongly in the area of response interventions. This chapter noted the problems that arise when response interventions specific to biological weapons are privileged (e.g., Project BioShield purchases of anthrax vaccine and antitoxin for botulinum toxin) over more generalized public health response capabilities. Further, a response gap exists, and is widening, between developed and developing countries with respect to the ability to respond effectively to pathogenic threats. The difficulties of improving response intervention capacity internationally may encourage developed states to concentrate on making their own response capabilities as effective and resilient as possible. The challenge of globalizing governance for biosecurity again looms large.

As with the historic changes that have transformed policy approaches to the threat of biological weapons, the implications of the securitization of public health for public health governance are radical, far-reaching, and still unfolding. The new world of public health governance is a work in progress that includes both revolutionary steps (e.g., the IHR 2005) and serious potential for stagnation and regression. Analysis of the synergy thesis demonstrates that it is not the "magic bullet" that cuts through the difficulties of biosecurity policy to produce a new world order conducive to effective, sustainable biosecurity for all. Moving public health governance more effectively toward this goal requires more than ritual incantation of the synergy mantra. Harder choices await.

Part III

BIOSECURITY, THE RULE OF LAW, AND GLOBALIZED GOVERNANCE

6 BIOSECURITY AND THE RULE OF LAW

I. INTRODUCTION

The rise of biosecurity as a policy concern tells the tale of the rise and fall of various rules designed to protect against biological weapons or naturally occurring infectious diseases. Previous chapters have, for example, analyzed what the emergence of biosecurity has meant for the Biological Weapons Convention (BWC) and the International Health Regulations (IHR). In addition, the development of biosecurity has stimulated attention on new types of rules to replace or supplement traditional strategies.

To this point, we have examined these rules-based issues in the context of the new worlds of biological weapons and public health governance. The frequency with which biosecurity connects to various domestic and international rules raises the third challenge of biosecurity identified in Chapter 1—embedding biosecurity in the rule of law. This challenge is, however, of deeper significance than understanding that biosecurity affects rules of domestic or international law.

This chapter focuses on the challenge of embedding biosecurity in the rule of law. Our identification of the rule of law as normatively and practically critical indicates that we believe that biosecurity should, as much as possible, be achieved within the rule of law. The rule of law approach provides a framework for contributing to integrating security and public health, supervising science for biosecurity, and crafting globalized governance on biosecurity threats. Achieving biosecurity under the rule of law represents a difficult challenge, especially given the need to globalize governance for biosecurity.

Demonstrating the need for biosecurity under the rule of law does not automatically resolve the rule of law challenges biosecurity faces.

We begin our analysis by addressing why the rule of law should play a major role in biosecurity policy. We describe tensions between the pursuit of security and the rule of law and explore existing rule of law controversies in the biosecurity area to demonstrate how much the new governance worlds of biosecurity intertwine with concerns fostered by the rule of law.

After establishing the relevance of the rule of law to biosecurity debates, we provide a rule of law primer for the biosecurity–rule of law relationship. Like the synergy thesis, the "rule of law" is often used in loose, abstract ways that cloud the important philosophy of governance represented by the principles enshrined in the rule of law approach.

The rule of law primer provides the background for the examination of pursuing biosecurity under the rule of law. We connect biosecurity with the key elements of the rule of law approach, especially the protection of individual rights and liberties, the pursuit of natural and distributive justice, and the importance of transparency and accountability in governance.

The analysis of biosecurity under the rule of law introduces the difficulties globalized governance presents for the rule of law strategy presented in the chapter. The need for globalized governance confronts the rule of law approach with obstacles generated by the anarchical structure of international relations. Consideration of the challenge of globalized governance for biosecurity then continues in Chapter 7.

II. WHY THE RULE OF LAW?

A. Biosecurity's New Governance Worlds

Most discussions about biosecurity do not consider the rule of law. Our approach does not follow the usual pattern, so clarifying why the rule of law is critical in analyzing biosecurity is important. Our starting point can be located in the emergence of the new governance worlds for biological weapons and public health.

As explored more later, the rule of law emphasizes the importance of embedding the exercise of political power in a framework of rules. The new governance worlds for biological weapons and public health are novel contexts in which political power will be exercised. How such power is exercised is a primary question as these new governance worlds develop. Answering this question involves not only understanding what objective is sought but also how those with power determine that goal and pursue it. Biosecurity governance cannot exist outside the larger philosophical and legal framework that applies to the exercise of political power.

The rule of law provides that framework for biosecurity, as it does for other aspects of governance. This framework is especially important for the unprecedented governance changes affecting biosecurity. As previous chapters illuminated, the new world of biosecurity is complex, fluid, and fraught with controversies. In such environments, the rule of law provides a stabilizing approach amidst the torrent of change. The rule of law does not answer every hard question, resolve every quandary, or eliminate the inevitability of difficult politics in connection with biosecurity. The rule of law is no more a "magic bullet" for biosecurity than the synergy thesis. Although not sufficient, the rule of law is necessary in a context where societies have to operate in novel governance contexts to achieve policy goals not previously pursued.

B. Friction Between Security and the Rule of Law

Another reason why the rule of law is important to biosecurity involves tensions that have existed between the pursuit of security and the rule of law. Accusations that governments have violated the rule of law often arise with respect to matters of national security. Most recently, such accusations have proliferated concerning President George W. Bush's administration's policies in the war on terrorism. Critics lament the Bush administration's violation of the rule of law in connection with a number of actions, including the invasion of Iraq, the detention of enemy combatants at Guantanamo Bay, the abuse of prisoners at Abu Ghraib, the practice of extraordinary renditions, the use of secret prisons, and the use of electronic surveillance in the United States without court approval or oversight.

These contemporary examples have historical antecedents when exigencies of security stressed the rule of law. The classical debate triggered by such stress has involved whether individual liberty should or must, at times, yield to the security imperative. Security claims may also clash with notions of justice important to the rule of law, such as the principle of nondiscrimination. Arguments based on the exigency of security also often favor the exercise of unconstrained, discretionary power through secretive, non-transparent mechanisms.

Heightened fears about biological weapons and the securitization of public health recognize the need for strengthened security and thus feed into the power and appeal of security arguments. Historical sensibilities should make us aware that increased demands for security will, in all likelihood, create friction with existing, or proposed, rules of law designed to discipline political power. The nature of the biosecurity enterprise should, thus, make us sensitive to rule of law issues.

C. Rule of Law Controversies in Biosecurity

A third reason why the rule of law is important involves acknowledgment that rule of law controversies have already arisen in biosecurity policy. How much transparency should expanded U.S. biodefense activities have? When should the needs of security trump the scientist's freedom to publish and disseminate research? When is compulsory vaccination as part of stopping an outbreak justified? How much process is due someone subjected to isolation or quarantine? What privacy protections should be accorded information gathered by governments conducting disease surveillance?

These, and other questions, have arisen as biosecurity policy emerged in the past ten years. As with much concerning biosecurity, these questions arose in the wake of crises. The anthrax attacks catalyzed efforts to think more rigorously about the emergency public health powers governments possess, and these efforts grappled with appropriate ways to balance robust government responses with protection of individual rights. The severe acute respiratory syndrome (SARS) outbreak stimulated similar attention on isolation and quarantine as public health measures in a policy environment informed by human rights principles. The infamous Australian mousepox experiment triggered arguments for and against greater government control over scientific publications in the biological sciences.

Given the upheavals affecting policy on biological weapons and naturally occurring infectious diseases, the appearance of hard issues that require balancing the exercise of government power and the enjoyment of individual rights and liberties should not be surprising. The rule of law provides a framework for working through such difficult issues. We should also expect such issues to continue to emerge, which reinforces our sense that the rule of law is important with respect to biosecurity in the twenty-first century.

D. What Kind of Biosecurity?

The rule of law is also important for the study of biosecurity because it contains normative values and aspirations that inform governance. As explored later, the rule of law promotes forms of justice and thus connects to conceptions of what constitutes the good society. Taking the rule of law into account ensures that we think about what kind of biosecurity we want.

Biosecurity policy is not devoid of considerations of fairness and justice that give the rule of law normative power and purpose. To be sure, biosecurity policy is complex and difficult enough without layering it with normative questions at the heart of the rule of law ideology. These questions are, however, necessary, and they are stubborn. Whether we acknowledge it or not, considerations of fairness and justice permeate the challenges of integrating security and public health, supervising science, and globalizing governance. The security and public health that biosecurity aims to achieve intertwine with commitments to advance individual freedom, collective solidarity, and social justice. Ignoring biosecurity's rule of law implications cheapens this important human enterprise.

III. A RULE OF LAW PRIMER FOR BIOSECURITY

A. Rule of Law as a Philosophy of Governance

The rule of law is the source of soaring rhetoric and intense frustration. It is a complex concept that does not enjoy consistent usage in jurisprudence or public discourse. Both sides of debates invoke its majesty and its mystery (Cass 2001), making the concept appear fluid to the point of being illusory. The rule of law idea has, however, a core, and this core expresses a philosophy of governance increasingly embraced around the world.

The essence of the rule of law is captured in the argument that people should live under "the rule of law, not the rule of men." This famous phrase refers to the philosophy that legal rules have supremacy with respect to the exercise of political power. The supremacy of legal rules means that no one is above the law. All political power is exercised within a framework of rules that determines how such power is wielded and for what purposes. Leaders who exercise power outside their legally defined competencies, or in defiance of substantive legal limitations, violate the rule of law. The supremacy of legal rules ensures that the arbitrary desires, passions, and whims of politicians do not determine the destiny of the populace.

The rule of law also means that no individual is below, or not entitled to, the law's application. All persons are equal before the law and deserve its protection. The supremacy of legal rules empowers the governed and restrains those governing, all with the objective of creating order and justice within society. The rule of law envisions a government that exercises power effectively but not at the cost of sacrificing human dignity for the sake of political expediency. See Figure 6.1.

As a philosophy of governance, the rule of law requires that legal rules authorize government actors to exercise delineated powers to achieve, in the words of the U.S. Constitution, a "more perfect union." The structural and substantive features of legal empowerment are most commonly found in national constitutions, which assign different branches of government competencies in the exercise of political power. Statutes, administrative acts, and court decisions of the legislative, executive, and judicial branches of government record the utilization of these competencies.

Equally important is the rule of law's function of limiting the exercise of authorized power. A constitution may empower only the legislative branch to pass laws, but it may also prevent the legislature from passing certain kinds of laws in certain areas (e.g., laws restricting free speech) or with certain content (e.g., discrimination against racial minorities). Restraining government power is at the core of the rule of law philosophy. A key objective of restraints on government power is protection of individual liberties.

The rule of law approach posits that government officials cannot always be trusted to place the greater good over their own interests. "The essence of

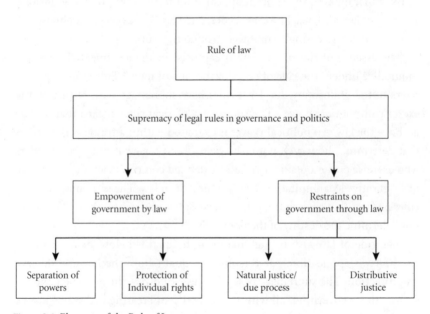

Figure 6.1 Elements of the Rule of Law

government is power," wrote James Madison (1865, 51), and "power, lodged as it must be in human hands, will ever be liable to abuse." Legal rules discipline government officials and institutions, forcing them to adhere to procedures and substantive standards, even if doing so negatively affects their agendas or effectiveness. Legal restraints on the exercise of power protect individual and community freedom amidst the ebb and flow of challenges, crises, and controversies that cascade through the life of a society.

Rule of law constraints on government power come in many forms. Clearly articulated, previously promulgated legal standards and procedures guide government decision making, thus channeling government actors into processes that deter politicians and bureaucrats from overstepping their authorities. Restraint also arises when the law insists that officials move through rigorous procedures before taking coercive action. Substantive and procedural constraints move governance in a direction where the exercise of power is more predictable, even-handed, and orderly—all of which guards against abuse inherent in unfettered power.

The role of law in empowering and restraining political power protects individual rights and liberties, and the rule of law is inseparable from this normative objective. The rule of law philosophy supports other normative values that shape this philosophy's vision of the role of government in the good society. These values include transparent and accountable government and the pursuit of justice. A government's transparency and accountability reflect the vibrancy of democracy in a society. These principles reflect the belief that the people, not the state, are sovereign in terms of ultimate political power. When government shields its actions from public scrutiny—as often happens in the name of national security—transparency and accountability suffer, creating potential threats for the rule of law's effectiveness in restraining political power.

The rule of law's attachment to the pursuit of justice flows from its commitment to the principle that no one is above or below the law. Like the rule of law, justice is complex and controversial. Nevertheless, three elements of the concept of justice have special resonance for the rule of law. First, the rule of law stresses the importance of nondiscriminatory treatment of similarly situated people. The nondiscrimination principle guards against the temptation that arises in the exercise of political power—to discriminate against those who are different.

Second, the rule of law seeks natural justice or due process—according individuals faced with coercive government actions the right to challenge such actions and to have such challenges heard by an independent decision maker. The due process aspect of justice recognizes both the need for the government to exercise political power and the right of individuals to ensure that the exercise of power happens in accordance with the law. Due process also serves the normative values of government transparency and accountability.

Third, the rule of law incorporates a broader notion of justice focused on the fair disbursement of the common advantages and burdens of a society. Distributive justice scrutinizes whether a society, through its governmental institutions, fairly and equitably allocates political and economic risks, burdens, and benefits. Unlike the individualized context of due process, distributive justice has a community orientation and thus raises questions about how a society should distribute opportunities and wealth its people create. More political controversies arise within distributive justice than within the other justice ideals connected with the rule of law.

The rule of law is, as we have said, a philosophy of governance. It is an idea, a belief, a faith. As such, its power depends on whether and how societies observe and preserve its tenets. A system based on the rule of law will not prevent, and never has prevented, all abuses of power. History is replete with the rule of men rather than the rule of law. Societies frequently confront crises that test their commitment to the rule of law. The September 11th attacks and the subsequent war on terrorism have, for example, triggered actions by the U.S. government that many believe deviate from the rule of law to promote an ideology that seeks to aggregate power in the hands of the commander in chief and the office of the president. Historical and contemporary episodes teach the lesson that the rule of law can never be taken for granted.

B. The Rule of Law as a Philosophy for Biosecurity Governance

We outlined earlier reasons why connecting the rule of law with biosecurity is important, but the significance of this connection goes deeper. The rise of biosecurity has transformed the governance contexts for biological weapons and public health, and many controversies examined in previous chapters involved policy makers, experts, and academics trying to reorient politics, science, and law to address the challenges this new world order creates. The novelty of biosecurity as a governance challenge should not, however, tempt us to be complacent about the rule of law or to look for ways to escape its scrutiny. Instead, we need to subject biosecurity to the rule of law.

This task requires examining the controversies and challenges of biosecurity through the rule of law's interest in protecting individual rights and liberties, pursuing justice, and promoting transparent and accountable governance. This examination reveals not only the normative values the rule of law approach preserves but also the practical value it produces for generating more effective and sustainable biosecurity governance. What we seek as a nation and as an international community is biosecurity under the rule of law.

IV. BIOSECURITY UNDER THE RULE OF LAW

A. Empowering Governance for Biosecurity

Two fundamental responsibilities of governments are to provide for the security and health of their populations. Without security and health, individuals cannot enjoy political, economic, social, and other freedoms and material benefits critical to personal well-being and thriving societies. To fulfill these responsibilities, governments require appropriate powers to take actions necessary for providing security and protecting health. A rule of law task, therefore, involves sufficiently empowering governments to achieve security and health protections for their peoples.

This point may seem obvious, particularly because governments have long been authorized to take actions concerning national security and public health. The convergence of the policy worlds of security and public health has, however, raised questions about whether governments are adequately empowered to address biosecurity threats. Examples from both the biological weapons and public health contexts illustrate this point.

Three trends in the new world of biological weapons governance analyzed in Chapter 3 were the criminalization of biological weapons development and use, regulation of the biological sciences, and preparing to respond to biological attacks. These trends highlight the need for governments to adopt new legislation to create the specific authority and frameworks necessary to accomplish criminalization, science regulation, and public health response preparedness. General governmental competence in security and public health existed, but governments have sometimes needed new law to channel general competence into effective action for each of these biosecurity objectives.

The same dynamic has appeared in the new world of public health governance. With public health personnel being the first responders for biological attacks or serious infectious disease epidemics, governments needed to make sure such personnel had the appropriate legal authority to respond effectively. Emergency preparedness had to include legal preparedness at both national and subnational government levels (Matthews, Abbott, Hoffman, and Cetron 2007).

In the United States, the U.S. Centers for Disease Control and Prevention (CDC), aided by outside experts, worked quickly in the wake of the anthrax attacks to provide state governments in the United States with a template—the Model State Emergency Health Powers Act (2001)—against which to review and, if necessary, revise their laws governing public health responses to serious pathogenic events. As of April 2006, forty-four state legislatures have revised or added to their public health laws after reviewing the Model Act (Center for Law and the Public's Health 2006). The rule of law philosophy informed the Model Act effort because it aimed to make sure that, in an emergency, law guided the exercise of emergency powers. Without advance legal preparedness, the exigencies of the crisis could marginalize the role law should play in regulating the exercise of emergency powers.

The need for the empowerment of governance through law is not confined to the governments of states but also arises with respect to international organizations. The effort to negotiate a protocol for the BWC sought to create a new international organization—the Organization for the Prohibition of Biological Weapons—authorized to engage in BWC compliance verification. The failure of this effort provides part of the background for the UN Security Council's adoption of Resolutions 1373 and 1540, which required all UN member states to take action against terrorism and to prevent non-state actors from obtaining weapons of mass destruction (WMD), WMD-related materiel, and WMD delivery systems.

As commentators noted, Resolutions 1373 and 1540 constituted unusual exercises of the Security Council's power to maintain international peace and security. Rather than the traditional arms control approach, the Security Council adopted something more akin to international legislation. The Security Council broke new ground with its Charter authority to strengthen biosecurity. As noted in Chapter 3, some proposals for shoring up the BWC's role in biosecurity involve increasing the Security Council's role in investigating unusual infectious disease events.

Novel issues of empowerment also arose with respect to the new International Health Regulations (IHR 2005). The IHR 2005 granted the World Health Organization (WHO) new legal authority, which strengthened WHO's ability to address disease events of international concern. The

IHR 2005 empowers WHO to (1) use nongovernmental sources of surveillance information (Article 9), (2) declare the existence of a public health emergency of international concern (Article 12), and (3) issue temporary recommendations to WHO member states about how to deal with such an emergency (Article 15). WHO undertook all these actions during the SARS outbreak, but it did not have legal authority to do so at that time. The IHR 2005 provided the rule of law framework for expanded WHO powers in the new world of public health governance.

As these examples demonstrate, empowerment of governments and international organizations form an important aspect of biosecurity under the rule of law. The need for empowerment is not surprising given the challenges biosecurity creates. Increasing the power of governments or intergovernmental organizations raises, however, rule of law concerns about ensuring that such power does not threaten individual rights and liberties, the pursuit of justice, or transparent and accountable governance.

B. Biosecurity and the Protection of Individual Rights and Liberties

Rule of law issues concerning the protection of individual rights and liberties are not strangers to the policy worlds of security and public health. A classical feature of national security law is, for example, the "security versus liberty" debate. Governments, understandably, consider national security as one of their most important obligations, especially with respect to threats of aggression emanating from foreign sources. Terrorist violence is particularly brutal and psychologically disturbing because it targets the innocent with no warning. Public fear is greatest when violent acts are unusual and highly visible (Kunreuther 2002)—the classical hallmarks of terrorist attacks. Faced with these threats, governments are likely to exercise existing powers to their fullest extent and seek new authority to use against the terrorist menace.

The post–September 11th period has seen the United States, and other countries, confront controversies about the impact on individual rights and liberties of exercises and expansions of government power for national security purpose. Political firestorms involving the security versus liberty debate have erupted in the United States over the USA PATRIOT Act (2001); the detention of enemy combatants in the United States (*Hamdi v. Rumsfeld* 2004; *Padilla v. Hanft* 2005) and at Guantanamo Bay (*Rasul v. Bush* 2004); the treatment of detained persons in Iraq, Guantanamo Bay, Afghanistan, and elsewhere; the practice of extraordinary renditions; the operation of secret prisons and detention facilities; plans to try illegal enemy combatants by military commissions (*Hamdan v. Rumsfeld* 2006); and the Bush administration's domestic electronic surveillance program.

Similarly, public health has confronted controversy concerning governmental infringements on individual rights and liberties. Even a cursory examination of traditional public health powers reveals the burdens governments can place on individuals. Reporting and monitoring health records for surveillance purposes entails government acquisition, storage, and use of sometimes personally sensitive information, implicating privacy. Compulsory vaccination, medical examination, and treatment invade bodily integrity by forcing people to submit to medical interventions. Isolation and quarantine affect the rights to free association and freedom of movement. Individuals or groups singled out through government public health actions have legitimate concerns about potential stigma, embarrassment, and discrimination (Gostin 2000).

The exercise of public health powers can also burden economic interests. Health-related licensing affects professional freedoms, inspections affect free enterprise, and nuisance abatements affect the freedom of contract and the right to use private property (Gostin 2000). Public health decisions may also require the destruction of economically valuable property, as seen in the mass culling of animals undertaken in response to outbreaks of bovine spongiform encephalopathy and avian influenza. Warnings and travel advisories issued by public health entities can adversely affect trade and tourism, as occurred during SARS. Compulsory licensing of pharmaceutical products (e.g., antiretrovirals for HIV/AIDS; Tamiflu for avian or pandemic influenza) affects intellectual property rights protected in international trade law.

Given the relationship of security and public health with the protection of individual rights, the convergence of these areas in biosecurity policy should raise rule of law concerns. Individual rights are not always absolute, and a government may sometimes infringe on a person's enjoyment of them to protect or promote the greater public good. Security and public health have both separately involved the need to infringe on individual rights to achieve the greater good for society. Combined through biosecurity, these policy areas present a formidable force for those concerned about protecting individual rights and liberties.

The pressures biosecurity policy can create for the protection of individual rights and liberties appear in many contexts. One obvious context involves responses to public health emergencies, which provide fertile environments for governments to overreact and thus unnecessarily infringe on civil and political rights. Embedding legal preparedness into emergency preparedness and response planning can minimize potential for government overreaction, but legal preparedness does not prepare governments for every contingency. Hard decisions with wrenching trade-offs in crisis situations will be needed. Rights will still be at risk.

Threats to individual rights and liberties may also arise with respect to efforts to prevent biosecurity problems. The criminalization of biological weapons development and use and the regulation of the biological sciences may encourage the government to scrutinize, and even restrict, scientific and public health activities once thought benign. Biosecurity concerns have already reshaped the world of research on pathogenic microbes through regulation of access, possession, storage, and transfer of biological agents, and those engaged in biological research have not universally welcomed this transformation. Missteps by researchers today could produce more than a negative report from a peer-reviewed journal; they could produce a prison sentence, as Dr. Thomas Butler learned (see Chapter 3).

The argument that the government needs to control more rigorously the conduct and publication of some types of scientific research involving biological agents has been particularly controversial. The principles of scientific freedom, innovation, and open dissemination of research have their moorings in the rights to free speech and freedom of association. The mere fact that we now debate how much biosecurity policy should affect core principles of the scientific endeavor, which are themselves grounded in bedrock individual rights, is indicative of the stress biosecurity can create for the protection of rights and liberties at the heart of the rule of law.

For biosecurity under the rule of law to be achieved, the first task is to ensure that the exercise of new or existing government power is subject to scrutiny from the perspective of protecting individual rights and liberties. The process of empowerment discussed earlier provides examples to illustrate this point. The Model Act (2001) was, for example, designed to ensure that state legislatures and public health officials examined how well their existing or proposed legal powers protected individual rights and liberties. How the Model Act balanced effective government responses and civil rights proved controversial (American Civil Liberties Union 2002; Heritage Foundation 2002), but the Model Act put the spotlight on this critical issue.

Similarly, at the international level, the IHR 2005 radically breaks from predecessor treaties by including provisions that protect human rights when governments act to protect themselves from disease threats. See Annex 4. How well the IHR 2005 embedded human rights protections remains contested (Fidler and Gostin 2006), but this rule of law question is now part of the discourse concerning the IHR 2005's contribution to biosecurity.

Another example comes from the U.S. federal government's effort to revise its federal quarantine regulations. This revision sought to upgrade federal law protections for civil liberties, especially due process, in the context of the exercise of federal quarantine power. The proposed regulations (Department of Health and Human Services 2005) were praised for improving the protections for individual rights and criticized for not including sufficient protections (Gostin 2006; Gostin, Berkman, and Fidler 2006).

The second task required to achieve biosecurity under the rule of law with respect to individual rights and liberties is to scrutinize strictly any government action that potentially infringes on rights and liberties. This approach is familiar to both constitutional law and international human rights law, and it involves three tests: the risk threshold test, effectiveness test, and least-restrictive measure test.

Under the risk threshold test, the rule of law requires that the exercise of power be directed at a threat or risk the severity and probability of which justifies action. Government has the burden of demonstrating that its action meets this threshold justification. Coercive action that adversely affects individual rights is not justified unless the government can show the existence of a probable and severe threat, risk, or danger to the population.

The Model Act includes, for example, the threshold justification test. The Model Act requires that a state governor declare a "public health emergency" before being granted special, more robust, powers, such as compulsory medical examination, vaccination, treatment, or quarantine. The governor must demonstrate the existence of three conditions before declaring a public health emergency: (1) an occurrence or imminent threat of an illness or health condition, that (2) is believed to be caused by bioterrorism or a new or reemerging infectious agent or biological toxin that (3) poses a high probability of a large number of deaths, a large number of serious or long-term disabilities, or widespread exposure to an infectious or toxic agent that poses a significant risk of substantial harm to a large number of persons (Model Act 2001, Article I, §104(m)).

Furthermore, the Model Act (2001, Article IV, §402) requires that the governor provide information in the emergency declaration that supports the existence of emergency conditions. As a check against arbitrary action, the legislature may vote to discontinue a declared emergency (Article IV, §405[c]). Similarly, the courts can review whether the governor established the existence of emergency conditions. The Model Act was crafted to give states the powers necessary for confronting a public health emergency, but the legislation only allows the exercise of those potentially coercive powers when they are absolutely necessary. A governor's power is limited by the requirement that he or she demonstrate the existence of a real threat to the population.

The effectiveness test requires the government to show that the intervention chosen will be effective in eliminating or mitigating the expected harm. Interventions that will not work against the identified threat protect nobody and erode public confidence and trust in the government. Implementing community quarantine in the wake of an anthrax attack would not, for example, be an effective intervention because anthrax is not contagious. The efficacy test is hardest to apply when scientific evidence about the threat or risk is incomplete.

The SARS outbreak provides interesting material on this issue. In responding to SARS, public health professionals used interventions from the "pretherapeutic" era of public health because, when the outbreak occurred, no diagnostic test, vaccine, or treatment for the SARS virus existed. The modes and efficiency of the virus' transmission were poorly understood. Armed with incomplete information, governments used old public health techniques, such as border screenings, travel advisories, and quarantine. Public health officials hoped, but did not know, that these measures would help in bringing SARS under control. Researchers subsequently questioned whether some of the interventions, such as border screenings, were effective.

Some experts believe that the precautionary principle offers a way to ease the tension between the efficacy test and situations in which government officials have incomplete information about a pathogenic threat. Articulated most comprehensively in environmental policy making, the precautionary principle involves four components: (1) preventive action is legitimate in the face of uncertainty, (2) the burden of proof shifts to the proponent of the activity the environmental effect of which is uncertain, (3) a wide range of alternatives to the potentially harmful activity should be explored, and (4) public participation in the decision should be increased.

Despite intuitive appeal, the precautionary principle only awkwardly applies to threats posed by pathogenic microbes for two reasons. First, precautionary action against pathogens would involve broader restrictions on individual rights and liberties than the precautionary principle creates in the environmental context. The major burden the precautionary principle creates in environmental protection is economic because precautionary action increases transaction costs or reduces profitable opportunities for private enterprises. Precautionary action against infectious diseases capable of disrupting societies would require interference with more than economic freedoms.

Second, public health's need for better scientific information on pathogenic threats creates urgency for getting beyond precautionary action not always present in the environmental context, which typically involves noncommunicable disease problems. The rapidity with which scientific researchers, coordinated by WHO, identified and analyzed the SARS virus was unprecedented, and this scientific information led to more informed public health interventions as the science on the virus improved.

These facets of the precautionary principle's application to biosecurity mean that the key rule of law strategy is to calibrate scientific uncertainty with effective government action through transparency and flexibility by the government. Governments must be willing to make clear the bases for their interventions, attempt to clarify uncertainty, and acknowledge when new scientific evidence warrants changing policies.

The third rule of law test used to scrutinize government actions that infringe on individual rights and liberties requires that all right-restricting measures be the least restrictive measures possible. If a government has a choice between two interventions that will effectively address a pathogenic threat, then it must select the option that least restricts rights and liberties of affected individuals. The Model Act and the IHR 2005 both use this test. The Model Act only permits mandatory isolation or quarantine if no other less restrictive intervention is available (Article VI, §604[b][1]). The IHR 2005 contains provisions that require states parties to use the least invasive or intrusive measures possible with respect to travelers (Articles 23.2 and 43.1).

The threshold, efficacy, and least-restrictive measure tests represent a tried-and-tested rule of law approach that balances the need for robust government actions with due respect for and protection of individual rights and liberties. The tests do not ensure that the government will strike the right balance in any given case, whether the issue involves restrictions on scientific research or infringements of civil and political rights. The tests form, however, a framework that structures the exercise of political power in a way that deters government actors from justifying rights-damaging actions under expansive, non-transparent notions of "security" or "emergency powers." The framework should be deeply embedded in all aspects of biosecurity policy that affect liberty interests.

C. Biosecurity and Justice

Justice is a complex, subtle, and controversial concept with multiple meanings and is never a subject approached lightly. It is, however, an ideal interwoven with the rule of law as a philosophy of governance. Justice is also of particular concern for biosecurity because the pursuits of security and public health have historically produced unjust treatment of individuals and groups. One of the darkest marks in U.S. constitutional jurisprudence is the Supreme Court's decision in *Korematsu v. United States* (1944), in which the Court let stand— under the banner of national security—a blatantly racist detention program aimed at Japanese-Americans. By triggering fear and prejudices, disease epidemics have also brought out the worst in governments and communities. Too often societies have blamed and vilified outsiders, minorities, or those too vulnerable to defend themselves for the illness, death, and dread caused by traumatic health events.

Biosecurity under the rule of law needs, therefore, to confront issues of justice, and we examine three aspects of the rule of law's relationship with justice—the imperative of nondiscrimination, the importance of natural justice or due process, and aspiration for distributive justice. Each aspect of justice is interconnected in the new worlds of governance created by the rise of biosecurity.

1. The Nondiscrimination Imperative

One of the most important aspects of justice is the principle of nondiscrimination. The connection of justice with nondiscrimination extends back at least to Aristotle, who expressed the ideal of justice as the equal treatment of equals and the unequal treatment of unequals. In its simplest formulations, the principle of nondiscrimination opposes treating an individual differently merely because of his or her membership in a distinct group or category of persons, such as race, ethnicity, gender, religion, age, or disability. Nondiscrimination mandates that people be treated according to their individual characteristics and situations and not on the basis of their association with a group or collectivity. The principle rejects prejudices, stereotypes, and fears about people and forces politics and the law to strive for the point where similarly situated individuals receive equality of treatment.

As indicated earlier, security and public health have often gravitated toward discrimination historically and in contemporary times, which makes nondiscrimination a key concern for biosecurity. More than once *Korematsu* has been raised as a warning against post–September 11th animosities toward Arabs and Muslims affecting U.S. national and homeland security policies. Concerns have been raised in the U.S. scientific community that prejudices against foreign scientists inform how the regulation of the biological sciences is unfolding.

Public health governance has also adopted discriminatory policies and practices. Several public health campaigns involving compulsory measures in the nineteenth and twentieth centuries in the United States reeked with prejudice: isolation of persons with yellow fever, despite its mode of transmission by mosquitoes (Musto 1986); arrests of alcoholics, especially poor Irishmen, in the false belief that intemperance caused cholera (Risse 1988); mass confinement of prostitutes suspected of having syphilis (Brandt 1985); and forced removal of children thought to have poliomyelitis (Risse 1992). In one of the most famous phrases from public health jurisprudence, a federal court struck down a quarantine implemented against Chinese Americans in San Francisco because public health authorities acted "with an evil eye and an unequal hand" (*Jew Ho v. Williamson* 1900).

These historical examples do not mean that discrimination in public health is a relic of less enlightened generations. The hand of discrimination has been at work in the HIV/AIDS pandemic, particularly in how government policies have targeted vulnerable groups such as injection drug users, sex workers, and gay men (Gostin 2004). The SARS outbreak saw hateful and hurtful stereotypes emerge in the West about persons of Asian descent being unhygienic vectors of infection (Chang 2003).

Discrimination is sometimes not blatant but takes the form of the neglect of the vulnerable. The anthrax attacks in 2001 saw the government lavish attention on staffers in the U.S. Senate while initially ignoring postal workers, many of whom were African American (Lipton and Johnson 2001). The images of poor, mostly African American survivors of Hurricane Katrina in 2005 are seared into the memories of people around the world as an image of justice denied in the United States.

The rule of law's nondiscrimination imperative applies equally to the new worlds of biological weapons and public health governance. Post–September 11th concerns about racial and religious discrimination in the application of U.S. national and homeland security law stand as a warning for biosecurity policy's pursuit of the criminalization of biological weapons development and use and regulation of the biological sciences. The temptation to engage in racial or religious profiling in connection with trying to prevent biological attack may be strong, but the embrace of discriminatory security and law enforcement strategies typically produces lost liberty without achieving greater security.

The nondiscrimination imperative is also important for surveillance and intervention. The public health infrastructure works best when its actions are based on neutral, scientifically informed criteria and evidence rather than on irrational fears and stereotypes. Nondiscrimination is also important in responses to severe disease risks to make sure that the response does not neglect minorities, the poor, and the vulnerable. Damaging discrimination also occurs when authorities act with a complacent eye and a neglectful hand.

2. Natural Justice: Procedural Due Process

The second component of justice to consider for purposes of achieving biosecurity under the rule of law is what Europeans call "natural justice" and North Americans refer to as "due process." This aspect of justice concerns the process through which governments exercise power against individuals to achieve the public good. This process must be fair and must accord the individual the opportunity to challenge the government's actions. Basic elements of natural justice or due process include notice from the government of the impending action, the right to contest the action or defend oneself against the government's exercise of power, the right to the assistance of legal counsel during the process, and the right to have the dispute decided by a neutral decision maker in a timely manner. Procedural due process is not only an independent aspect of justice but also is interdependent with the protection of individual rights and liberties.

Most people are familiar with justice's connection to procedural due process through the operation of criminal law. Many domestic legal systems and international human rights law have enshrined procedural due process in their rules. For example, the International Covenant on Civil and Political Rights (1966, Article 9) provides, "No one shall be deprived of his liberty

except on such grounds and in accordance with such procedure as are established by law. . . . Anyone who is deprived of his liberty by arrest or detention
shall be entitled to take proceedings before a court, in order that that court
may decide without delay on the lawfulness of his detention and order his
release if the detention is not lawful."

Procedural due process has great importance in connection with biosecurity policy. Again, historically, exigencies of security and public health have
encouraged governments to ignore procedural due process, thus shortchang-
ing this critical aspect of the rule of law. The controversies in the United States
concerning the process due enemy combatants detained in the war on terrorism illustrate the pressures national security imperatives can place on a
government's willingness to accord due process to persons deprived of their
liberties. The Supreme Court decisions in *Hamdi v. Rumsfeld* (2004), *Rasul v.
Bush* (2004), and *Hamdan v. Rumsfeld* (2006) particularly involved judicial
intervention to force the executive branch to provide some due process for
persons detained by U.S. military forces.

Public health too has experienced controversy over the adequacy of procedural due process when public health authorities applied compulsory measures against individuals. A frequent theme in public health law during the
past ten years has been the need to improve due process protections for persons subject to the public health powers of the government. This goal was
high on the list of the Model Act project, arose in connection with the isolation and quarantine used during SARS, and has also featured in the federal
government's proposed new quarantine regulations.

The new worlds of biological weapons and public health governance will,
in all likelihood, involve governments taking compulsory measures against
individuals and thus infringing on their rights. Governmental powers exercised with respect to the criminalization of biological weapons development
and use, regulation of the biological sciences, conduct of biodefense, and responses to biological attacks may well be coercive with respect to individuals, creating the need for procedural due process. The government may, for
example, prevent a researcher from conducting research on certain biological
agents or toxins, thus constricting the researcher's ability to practice his or
her profession. The researcher must be able to challenge this decision, with
the assistance of legal counsel, before a neutral decision maker. Although due
process is most often connected with governmental actions, the increasingly
important role played by non-state actors in the supervision of science for

biosecurity purposes means that any procedures such actors apply that might deprive researchers of the benefits of scientific freedom, innovation, and wide dissemination of research should also be subject to due process criteria.

Governments faced with the challenges of the new world of public health governance will also confront situations that require them to take coercive actions that restrict or infringe upon individual rights, liberties, and well-being. This reality is especially true with respect to interventions believed necessary to address serious infectious disease outbreaks, such as compulsory medical examination, vaccination, isolation, or quarantine (see box). Reaching satisfactory levels of procedural due process in public health was often difficult

---

THE EMERGENCE OF XDR-TB AND THE POTENTIAL NEED FOR COMPULSORY MEASURES

Global health concerns about the emergence of extensively drug-resistant tuberculosis (XDR-TB) worsened in September 2006 with the appearance of a new deadly strain of XDR-TB in the province of KwaZulu-Natal in South Africa. WHO called for a strengthened response to this XDR-TB emergence to prevent the global spread of this virtually untreatable threat (WHO 2006d). The threat has become so serious that public health experts are considering compulsory measures as part of the global strategy against XDR-TB. Singh, Upshur, and Padayatchi (2007) asserted, "We must come to terms with the extent to which judicially sanctioned restrictive measures should be employed to bring about control of what could develop into a lethal global pandemic." Public health authorities have used compulsory isolation and treatment in efforts to control multi-drug resistant tuberculosis (MDR-TB), so debate about using such measures to deal with the more frightening threat of XDR-TB comes as no surprise. Experts raising the potential need to apply compulsory measures to persons infected with XDR-TB stress the importance of doing so in accordance with human rights principles. As Singh et al. (2007) argued, "Human rights doctrine . . . recognises the limitation of many rights in a public health emergency, provided the measures employed are legitimate, non-arbitrary, publicly rendered, and necessary." In January 2007, WHO issued guidance on human rights and involuntary detention for XDR-TB control (WHO 2007b). The application of a compulsory isolation order in May 2007 against a citizen of the United States diagnosed with XDR-TB significantly raised the profile of XDR-TB as a global problem and the debate about the use of mandatory isolation as a public health measure to address the XDR-TB threat (Markel, Gostin, and Fidler 2007).

---

before the rise of biosecurity. The convergence of public health and security rationales do not ease the pressure on governments to water down due process protections when disease threats appear. Biosecurity under the rule of law requires heightened concern and vigilance about ensuring that governments, non-state actors, and societies respect natural justice.

3. Distributive Justice

The final component of justice important to the rule of law is distributive justice. This aspect of justice requires that the risks, benefits, and burdens of governmental action be fairly, equitably, and appropriately distributed across a population to avoid the unjustified targeting or neglect of socially vulnerable segments of the community. For biosecurity policy, distributive justice means ensuring that the benefits and burdens of biosecurity activity are fairly, equitably, and effectively distributed within a population, particularly in such a way that the poor and vulnerable are not left disproportionately exposed to the harm disease events can cause.

Thinking about national security through the lens of distributive justice has typically raised questions about the level and nature of spending on national defense against external state enemies. Even during the height of the Cold War, political battles were waged over whether the amount of military spending was enough to keep the United States safe from the Soviet threat. The security provided against the Soviet Union was a public good that extended to all Americans. The threats of biological attack and naturally occurring infectious diseases change, however, the traditional dynamic. Security is no longer just national security against foreign enemy states; it involves homeland security against terrorism and health security against epidemic diseases. The government has to deliver security internally to all aspects of its population across multiple policy areas. As discussed later, this context brings distributive justice more directly to bear on security considerations because now the government has to respond at home and protect all parts of its population from intentional, accidental, or naturally occurring harm.

Public health has, historically, had a closer relationship with distributive justice because, unlike national security, its primary concern was domestic health. In fact, many commentators have viewed distributive justice as a core public health value. As Beauchamp (1999, 105) put it, "The historic dream of public health . . . is a dream of social justice." As Chapter 4 noted, public health's focus on population health gives it an over-arching perspective on social determinants of health, which provide clues about the fairness, equity, and justice of a society's functioning.

Given this background, distributive justice's complex relationship with biosecurity policy should hardly be a surprise. Distributive justice essentially asks three questions of biosecurity policy. First, is public money being appropriated in a manner that will produce the most equitable distribution of security and public health benefits possible in a population? This question connects to concerns public health experts raise that the United States spends too much on narrowly tailored biodefense programs and not enough on more broadly based public health improvements, especially when investments in the latter are more likely to bolster security and public health simultaneously. Distributive justice favors policies that maximize the security and public health benefits achieved through government actions.

Second, distributive justice forces us to enquire how vaccines, antimicrobial drugs, or other biosecurity goods and services will be equitably distributed and used in the event of biological attack or a severe infectious disease event. This enquiry has been stimulated by experts' acknowledgment that supplies of vaccines, antivirals, and even medical items such as masks and gloves will rapidly be exhausted during the early stages of pandemic influenza. Will rationing of scarce biosecurity supplies be determined by an individual's socioeconomic status or public health rationale informed by concepts of distributive justice?

The tragedy of Hurricane Katrina underscores the propriety of scrutinizing biosecurity preparedness and response policies from the distributive justice perspective. Local, state, and federal government authorities knew long before the hurricane hit that tens of thousands of poor, mainly African American residents would not be able to evacuate New Orleans without government assistance (Glasser and Grunwald 2005). But virtually nothing was done to address this problem. This complacency, neglect, and insensitivity produced injustice on a massive scale, played out for the entire world to see. Biosecurity policies face the same fate if they do not incorporate the distributive justice perspective the rule of law advocates.

Third, distributive justice asks countries and their governments to look beyond their shores to understand the unfairness and inequities that exist around the world with respect to the integration of security and public health. As Chapter 7 explores, so many aspects of biosecurity require a global approach that distributive justice cannot confine its attention to national and subnational problems. The controversies regarding access to antiretro-virals in the developing world for persons living with HIV/AIDS provide a glimpse at the global nature of distributive justice concerns with respect to serious infectious disease epidemics. Chapter 5 emphasized the problems biosecurity faces with respect to the surveillance and response gaps that exist between developed and developing countries, a gap that money spent on national biodefense often does little to reduce. The distributive justice aspect of the rule of law approach to biosecurity encourages, thus, greater scrutiny of the biodefense imperative, particularly the potential rise of a biodefense industrial complex.

4. Summary on Justice and Biosecurity Under the Rule of Law

Achieving biosecurity under the rule of law requires policy makers nation-ally and internationally to heed the nondiscrimination imperative, fulfill the requirements of natural justice or due process, and integrate considerations of distributive justice into planning and action. Security and public health have each had difficulty in the past incorporating and staying true to these aspects of justice. The convergence of these policy spheres in the form of biosecurity does not leave past difficulties with justice behind but does unfortunately cre-ate new incentives to downplay, dilute, or marginalize aspects of justice. A rule of law approach to biosecurity will ensure, at the very least, that justice issues do not fall by the wayside because of the pressure governments feel to act boldly and ask questions later in the face of serious disease threats.

D. Biosecurity, Transparency, and Accountability in Governance

The last major component of biosecurity under the rule of law is securing transparency and accountability in governance nationally and globally. Trans-parency and accountability are enormous topics that we only briefly address with respect to biosecurity. The development of biosecurity policy to date has, however, already demonstrated how critical transparent and accountable gov-ernance is and how difficult it is, and will be, to achieve.

Briefly, transparent governance requires that the information used and criteria applied by decision makers, and the substantive content of deci-sions, be available for public scrutiny. Transparency is critical for oversight of whether governments respect individual rights and liberties and whether leaders have properly considered questions of justice. In short, critical aspects of biosecurity under the rule of law cannot be achieved without transparency in governance.

Transparency has more specific roles to play in biosecurity policy as well. Transparency is a core requirement for effective surveillance and interventions. History shows how public health suffers when governments hide, cover up, or tell less than the whole truth when disease threats appear. China's dishonest and dissembling behavior during its initial responses to SARS jeopardized public health, not only in China, but also in countries around the world. This lesson informs the efforts made in the IHR 2005 to increase the transparency of surveillance information concerning public health emergencies of international concern.

China's behavior can be explained, at least in part, by its fears about domestic security and order. The Chinese reaction to SARS followed the pattern typically seen from states concerned about the security implications of dangerous or disturbing information. As disease risks mount in frequency and potential seriousness, the need for transparency increases, especially in the new world of public health governance. In addition to transparency in surveillance, the criteria determining how and when governments and international organizations should intervene also needs to be transparent so that those affected can understand, cooperate with, and monitor how public authorities are exercising power. Biosecurity under the rule of law cannot tolerate governments, international organizations, or non-state actors behaving non-transparently because of security or other fears in connection with the operation of public health infrastructures.

Tensions arise, however, in biosecurity policy concerning the demand for greater transparency, and these tensions connect to the biodefense imperative. Chapter 3 mentioned controversies concerning the shift in the U.S. biodefense program in the last decade from more to less transparency. This shift is a significant rule of law concern because it takes biosecurity policy in directions that prefer secrecy, expansive discretionary power for the executive branch, and minimal to nonexistent oversight by the legislature, courts, and the people being governed. Calls for the U.S. biodefense program to increase its transparency reinforce how serious transparency is for biosecurity policy under the rule of law.

Accountability in governance refers to the idea that those who exercise political power have to answer to the governed. Democracies function on the basis of periodic opportunities for the people to hold elected leaders accountable. Accountability in governance goes, however, beyond the democratic principle. Accountability arises as well when different branches of the government check and balance each other, which means that biosecurity has to be a key legislative and judicial matter and not just left to the discretion of the executive branch. Natural justice or due process itself provides a critical accountability mechanism because it subjects executive branch actions to judicial scrutiny. People within governments who speak out against illegal or improper conduct—whistleblowers—also serve an accountability function and deserve, in most situations, legal protection.

In addition to traditional forms of accountability, the emergence of biosecurity has produced interest in new accountability mechanisms that can perhaps increase the sensitivities of governments to the needs of biosecurity. These mechanisms reside mainly in the hands of non-state actors but can bring pressure to bear on governments. One such mechanism is the global market. Countries have learned through SARS and avian influenza that companies, traders, and investors value openness in government responses to disease events. When disease strikes, a government's failure to behave transparently and cooperate with other countries, international organizations, and non-state actors is bad for business, and the global market punishes transgressors.

The other set of non-state actors that can bolster accountability are nongovernmental organizations (NGOs), which operate on both the security and public health sides of biosecurity. NGOs focused on arms control keep a watchful eye on governments' BWC compliance and are quick to raise concerns about potential noncompliance. On the public health side, NGOs facilitate the flow of epidemiological information worldwide, thus functioning as an early warning and surveillance resource.

Chapter 5 noted the IHR 2005's radical provision that permits WHO to consider nongovernmental information when WHO conducts global surveillance. This provision allows WHO to bring such information to the attention of states parties and ask for verification, and the IHR 2005 mandates that the states parties respond (Article 10). NGOs that facilitate flows of global epidemiological information, such as the Program for Monitoring Emerging Disease (ProMED-mail), contribute to making biosecurity governance more transparent and accountable.

ProMED-mail is particularly interesting and influential in this respect. It is "an Internet-based reporting system dedicated to rapid global dissemination of information on outbreaks of infectious diseases and acute exposures to toxins that affect human health, including those in animals and in plants grown for food or animal feed" (ProMED-mail 2006). ProMED-mail collects information from many sources (e.g., media, official documents, reports from ProMED-mail subscribers), has the information screened, reviewed, and investigated by expert moderators, and then disseminates the vetted information through e-mail to more than 30,000 subscribers in 150 countries and by posting on the Internet. This nongovernmental endeavor aims "to promote communication amongst the international infectious disease community, including scientists, physicians, epidemiologists, public health professionals, and others interested in infectious diseases on a global scale" (ProMED-mail 2006).

The growing interest among scientists to formulate codes of conduct for doing research in the biological sciences discussed in Chapter 3 also envisions a different kind of non-state actor accountability mechanism. Applied seriously by scientists in their individual and collective capacities, the codes could empower scientists to raise questions and, if necessary, objections to scientific research that is illegal or improper. Analyses of the potential dangers of research in the biological sciences often emphasize the governance importance of the responsibility of individual scientists and scientific communities to make sure that their research does not create biosecurity threats. Codes of conduct for scientists could make the global scientific community a watchdog and whistleblower on government and nongovernmental behavior that threatens biosecurity. Researchers in Canada exploited this idea by proposing the establishment of a global network of scientists to promote biological research and to maintain vigilance against any misuse of such research (Canadian Program on Genomics and Global Health 2006).

The potential for security and public health to move in opposite directions creates problems for achieving transparency and accountability in biosecurity policy. Less transparent, less accountable biodefense programs contrast with the increasingly transparent and accountability-laden world of public health governance. This tension does not mean that biodefense activities have to end because such an outcome is not realistic or advisable. It means, however, that biodefense programs should value transparency and accountability as strengths rather than as threats to achieving protection against biological weapons. The rule of law approach to biosecurity supports, thus, efforts underway to ensure that the biodefense imperative does not weaken, nationally or internationally, the principles of transparency and accountability.

E. Instrumental Advantages of Biosecurity Under the Rule of Law

Discussions about the rule of law can, at times, seem abstract, overly interested in normative values, and disinterested in the governance practicalities that arise in the variable, complex, unpredictable, and often urgent scenarios that governments face when biosecurity threats occur. From this perspective, biosecurity under the rule of law appears more like a recipe for restraining political power rather than facilitating its effective use. We challenge this sentiment because working toward biosecurity under the rule of law brings significant practical benefits to governance that supplement its concern with normative values.

To begin, as discussed earlier, the rule of law recognizes the need to empower governments adequately to address serious threats to the security and health of their populations. The rule of law is not simply about restraining power. Under the rule of law, the power to achieve biosecurity should be the power to do so effectively. For the rule of law, the empowerment process is an opportunity for ensuring that the political power authorized is tailored properly to address the threat in question. Legislation can guide policy makers toward making more effective and efficient decisions when they exercise the power the legislature grants them.

Authorizations for action that are too general inevitably raise questions when implementation becomes necessary, which inhibits swift and effective action. In tabletop exercises involving biological attacks or naturally occurring disease outbreaks, decision makers have repeatedly been plagued by questions about the scope and substance of their legal authorities. Biosecurity under the rule of law supports robust legal preparedness in advance of the disease crisis. Such preparedness can contribute to more effective biosecurity responses when the emergency is at hand.

The contributions of the rule of law to biosecurity preparedness go deeper than supporting effective responses to actual disease crises. The rule of law encourages policy making to seek and maintain a balanced integration of security and public health. This balanced approach counters two tendencies seen in how governments respond to intentionally caused and naturally occurring infectious diseases. The first tendency is to focus more attention and resources on security conceived in a narrow way. Defense against biological weapons has received more policy attention and resources in the United States than has public health infrastructure improvement. The sustained continuation of this tendency will harm biosecurity in the long run.

The second tendency involves privileging technological solutions over basic public health infrastructure. This tendency includes the biodefense emphasis on developing new technologies—vaccines, antimicrobials, sensors—for specific, very low probability biological attacks at the expense of designing and funding generally applicable public health surveillance and intervention capabilities. The tendency also appears with respect to naturally occurring infectious diseases because, at times, policy makers embrace technological solutions (e.g., privileging antiretroviral treatment over HIV/AIDS prevention; stockpiling Tamiflu for pandemic influenza) without paying enough attention to building robust public health capabilities that can withstand outbreaks without being overly dependent on technological fixes.

The tragedy that unfolded after Hurricane Katrina underscores benefits the rule of law offers in the context of pushing public officials to achieve balance between security and public health. September 11th caused a flurry of policy activity in Washington, D.C., which eventually produced, among other things, the Department of Homeland Security (DHS). Congress folded the Federal Emergency Management Agency (FEMA) into DHS, linking it to the DHS main mission of fighting terrorism. When an entirely predictable, and frequently predicted, natural disaster occurred, the DHS response was shockingly inadequate and completely unacceptable. This situation left many people wondering what kind of security all the billions of dollars for homeland security had actually produced.

The nightmare Hurricane Katrina became for the federal government helped spark the policy frenzy in the fall of 2005 about the serious lack of preparedness in the United States for pandemic influenza. Here was another predictable, and frequently predicted, naturally occurring disaster waiting to happen for which the United States and most other countries were not prepared. Despite shifting some public health functions from the Department of Health and Human Services (DHHS) and CDC to DHS after September 11th, most of the money allocated to DHS to fight terrorism generally and bioterrorism specifically was of little, if any, value to the challenge of pandemic influenza preparedness. None of the money spent, for example, on smallpox and anthrax after September 11th has contributed much, if anything, to the nation's readiness for a naturally occurring epidemic. Recognition of this fact is found in Congress' appropriation of $6.1 billion for pandemic influenza preparedness (U.S. DHHS 2006a).

Achieving biosecurity under the rule of law also offers instrumental benefits in connection with the government's relationship with the governed. As most public health experts have argued, critical to a successful response to a frightening disease event is the trust, confidence, and cooperation of the people in the government. Such trust, confidence, and cooperation can help governments rely on voluntary actions by the population rather than having to use compulsory measures.

Respecting individual rights and liberties through due process mechanisms in the event compulsory measures are needed demonstrates to the populace that, in the crisis, the government has not forgotten to respect justice and human dignity. Keeping the government's approach to the disease event transparent and accessible also adds to the people's willingness to follow the government. This willingness is not the product of some exercise in "feel good" politics but is a practical instrument that helps the government deal with the disease threat more effectively. Reaching the point where the government can create and sustain the people's trust, confidence, and cooperation takes hard work over many years. Losing these assets when the crisis arrives takes hours if not minutes if the government is not prepared.

Reaching the point at which biosecurity policy can support the normative values and instrumental advantages of a rule of law approach is a daunting challenge. Sustaining political support for public health has always been difficult because effective public health makes politicians believe that the job is done, enticing them to shift resources toward resolution of other problems. Such complacency cannibalizes public health infrastructures until a new crisis reveals the inadequacy of underfunded and understaffed public health capabilities.

Having a rule of law approach to biosecurity is not, however, the solution for all the problems arising in the new worlds of biological weapons and public health governance. The rule of law approach does not answer every hard question or clarify every difficult choice that has to be made in making biosecurity policy. Nor does the rule of law eliminate the sharp politics that permeate all areas of biosecurity. It does, however, provide a framework to use to inform the choices that must be made and to improve the quality of what politics produce. This framework can be particularly useful when contexts for governance change so radically that policy makers lack experience and precedents to guide fulfillment of their heavy responsibilities.

F. The Globalized Governance Problem
for Biosecurity Under the Rule of Law

Although we have mentioned international and global issues, this chapter has not grappled directly with perhaps the biggest rule of law problem affecting biosecurity—the need for globalized governance in the realm of biosecurity. The rule of law as a governance philosophy originates in thinking about politics within sovereign states. Its structure and substance make assumptions about the hierarchical nature of political power within states. The rule of law approach transfers awkwardly to a political environment that is anarchical. As international lawyers know all too well, efforts to superimpose the rule of law ethos directly on international relations without considering the effects of the anarchical nature of international politics have never fared well. Further, the global scope of biosecurity policy requires that the rule of law approach be harmonized across many countries.

This book identifies the need for globalized governance as one of the main challenges of twenty-first century biosecurity politics. We have discussed frequently how the demands of the new worlds of biological weapons and public health governance force policy to "go global" to address effectively the problems at hand. Integrating security and public health, supervising science for biosecurity, and embedding biosecurity in the rule of law each must be achieved in a world characterized by globalization. This task is so significant and difficult that we devote the next chapter to the challenge of crafting globalized governance for biosecurity.

V. CONCLUSION

This chapter addressed the challenge of embedding biosecurity policy in the rule of law. We argued for a strategy that integrates biosecurity politics within the governance framework provided by the rule of law, or what we called biosecurity under the rule of law. The rule of law framework is critical because the emergence of biosecurity signals the development of new worlds of governance for biological weapons and public health. These new governance worlds need the rule of law as much as the previous, distinct worlds of security and public health did, and perhaps more so.

To clarify this need, the chapter broke out the elements of the rule of law and applied them to the challenges biosecurity policy faces. Biosecurity under the rule of law requires empowering governments to handle biosecurity threats effectively, protecting individual rights and liberties in dealing with such threats, grafting notions of justice onto biosecurity endeavors, and ensuring that biosecurity governance is transparent and accountable. The extent and seriousness of these tasks reinforces the notion that embedding biosecurity in the rule of law presents a difficult, never-ending challenge.

Nevertheless, the challenge is critical to shoulder because biosecurity under the rule of law supports deeply held normative values that deserve heightened commitment, even in the face of the manifold difficulties biosecurity creates for societies. In addition, biosecurity under the rule of law can produce practical benefits that are often under-appreciated in discourse about the rule of law.

The normative and practical benefits do not, however, make the rule of law approach one that simplifies biosecurity policy. As the histories of security and public health demonstrate, application of the rule of law in the real world is a harder task than ideological genuflection to the rule of law as a philosophy of governance. As the next chapter explores, the global context in which biosecurity must be pursued creates one of the most formidable challenges to achieving biosecurity under the rule of law. These, and other, difficulties should not stand in the way of the convergence of rule of law thinking with biosecurity policy. The rule of law holds that no one is above the law. Similarly, no policy realm—no matter how recent, complex, and difficult—stands outside the rule of law as a philosophy and instrument of governance.

7 GLOBALIZING GOVERNANCE
Toward a Global Biosecurity Concert

I. INTRODUCTION

Previous chapters of this book have repeatedly argued that globalization's impact on biosecurity requires governance beyond national governments and conventional forms of intergovernmental cooperation. Biosecurity policy confronts transnational phenomena, such as terrorism and the globalization of the biological sciences, that place incredible stress on traditional governance approaches to biological weapons and naturally occurring infectious diseases. In addition, these transnational phenomena underscore how new governance approaches must be global in scope to avoid gaps or "weak links" in the chain of efforts created to prevent, protect against, and respond to pathogenic threats. The global nature of the potential threats demands policy and governance actions that are also global in scope and substance.

This chapter explores the challenge of globalizing governance to achieve biosecurity in the twenty-first century. At one level, little disagreement exists that transnational forces require states and non-state actors to work together to overcome obstacles to robust and sustainable biosecurity. Consensus breaks down when experts debate strategies to globalize governance for biosecurity purposes. This breakdown flows from not only divergent ideas about how to advance globalized governance but also different levels of skepticism about the effectiveness of globalized policy. The difficulties of globalizing governance for biosecurity—the fourth key challenge for biosecurity policy in the twenty-first century—cast shadows over the entire biosecurity enterprise.

We begin by reviewing how the need for globalized governance on biosecurity cuts across the challenges of integrating security and public health, supervising science for biosecurity, and embedding biosecurity governance in the rule of law. The normative importance of globalizing governance also appears with respect to more specific policy trends and needs, including criminalization of biological weapons development and use, regulation of the biological sciences, managing the biodefense imperative, and improving public health infrastructure through strengthening surveillance and intervention capabilities.

Having established the crosscutting normative importance of globalized governance, we consider conceptual aspects of this challenge. In essence, the transnational problems of biological weapons and naturally occurring infectious diseases can no longer be adequately addressed through mechanisms found within the hierarchical political structures of states or those traditionally used among states in their anarchical relations. Globalizing governance for biosecurity represents a collective action problem that existing theories of international relations only handle awkwardly.

The conceptual difficulties are reflected in the proliferation of new governance initiatives related to biosecurity that has occurred in the past decade. This proliferation contains patterns at national, international, and global levels that provide insights into how state and non-state actors are addressing the challenge of globalizing biosecurity governance. These patterns underscore the normative importance of globalizing biosecurity governance and support the prominence this particular challenge has for biosecurity policy.

The patterns are not enough, however, to take biosecurity governance where it needs to be. We posit the need for a global biosecurity mechanism that links governance changes and initiatives more productively. We call this mechanism a "global biosecurity concert," and we analyze what the substantive objectives of this concert should be and how such a concert could work.

II. GLOBALIZING GOVERNANCE AS A CROSSCUTTING AND COMPREHENSIVE BIOSECURITY CHALLENGE

In introducing the biosecurity challenge, Chapter 1 argued that one of four main tasks for biosecurity policy is how to organize governance of transnational threats through a political structure dominated by sovereign states. Addressing this problem creates the need to move beyond traditional national and international strategies and to globalize governance. This need acknowledges that past approaches, including collective action through international law and international organizations, are not sufficient for the task at hand. Globalization affects security and public health in ways that call for strategies tailored to the globalized nature of biosecurity threats.

Previous chapters frequently noted that the task of globalizing governance is interdependent with the other three main biosecurity challenges. Integrating security and public health is a policy challenge that operates within a global context. Security and public health policy separately experienced different degrees of international governance during the twentieth century, but the international legal regimes adopted for these realms never connected. Events in the last decade destroyed security's and public health's splendid isolation and the task of integration forces policy makers to think beyond traditional forms of international cooperation.

Globalization likewise complicates the challenge of supervising science for biosecurity. The global spread of the biological sciences both heightens the need to regulate scientific research and makes achievement of effective regulation difficult. In addition, transnational diffusion of biotechnology relevant to manipulating microbial life makes the traditional arms control technique of verification by a standing international organization difficult to apply, as the Biological Weapons Convention (BWC) Protocol negotiations revealed.

The global context for biosecurity also affects the criminalization of biological weapons development and use. The globalization of the biological sciences requires that criminalization be done as universally as possible. Achieving universality is, as Chapter 3 explored, difficult, even with the obligations imposed on states by the BWC and Security Council mandates on terrorism and weapons of mass destruction. Getting to a more universal level of criminalization requires globalizing this governance effort.

The crosscutting nature of the challenge of globalizing governance appears as well in public health's new governance world. Chapter 5 emphasized the importance of improving surveillance and intervention capabilities from local to the global levels. Strategies for improving public health infrastructure include building the participation of non-state actors into the governance frameworks for surveillance and intervention. Attempts to build global governance mechanisms for surveillance and interventions have not, however, overcome the surveillance and response gaps that exist between developed and developing countries, gaps that undermine biosecurity nationally and globally.

The challenge of globalizing governance also affects the objective of embedding biosecurity in the rule of law. The rule of law as a philosophy of governance encounters difficulties when applied in a political context characterized by sovereign states that recognize no common, superior authority. All the major challenges of biosecurity governance require policy to leave the confines of the state and engage in globalized politics. Integrating the need for the rule of law and the need to globalize biosecurity governance represents a complex task.

Given how comprehensively the challenge of globalizing governance cuts across biosecurity policy, the relationship between biosecurity and globalized governance takes on paramount importance. Capturing all facets of this relationship proves difficult, and we do not pretend that we have done all past, present, and future aspects of this relationship justice. This chapter attempts, however, to provide some sense of how normatively critical and difficult globalizing governance for biosecurity is and will be in the twenty-first century.

III. THE CRUX OF THE GLOBALIZING GOVERNANCE CHALLENGE

A. Transnational Problems Meet Anarchical Politics

The pervasiveness of the globalizing governance challenge creates the need to get at the heart of this challenge. This task requires understanding the problems biosecurity policy confronts and the instruments at hand. In essence, the problems outstrip the capabilities of traditional governance instruments and approaches, forcing policy makers to contemplate new ways to address biological weapons and naturally occurring infectious diseases. Implementing new strategies runs, however, headlong into the traditional structure and dynamics of international relations, which are based on the division of humanity into approximately 200 sovereign states. These states interact in a condition of anarchy, meaning "that international politics takes place in an arena that has no overarching central authority above the individual collection of sovereign states" (Dunne and Schmidt 2001, 143).

Problems that escape the traditional political architecture of international relations must be addressed largely from within that architecture. Put another way, transnational problems have to be confronted through anarchical politics. Biological weapons proliferation and naturally occurring infectious diseases are transnational problems, which mean they escape the ability of any individual state or limited collectivity of states to manage effectively. The threat biological weapons present is a problem that not even the United States can adequately address on its own or through the traditional mechanism of arms control. Similarly, public health challenges today transcend the state-centric, Westphalian architecture used to organize international relations since the mid-seventeenth century (Kickbusch 2003).

Another way to think about transnational problems is to consider how globalization affects sovereignty and the traditional tools of international governance (e.g., international law, international organizations). Although many definitions of globalization exist, common to most of them is the idea that globalization diminishes the ability of the state to control what happens in its territory. The state's hierarchical configuration of political power becomes increasingly unable to manage transnational problems, threats, and issues. Globalization perforates sovereignty across a range of political, economic, and social realms. The resulting "Swiss cheese sovereignty" encourages states to try to cooperate through international law and international organizations. The traditional dynamics of anarchical politics among states tends, however, to produce lowest common denominator outcomes that do not impinge significantly on state sovereignty. Such outcomes often contribute little to helping states reign in transnational problems fueled by ever-accelerating globalization.

The difficulty of achieving international responses, and the often-minimal contributions such responses make, generates incentives for powerful states to concentrate on their needs, interests, and vulnerabilities. This move acknowledges that a powerful state cannot, by itself, handle transnational threats but posits that self-help might produce better results than diluted half-measures generated by international governance mechanisms.

This pattern is visible in biosecurity politics. Recall Chapter 5's discussion of the fault lines in biosecurity policy. The first fault line involves tension between focusing on biological weapons or infectious diseases. The second fault line concerns whether national interests or international needs will be the primary focus. The United States has emphasized national biodefense against biological weapons over international action against naturally occurring infectious diseases. Part of this emphasis involves President George W. Bush's administration's skepticism about international legal regimes and institutions, skepticism, which is not entirely without empirical support in the area of biosecurity.

Previous chapters highlighted how the international legal regimes built during the twentieth century to address biological weapons and naturally occurring infectious diseases proved significant failures. We reviewed how experts have concluded that the Geneva Protocol and the BWC do not offer an adequate approach to contemporary threats from biological weapons. We analyzed the failure of the traditional international law relating to the control of the international spread of disease and the efforts made to revise these rules radically in the form of the new International Health Regulations (IHR). In short, history provides plenty of evidence that merely adopting more treaties among states is not an effective strategy against the threat of biological weapons or naturally occurring infectious diseases.

B. The Collective Action Problem and International Relations Theory

The problems that transnational threats present for states interacting in anarchy bring to mind attempts to explain the success or failure of collective action among states. This chapter is not the place to engage in detailed theoretical analysis of the biosecurity problem, but general theoretical considerations can help communicate why biosecurity proves such a difficult challenge for states and their international relations.

State-centric theories of international relations, such as realism and institutionalism, analyze international politics as the clash and convergence of the material interests of states. Realists and institutionalists differ regarding the extent to which international law and international organizations can ameliorate competition for power, influence, and survival among states (Keohane and Martin 1995; Mearsheimer 1994/1995). In terms of biological weapons, an institutionalist would emphasize the Geneva Protocol and the BWC as important variables in explaining how rarely states used biological weapons against each other during the twentieth century. A realist would explain this absence of biological attacks by emphasizing bio-deterrence and state calculations that use of biological weapons produced few if any military or political advantages in the struggle for power with rival states.

Although concerns about state interest in biological weapons remains, these concerns have not driven the growth in policy attention on biological weapons in the last decade. Governments in many countries are worried about terrorist interest in biological weapons. The threat of terrorism proves difficult to slot into theories that assume that the only actors of consequence are states. Difficulties also arise with respect to the threat to states' material well-being presented by epidemic infectious diseases, which is a threat that does not flow from the actions of states or terrorists. State-centric theories struggle, therefore, with critical features of the biosecurity problem.

Other theories, such as liberalism and constructivism, integrate non-state actors and transnational phenomena into their frameworks. Liberal theory posits that non-state actors and processes, especially domestic politics and international economic intercourse, determine the nature of international relations (Dunne 2001; Moravcsik 1997). Constructivism creates space for non-state actors, such as human rights advocacy groups, and transnational phenomena, such as the globalization of culture, to shape and reshape how states socially construct the anarchy in which they interact (Wendt 1992, 1999). Theories not fixated on states and their interactions favor moving governance domestically and globally toward greater participation by non-state actors. In fact, most definitions of "global governance" distinguish it from "international governance" by emphasizing how the former builds non-state actors into governance mechanisms whereas the latter involves only states and their state-based creations, international organizations.

Although global governance features in biosecurity policy, theories that emphasize non-state actors and phenomena pose problems for core features of biosecurity. As Chapter 4 noted, security and public health are quintessential public goods. Typically, governments have to produce public goods because private actors have insufficient incentives and resources. The production of public goods is, thus, conceptually anchored in governmental responsibilities, resources, and action. Not surprisingly, the production of both security and public health has been practically anchored in states and their governments.

Various features of the new governance worlds of biological weapons and public health illustrate this point. The four trends of the new world of biological weapons governance—criminalization, regulation of the biological sciences, managing the biodefense imperative, and public health preparedness and response—represent activities that governments must predominantly shoulder. States cannot delegate these functions in the manner that they might outsource management of airports or seaports to private companies. The same situation applies to the public health functions of surveillance and intervention. Public authorities must primarily undertake, regulate, and oversee these functions. In addition, the rule of law also weighs in here because the various functions for biological weapons and public health governance must adhere to rule of law principles applicable to the exercise of political power.

Security and public health both contain, thus, a Westphalian core that forces states to remain key players. This reality forces states to engage with each other in the realm of anarchical politics. This anarchical realm creates obstacles and inefficiencies for coordinating state interests, and these difficulties are meat and potatoes for state-centric theories of international relations.

Although the problems of biological weapons and naturally occurring infectious diseases are transnational in nature, policy responses have to rely on state-based, hierarchical governance because security and public health are classical public goods. State-based responses to transnational problems are, however, embedded in the anarchical system of international politics, which constrains what states can collectively agree to do. The transnational problems, thus, outstrip the response capabilities of the hierarchical and anarchical governance frameworks. Biosecurity faces the conundrum of needing to globalize governance by involving non-state actors in the production of public goods that remain primary responsibilities of hierarchical governments forced to engage in anarchical politics.

The task of globalizing governance implies, therefore, that state and non-state actors from the local to the global levels must fulfill governance responsibilities to integrate security and public health, supervise science for biosecurity, and embed biosecurity governance in the rule of law. As Littlewood (2005, 234) argued with respect to managing the biological weapons problem: "The new reality is quite simple. Action is required at all levels; individual, subnational, national, regional, like-minded, and international, public, private, government, and intergovernmental levels."

Biosecurity as a collective action challenge resembles a "global public good," the production of which involves state and non-state actors and the benefits of which extend to many countries and peoples. This perspective dovetails with arguments that effective management of globalization requires improved production of global public goods (Kaul, Grunberg, and Stern 1999; Kaul, Conceição, Le Goulven, and Mendoza, 2003b). The global public good concept also captures the global context in which integration of two classical public goods, security and public health, must occur for biosecurity to be robust and sustainable in the twenty-first century.

IV. PROLIFERATION OF GOVERNANCE INITIATIVES
RELATED TO BIOSECURITY: LOOKING FOR PATTERNS

One indicator of the normative significance of globalizing governance for biosecurity is the proliferation of initiatives during the past decade that relate to biological weapons and naturally occurring infectious diseases. Previous chapters mentioned many of these initiatives. Chapter 3 described, for example, the proposed treaty on the criminalization of the development and use of biological weapons. This proposal sought to embed in international law the idea that development and use of biological weapons were international crimes subject to universal jurisdiction. Chapter 3 also noted how UN Security Council Resolutions 1373 and 1540 constituted novel exercises of the Council's powers under Chapter VII of the UN Charter.

The new world of public health governance has also seen initiatives in the last decade. Earlier chapters acknowledged, for example, the radical breakthrough in global health governance that the new IHR (2005) represent. Global health has also seen an explosion of public-private partnerships, such as the Global Fund to Fight AIDS, Tuberculosis and Malaria, that seek to contribute to the fight against infectious diseases. Actually, the proliferation of initiatives, actors, and financial resources in global health during the past decade has reached a point where the proliferation may harm efforts to improve public health in developing countries (Cohen 2006; Garrett 2007).

Rather than describe all the initiatives relevant to biosecurity, we want to see whether these initiatives exhibit common patterns. Such patterns may provide clues about how states and non-state actors are approaching the challenge of globalizing governance for biosecurity. The following sections look for patterns at the levels of national, international, and global governance.

A. National Governance: Reconceptualizing State Responsibilities and Interests

The continuing importance of sovereign states for biosecurity means that globalizing governance cannot ignore national governance. How national governments approach biosecurity remains critical even as the problems of biological weapons and naturally occurring infectious diseases become more transnational. The national and subnational governments of states continue to manage most key governance functions in security and public health.

This reality correlates with the pattern discernable in the proliferation of governance initiatives related to biosecurity: the need for states to reconceptualize their responsibilities at home and interests abroad with respect to biological weapons and naturally occurring infectious diseases. The rise of biosecurity represents the emergence of a new challenge for states and their peoples. The old approaches to the problems of biological weapons and epidemic infectious diseases no longer work. This sea change means that the old ways of conceptualizing these problems also no longer retain value.

Chapters 2 and 3 demonstrated how significantly the problem of biological weapons has changed and what that change means for governance of this problem. The rise of biosecurity signals the death of the traditional arms control approach that prevailed throughout the twentieth century. The Geneva Protocol and the BWC operate within a radically transformed political and technological context. The evil of biological weapons these treaties sought to restrain and prohibit now has to be countered through more and different mechanisms. The four trends that characterize the new world of biological weapons governance—criminalization of biological weapons development and use, regulation of the biological sciences, managing the biodefense imperative, and public health preparedness and response—demonstrate that many states are reconceptualizing how to address the threat of biological weapons. They are rethinking their responsibilities at home and their interests in nonproliferation internationally.

A similar tale of reconceptualization appears in public health. The securitization of public health has transformed public health from a neglected endeavor to one intertwined with old and new conceptions of security. Those fixated on security as protection from physical violence realized that the prospect of biological attack made public health infrastructure a national security asset. Those more concerned with the global ravages of infectious diseases saw traction in thinking about them through security perspectives. The planetary plague HIV/AIDS became, the emergence of severe acute respiratory syndrome (SARS), the spread of avian influenza, the development of antimicrobial resistance, and the possibility of pandemic influenza have generated policy urgency that reinforces the conceptual shifts.

The reconceptualizations of state responsibilities and interests with respect to biological weapons and naturally occurring infectious diseases are critical for globalizing governance for biosecurity. Without the engagement of states at home and abroad, international and global governance on biosecurity suffers. Revolutionary change in the structure of international relations, such as the creation of world government, is not likely to happen in the twenty-first century. States and their national governance capabilities will be key building blocks of biosecurity.

The reconceptualization of state responsibilities and interests does not, however, mean that the engagement of all states is equal in intensity. Tensions examined earlier in the book bear witness to a more uneven reality at the level of national governance. Fears about biological attack may produce regulation of the biological sciences in ways scientists and public health experts believe harm science's potential contribution to health. Overemphasis on national biodefense may divert resources from improving public health infrastructures and may undermine governance transparency and accountability. Developed countries' worries about biological weapons may not overlap with developing countries' preference to battle naturally occurring infectious diseases. In short, the reconceptualizations apparent in state behavior do not produce the mythical "harmony of interests" among states concerning biosecurity.

B. International Governance: From Formal Pacts to Flexible Partnering

Reconceptualization of state responsibilities and interests is necessary but not sufficient for globalizing governance for biosecurity. The biosecurity challenge still involves the need for diplomacy to manage dissonance in state interests. Further, the transnational nature of the problems of biological weapons and epidemic infectious diseases makes international governance essential to effective management of these problems. Thus, initiatives that attempt to improve intergovernmental action on biosecurity are hardly surprising.

We need to identify more, however, than increased international governance activity. Does this activity reveal characteristics that provide a sense of the current and future direction of international governance? A pattern that has emerged is a preference to avoid binding, formal international legal regimes in favor of more flexible, innovative partnering efforts.

The last decade has seen many proposals for new treaties related to biosecurity issued and advocated. These include the BWC Protocol, a treaty to criminalize development and use of biological weapons (Meselson and Robinson 2004), a treaty to create an international regime for biosafety standards for biological research (Barletta, Sands, and Tucker 2002), and a binding regime to establish international oversight of dangerous biological research (Steinbruner, Harris, Gallagher, and Okutani 2005 and 2007). The BWC Protocol collapsed and will not be revived, and none of these other proposals for new international regimes has made progress in any diplomatic forum.

Instead of formal pacts, states have more often pursued nonbinding partnering arrangements concerning issues relevant to biosecurity. Such partnering efforts were not unknown in the past, as illustrated by like-minded states attempting to control exports of dual-use technologies through the Australia Group (2006), organized initially in 1985, and the Wassenaar Arrangement (2006), established in 1996. The last decade has, however, seen nonbinding partnering efforts expand in the areas of biological weapons and public health.

For example, the United States has used the partnership model to advance intergovernmental cooperation on biosecurity through the Global Health Security Initiative, the Group of Eight (G8) Global Partnership on Weapons of Mass Destruction, the Proliferation Security Initiative, the President's Emergency Plan for AIDS Relief, and the Global Partnership on Pandemic Influenza. The new world of public health governance also exhibits the pattern for partnering through such efforts as the Global Fund to Fight AIDS, Tuberculosis, and Malaria (Global Fund), Roll Back Malaria, Stop TB Campaign, the Global Outbreak Alert and Response Network, projects within intergovernmental organizations (e.g., the World Bank, Asia Pacific Economic Cooperation Forum [APEC], and the G8) on infectious diseases, the International Finance Facility for Immunization, UNITAID, and other efforts.

The preference for nonbinding, flexible partnering arrangements does not, of course, hold in all cases because states have developed legally binding commitments that contribute to biosecurity. States adopted, for example, the International Convention for the Suppression of Terrorist Bombings, which includes the duty to criminalize the use of biological weapons. Security Council Resolutions 1373 and 1540 created new international legal obligations binding on UN member states. The IHR 2005 contains new binding international legal rules.

Both the pattern of partnering and the exceptions are complex features of contemporary biosecurity politics, but they share an important political source—the biosecurity interests of the United States. The Bush administration's preference for informal partnerships and "coalitions of the willing" is well known, and the administration has applied this preference to its foreign policy interests in biosecurity matters, as noted earlier. As for the exceptions involving creation of new international legal rules, the United States strongly supported these new binding legal obligations, which facilitated the adoption of the respective commitments.

U.S. influence in international biosecurity governance is not surprising given its status as the world's leading power. Most major advances or changes in international governance opposed by the United States either die (e.g., BWC Protocol) or face difficulties without U.S. participation (e.g., Kyoto Protocol on climate change, Statute of the International Criminal Court).

Whether preferring partnering over formal pacts extends beyond the Bush administration as an aspect of U.S. foreign policy remains to be seen. We perceive that this pattern runs deeper in international politics and cannot be explained by the predilections of one administration. The reconceptualization of state responsibilities and interests in biosecurity is recent and still ongoing, which makes states hesitant to accept binding schemes of international governance, as envisioned by the BWC Protocol or various proposals for new treaties. Partnering arrangements allow states to engage in needed cooperation without the high transaction costs of negotiating and implementing formally binding legal rules. Of the new treaties recently adopted, only the IHR 2005 creates new authority for an intergovernmental organization that impinges on the exercise of state sovereignty. Given the controversies that surround what biosecurity policies are most appropriate, flexible, cooperative relationships have advantages in allowing states to navigate uncertainties present in the new worlds of biological weapons and public health governance.

Another reason why states may continue to prefer the flexibility of partnering arrangements involves the process of reconceptualizing their responsibilities and interests with respect to biological weapons and naturally occurring infectious diseases. A theme in both the partnering relationships and the new legally binding commitments concerns the need for states to implement biosecurity measures more rigorously at home. The BWC's New Process agenda, various partnership efforts, the Security Council resolutions, proposed treaties on criminalization and biosafety, and the IHR 2005 all focus attention on more domestic implementation of policies for enhancing biosecurity. This dynamic suggests some level of recognition that biosecurity begins at home.

Partnering arrangements are also conducive to the participation of nonstate actors in governance. Nongovernmental organizations (NGOs) cannot become parties to treaties, but they can participate in public-private partnerships geared to addressing biosecurity problems. These partnerships have exploded in the past decade, especially in the context of global health efforts on infectious diseases. Recognizing the need for global governance mechanisms to supplement national and international governance also feeds into the pattern of partnering.

Identifying the partnering pattern and understanding its logic does not mean that the pattern best serves biosecurity governance in the long run. Previous chapters argued that informal, ad hoc international cooperation does not well serve harmonization of substantive policies, whether involving criminalization, the regulation of biological sciences, or some other matter. Partnering may lead the two parts of biosecurity in different directions. In terms of biological weapons, partnering may induce policy to drift unproductively without sufficient direction or commitment from states. Some complaints about the BWC's New Process agenda, for example, focused on the lack of systematic follow-up to the issues discussed from 2003 to 2005. Similar concerns may arise with the intersessional meetings scheduled by the Sixth BWC Review Conference. As already indicated, partnering in global health has produced a plethora of projects and initiatives that strains public health capabilities, particularly in developing countries, without producing sustainable progress.

These concerns suggest that the partnering pattern might reflect and contribute to the development of "unstructured plurality" in international governance (Bartlett, Kickbusch, and Coulombier 2006). Unstructured plurality may produce governance that is quasi-medieval in fragmenting authority, resources, participation, and allegiance. Such patchwork governance might prove no match for the forces of globalization that drive biosecurity threats in the twenty-first century.

C. Global Governance: Harnessing the Potential of Non-State Actor Participation

The final level of globalizing governance for biosecurity involves global governance, or the integration of non-state actors into efforts to address threats posed by biological weapons and infectious diseases. The growing influence and roles of non-state actors in international relations has been an important topic in the post–Cold War period. Experts began to sense a transition from state-centric, Westphalian international politics to a more complex, post-Westphalian context in which non-state actors played important governance roles. These roles were sometimes viewed in a positive light (e.g., NGOs engaged in human rights and environmental advocacy) and sometimes negatively (e.g., growth in organized crime and terrorism). Key among the factors that heightened scrutiny of non-state actor participation was globalization, which empowered non-state actors in their transnational activities and their attempts to influence states and intergovernmental organizations.

The last ten years has seen a great deal of attention focused on global health governance, or the process of incorporating non-state actors into the governance of global health issues. This trend characterizes the new world of public health governance, and thus is significant for biosecurity purposes.

The proliferation of public-private partnerships (PPPs) in global health during the last decade provides the best example of harnessing the governance potential of non-state actors.

The explosion in PPPs in global health dovetails with the international governance preference for flexible partnering rather than formal treaty structures. For example, the Global Fund was established as a PPP to make sure that it was not housed within a traditional intergovernmental framework (e.g., World Health Organization [WHO]). States could participate without accepting binding obligations, and non-state actors could participate in the Global Fund's governance structure and activities.

The importance of integrating non-state actors into the new world of public health governance also appears in the IHR 2005. As Chapter 5 elaborated, the IHR 2005 allows WHO to collect and use nongovernmental information in global surveillance, which integrates non-state actors into global surveillance capabilities. The IHR 2005's surveillance provisions represent one of the best examples of global health governance built into binding treaty law.

The integration of nongovernmental surveillance information and capabilities reflects not only the globalization of new technologies, such as the Internet and e-mail, but also the success of non-state actor efforts (e.g., ProMED-mail) to create a global early warning system for infectious diseases. At the heart of WHO's Global Outbreak and Alert Response Network (GOARN) is the Global Public Health Information Network (GPHIN), which trolls the Internet for indications of significant disease events around the world. The Nuclear Threat Initiative (2004), a NGO involved in issues related to weapons of mass destruction, sponsored an upgrade so that GPHIN can search in more languages and increase its breadth and depth of coverage. More recently, the philanthropic foundation established by the founders of Google launched its Networked System for Total Early Disease Protection (*Wall Street Journal* 2006), which represents yet another nongovernmental effort to contribute to the surveillance mission of global health governance.

Historical precedents of NGOs, such as the Rockefeller Foundation, working on international health since the early twentieth century allow contemporary efforts to incorporate non-state actors into global health fit into a continuum. The same cannot be said for the history of governance on biological weapons. During the Cold War, the governance of biological weapons was almost exclusively the province of states. With the coming of a new world of biological weapons governance, the traditional state-centric instruments of bio-deterrence and arms control agreements became insufficient, and the potential governance role of non-state actors emerged as a result.

All the controversy about biological weapons in the 1990s stimulated more non-state actor activity than previously had been the case. Some of this activity flowed from NGOs' involvement in the BWC Protocol negotiations and other aspects of the new biological weapons threats, such as NGO concern about the development of so-called non-lethal biological weapons. The NGO community concerned about biological weapons developed "watchdog" attributes familiar from NGO participation in other aspects of international law and international relations. In the wake of the collapse of the BWC Protocol, a network of NGOs formed the BioWeapons Prevention Project (BWPP) to heighten civil society monitoring of BWC issues. As Tucker (2004, 34–35) observed, "The BWPP puts member states on notice that their behavior is being watched, providing a degree of accountability and reinforcing the international norm against biological weapons." The International Committee of the Red Cross (ICRC), long known for its work on international humanitarian law, also developed interest in the potential biosecurity threats created by advances in biotechnologies and began to exert its influence in this field (ICRC 2004a). The behavior of the United States in the BWC Protocol negotiations and its biodefense programs became targets for NGOs that favored the Protocol and feared the consequences of expanded state biodefense programs.

The BWC Protocol negotiations also brought pharmaceutical and biotechnology companies more directly into the governance arena because the Protocol would have applied to their operations. These non-state actors never concerned themselves with arms control politics before the end of the Cold War, but the BWC Protocol placed them in the thick of the controversies. These companies used their political influence in Washington, D.C., in connection with Protocol negotiations. One reason the Bush administration gave for rejecting the BWC Protocol was the threat it posed to the proprietary interests of pharmaceutical and biotechnology companies.

Another important feature of non-state actor involvement in the new world of biological weapons governance concerns scientists engaging in biological research. As previously argued, this community never really worried about how its activities related to the proliferation of biological weapons during the Cold War. The rise of bioterrorism, the rapid expansion of scientific research capabilities and possibilities, and the global spread of biological science knowledge and technologies combined to shine the proliferation spotlight on the biological sciences. As Chapter 3 mentioned, one consequence of these developments has been the increased engagement of the biological sciences community as a non-state actor in biological weapons governance.

This engagement can be seen in the interest shown in codes of conduct for scientists engaging in biological research. The BWC New Process agenda discussed such codes of conduct, nongovernmental scientific organizations have developed and promulgated such codes, and the Sixth BWC Review Conference has included these codes as a topic in its 2007 through 2010 intersessional meetings. Codes of conduct hold that individual scientists, not just governments, have the responsibility to ensure that their work does not intentionally or inadvertently contribute to the development or use of biological weapons. These ethical duties resonate with trend toward imposing legal obligations on individual scientists through criminalization of biological weapons development and use. The scientist is, in other words, a critical actor in the governance enterprise of preventing biological weapons proliferation and use. Here again we have a form of global governance that integrates the non-state actor into how the problem is managed.

The potential for non-state actor involvement in the new world of biological weapons governance does not stop with the individual scientist working in the laboratory. Scientists can form networks to contribute to the central issues confronting biosecurity policy. For example, the Canadian Program on Genomics and Public Health (2006) proposed the creation of a global network of scientists to promote biotechnology research while keeping vigilant against any misuse of biological science. One participant in this effort characterized the proposal as the establishment of "an [International Atomic Energy Agency (IAEA)] for biotechnology—not with a team of IAEA-type inspectors, but an expanding global network of scientists" (Joint Centre for Bioethics 2006). Influencing this proposal were fears that security concerns about biological weapons would adversely affect progress in the biological sciences that could improve the human condition. Global networks of scientists could act to ensure balanced policies of both the integration of security and public health and the supervision of science for biosecurity.

Codes of conduct for, and supervisory networks of, scientists link those engaged in the biological sciences to a common endeavor that transcends borders and the sovereignty of states. Traditional international governance regulated states, not transnational communities of non-state actors. Making scientists participants in their individual and professional capacities in biosecurity governance extends the norm against biological weapons to every laboratory bench and scientific experiment.

The pattern of increasing non-state actor involvement contributes to globalizing governance for biosecurity, but even the most ardent advocates of non-state actor participation do not believe that such participation is sufficient to address the problems biological weapons and infectious diseases present now and in the future. Such participation converges with changes at the national and international levels to produce the transformation of governance of biological weapons and infectious diseases.

D. From Unstructured to Purposeful Plurality in Globalized Biosecurity Governance

The patterns identified at national, international, and global levels reveal a complex environment in which biosecurity governance takes place. Globalizing biosecurity governance is not an exercise in centralization and simplification. Taken together, the patterns confirm the turn away from traditional approaches to biological weapons and public health toward multilevel, multivariable, and multi-actor strategies. Littlewood (2005, 234) observed that the traditional arms control tendency to aggregate governance on biological weapons under one treaty or international organization no longer controls and that "managing the biological weapons problems requires a rubric of measures from the individual to the international." Other experts and officials similarly note that the future of governance concerning biological weapons points away from consolidating strategies within the BWC. As noted in Chapter 3, the UN Secretary-General (2006b) premised his proposal for a UN forum on biosecurity on the need to see the BWC as part of an array of interlinked governance tools. Tucker (2007) noted, "the current approach of creating a web of mutually reinforcing biosecurity measures at the individual, national, and international levels will probably prevail for the next several years." Chapter 5 described similar dynamics in the new world of public health governance. Many experts have analyzed the proliferation and diversity of actors, organizations, and initiatives characterizing contemporary global health. Just as events have made the traditional arms control approach found in the BWC ineffective, developments in global health have moved beyond the traditional international health model, with its center of gravity in the WHO.

The emergence of "unstructured plurality" in the worlds of biological weapons and public health has stimulated worries and calls for imposing order on the pluralism to produce more effective governance strategies. In terms of biological weapons, some experts want to see the BWC restored "to its former position at the heart of the regime (Tucker 2007), whereas others argue the UN should play a more vigorous leadership role (Kellman 2006a). Discourse concerning global health frequently uses the metaphor of "architecture" to describe the desire to tame unstructured plurality. Reflecting on the new landscape of public health, the dean of the Harvard School of Public Health argued, for example, "There's one missing piece. There's no architecture of global health" (quoted in Cohen 2006, 162). NGOs have explored strategies for developing new architecture for global health governance (German Overseas Institute 2006; Open Society Institute 2005).

As the concerns about unstructured plurality in the governance worlds of biological weapons and public health demonstrate, globalizing governance for biosecurity must involve more than multiplying actors, initiatives, and financial resources. The new pluralism is a by-product of the governance transitions underway concerning biological weapons and public health. The trajectory of globalized governance does not bring policy back to the traditional arms control and international health approaches. The current plurality of biosecurity politics is not a temporary phenomenon. Where the trajectory will lead biosecurity policy is not clear, but unstructured plurality creates serious concerns that must be confronted. The strategy of globalizing governance for biosecurity must seek to transform unstructured plurality into purposeful plurality. The next part of the chapter discusses how this objective could be advanced.

V. BUILDING A GLOBAL BIOSECURITY CONCERT

A. Need for a Global Biosecurity Mechanism

Moving biosecurity governance from unstructured plurality to purposeful plurality will require new strategies and mechanisms. Suggestions in this direction are often, however, general in nature, such as "strengthen the BWC," "empower WHO," "improve coordination existing initiatives," or "build new global governance architecture." In the wake of the policy revolution biosecurity represents, such generality is understandable because we are grappling with challenges and political contexts for which past governance models are insufficient or inappropriate. In addition, specific ideas for change are always vulnerable to the accusation they are politically unrealistic, and, in a context where the politics remains volatile, identifying what is politically realistic is difficult. Developments in biosecurity politics suggest, however, that the utility of generalized proposals and hopes for the future is declining rapidly.

The urgent need for new global governance mechanisms leads us to propose what we call a "global biosecurity concert." Improving biosecurity in the twenty-first century requires strengthening governance in the areas of biological weapons and public health, and integrating these governance responses in a coordinated manner. This task calls for a flexible but directed mechanism capable of orchestrating the complex web of actors and activities that make up biosecurity politics. We will not see a single, comprehensive treaty that unifies the complicated dynamics of contemporary biosecurity governance. Nor will any existing international institution, including the BWC, WHO, or the UN, alone provide an adequate platform for managing the pluralism of biosecurity governance. Moving biosecurity from unstructured to purposeful plurality will not, however, happen without some concerted efforts to shape, frame, and monitor biosecurity governance. The goal is a mechanism that lies between architecture and anarchy.

The idea of a global biosecurity concert immediately brings to mind the nineteenth century's Concert of Europe, which was an attempt by European great powers (originally, in 1815, Great Britain, Prussia, Austria, and Russia and joined in 1818 by France) to manage international relations to prevent the kind of catastrophic armed conflict seen in the Napoleonic Wars. The Concert of Europe was not formally based in a treaty or a formal international organization, but it functioned as a diplomatic mechanism for achieving common goals shared by the European great powers. Historians regard the Concert of Europe as one of first serious attempts to establish a mechanism among states to maintain international order and peace (Hinsley 1967).

Our idea for a global biosecurity concert is linked with the Concert of Europe only through the notion of organizing international cooperation through a "concert" mechanism. Concert mechanisms in international relations pursue specific substantive objectives through diverse and flexible means. Although international law informs the operation of diplomatic concerts, the concerts themselves are not specifically created by binding legal instruments, such as treaties that serve as the charters or constitutions of formal international organizations. In contemporary parlance, a concert is a type of regime that operates through a dynamic mixture of "hard law" and "soft law." This mixture shapes the substantive objectives of the concert, and, typically, stronger powers provide political support and direction for the concert's diversified activities.

Experts have used the "concert" idea to formulate new governance approaches in contexts characterized by the perceived weakening or failure of existing regimes. For example, the changing nature of security challenges in Asia promoted experts to analyze the need for a "Concert of Asia" as a new strategy to address Asia's security problems (Acharya 1999; Khoo and Smith 2002; White 2006). In the context of uncertainty about the effectiveness of UN reform proposals, Ikenberry and Slaughter (2006, 25) argued for development of a "Concert of Democracies" that would work "to strengthen security cooperation among the world's liberal democracies and to provide a framework in which they can work together to effectively tackle common challenges." In the same vein, we propose moving beyond the failings of traditional governance approaches to biological weapons and public health through a concert of state and non-state actors focused on biosecurity challenges.

The global biosecurity concert idea also connects with another approach to global governance—networked governance or global issue networks. This approach seeks more effective governance responses to global problems than traditional intergovernmental organizations produce. Rischard (2002, 17, 20–21) argued, for example, "Traditional institutions are incapable of addressing the growing list of complex global issues" because none of the existing "international problem-solving architecture"—treaties and conventions, intergovernmental conferences, G8-type groupings of states, and global multilaterals (e.g., WHO)—"is very effective when it comes to seriously and proactively tackling inherently global issues—and tackling them fast." The global biosecurity concert should make use of networks in the new worlds of biological weapons governance and public health, but a leading concern with unstructured plurality is that existing networks are not coordinated or connected effectively. The concert idea seeks to have governance networks moving more effectively in consistent policy directions, particularly to ensure the integration of security and public health.

We acknowledge that thinking about the new worlds of biological weapons and public health governance through a concert mechanism is unusual. To provide a better idea of what we mean by a global biosecurity concert, we describe what the substantive objectives of this concert should be, consider precursors and precedents for a concert mechanism, and introduce a possible way to structure such a concert.

B. Substantive Concert Objectives

The scope of biosecurity means that a global biosecurity concert requires attention to both biological weapons and naturally occurring infectious diseases. A key concert task will be to ensure sustainable integration of security and public health. This integration task distinguishes the concert idea from concepts such as the "web of deterrence" (Pearson 1998) and the "web of prevention" (ICRC 2004b) (see box). Like the concert idea, these webs attempt to construct coherent strategies from pluralism in policies, initiatives, and actors. These webs focus, however, on the dangers of intentional misuse of biological agents and do not directly address the threat of naturally occurring infectious diseases. A global biosecurity concert should advance both aspects of biosecurity in an integrated manner.

1. Biological Weapons and a Global Biosecurity Concert
Integration of the security and public health elements of biosecurity means a concert mechanism should have two hubs that provide normative and practi-

---

THE WEBS OF DETERRENCE AND PREVENTION

Web of Deterrence

"The web of deterrence is made up of a series of strands which are mutually reinforcing and lead would-be proliferators to judge that acquisition of CBW [chemical or biological weapons] is not worthwhile. A single strand alone will not suffice yet together they make the benefits of CBW acquisition minimal. It is, however, vital to ensure that all the strands are strong.

- Comprehensive prohibition through international treaties and national legislation establishing the clear norm that development, production, storage, acquisition or use of CBW are totally prohibited;
- Broad monitoring and controls ensuring that materials or equipment are used only for permitted purposes thus increasing the difficulty of acquiring materials or equipment for prohibited purposes;
- Broad band protective measures, both active and passive, thereby reducing the effectiveness of CBW;
- Determined national and international responses to non-compliance with the prohibition ranging from diplomatic actions, sanctions through to armed intervention, making it clear that acquisition of prohibited weapons will not be tolerated." (Pearson 1998)

---

cal direction for orchestrating better biosecurity governance. For biological weapons, the BWC is the hub because it contains the anchor norms that inform all governance initiatives on biological weapons. The death of the traditional arms control approach does not mean that the BWC has ceased to be "at the centre of the legal, normative, and moral authority under which action is taken to counter biological weapons" (Littlewood 2005, 241). The biosecurity concert idea recognizes the BWC as a normative center of governance gravity but does not seek to make the BWC process the central mechanism for addressing the biological weapons problem. A biosecurity concert should, for example, advance the work undertaken in past and future BWC intersessional meetings not because they arose in the BWC process but because they correspond to key challenges in the new world of biological weapons governance. Concert activities should not necessarily seek to revise the BWC or adopt new

Web of Prevention

"The web of prevention is expressly designed to foster synergy of action among all people in a position to limit risk of poisoning and the deliberate spread of disease. The idea is that if individual actors in the life sciences are properly informed of the risk, rules and their responsibilities, they will make better decisions.

Steps to minimize the risks of poisoning and the deliberate spread of disease resulting from advances in the life sciences can only be truly effective if they result from 'joined-up' thinking across all responsible sectors, namely government, the scientific community and the biotechnology and pharmaceutical industries.

Such engagement requires three main stages of action:

1. to acknowledge that minimizing risks from the hostile use of advances in the life sciences is of concern to them and part of their responsibility;
2. to identify and implement the necessary actions within their own sphere of influence that will contribute to risk reduction and that complement being taken in other spheres; and
3. to ensure that their actions are known amongst and complement the actions of actors in other relevant sectors.

Individual preventive actions, while sometimes not appearing likely to be effective on their own, can add up to very important in combination with others. They do not have to be complex, expensive or onerous, and should reflect the particular circumstances of a situation. The benchmark is that they should be effective." (ICRC 2004b)

treaties, but the concert's purpose would be to engage states and non-state actors in activities that support the BWC's norms against development and use of biological weapons.

Our argument that the global biosecurity concert should not specifically aim to strengthen the BWC process itself may cause concern for BWC proponents. Such concerns may arise from the belief that the norms against biological weapons are only as strong as the formal BWC process. This perspective remains stuck in the mentality of the traditional arms control approach. The proliferation of governance activities on biological weapons, from the Security Council to the individual scientist, reveals that the prohibitions against the development and use of biological weapons are robust outside the four corners of the BWC. As we argued in Chapter 2, the norms against biological weapons are stronger today despite the lack of progress on strengthening the BWC process over the past decade.

Whether that strength continues remains, of course, an open question, but the BWC process is not the only means available to apply the prohibitions against biological weapons development and use. The willingness of more and more people and institutions to push the cause of preventing development and use of biological weapons in realms beyond the BWC suggests that this cause is too important to leave to the dysfunctional BWC process.

The four governance trends in the new world of biological weapons governance analyzed in Chapter 3 constitute policy tracks a global biosecurity concert could advance. As existing trends, they are already the subject of diplomatic and nongovernmental attention, as the New Process agenda and the planned 2007 through 2010 intersessional meeting topics attest. To date, however, these trends have developed independently in an ad hoc fashion. The global biosecurity concert should facilitate state and non-state actor activities so that progress on all four trends is systematically made. Such progress would bolster the norms against biological weapons.

The BWC's New Process agenda reveals the need for more concerted efforts on criminalization of biological weapons development and use, supervision of science, and public health preparedness and response. The 2007–2010 intersessional meetings offer an opportunity to continue concerted activities on these topics. An intersessional meeting strategy within the BWC can become an important way in which states, international organizations, and non-state actors focus integrated efforts on improving global biosecurity governance. This strategy can also help reorient the BWC process away from the modalities of the traditional arms control approach toward addressing the governance trends that give biosecurity policy shape.

Complaints that intersessional meetings do not have the power to adopt decisions suggest that the intersessional meetings represent little more than "meetings for the sake of meeting." Tucker (2007) argued, for example, "The intersessional process will once again be limited to exchanges of information, and any decisions will have to await the Seventh Review Conference in 2011. This pace of work is simply too slow to cope with the urgency of the biological weapons threat." This perspective views the BWC process as somehow isolated from the other venues in which biosecurity governance transpires.

Information presented and discussed at the intersessional meetings can, however, feed into processes taking place in the Security Council's 1540 Committee, Interpol's efforts on criminalization, the G8 and other regional organizations, WHO's activities on biosecurity, and NGO analysis and advocacy. The intersessionals can become events the importance of which extends beyond the BWC process itself. The world of biosecurity policy did not stagnate after the failure of the Fifth Review Conference. To the contrary, the period between the Fifth and Sixth Review Conferences saw more governance activity on biological weapons than at any other time in history. The idea that biosecurity governance must wait for decisions at the Seventh Review Conference does not reflect how much the BWC's role changed between the Fifth and Sixth Review Conferences. The global biosecurity concert views the BWC as a main hub of activity, but it recognizes that the world will, and should, have more than one center of gravity for governance concerning the threat from biological weapons.

The most difficult governance trend to address in a global biosecurity concert will be the biodefense imperative. As Chapter 3 explored, this imperative played a significant role in U.S. opposition to the BWC Protocol and in U.S. behavior at the Fifth and Sixth Review Conferences. Collective efforts inside and outside the BWC to manage the biodefense imperative will remain sensitive for many years to come. A global biosecurity concert need not achieve dramatic results on biodefense to advance governance on biological weapons. Simply increasing collective consideration of the challenges legitimate biodefense activities face would alleviate some tensions built up in the last ten years on this topic. Many concerned about the manner in which the biodefense imperative plays out in the United States and other countries are working to shore up the legitimacy of biodefense research in ways that minimize the potential for the emergence of a new kind of bio-deterrence among states.

A global biosecurity concert could engage with the biodefense imperative in three ways. First, a concert should seek to promote increased transparency in national biodefense activities. The principle of transparency is not new and has proven difficult to foster, but it remains a central technique for balancing the right to conduct biodefense research with the obligation to demonstrate that such research does not constitute development of a biological weapon. Transparency in biodefense also serves the important rule of law functions of transparent and accountable government that benefit biosecurity in the long run.

Second, a concert could promote more rigorous consideration of the dangers of highly secretive biodefense research involving threat characterization studies that involve creation and manipulation of possible biological warfare agents. Justifications that this type of biodefense research is legitimate because the intent of the research is defensive threaten the prohibitions in Article I of the BWC. The Bush administration has relied on the "defensive intent" test to justify its threat characterization research (Warrick 2006; Ruppe 2004), even though the prohibitions in Article I of the BWC do not hinge only on the intent of the states parties. The BWC makes no distinction between "offensive" and "defensive" activities, let alone "offensive" or "defensive" intent. The proper distinction in Article I is between permitted and prohibited activities.

If the Bush administration is correct, however, then every country has the right to engage in novel threat characterization research and keep it completely secret. This interpretation of the BWC paves the way for the new kind of bio-deterrence described in Chapter 3, a bio-deterrence not based on actual weapon stockpiles but on possessing and refining the most cutting-edge scientific capabilities in creating and manipulating dangerous pathogens. This type of bio-deterrence would encourage a dynamic among states that could render the general purpose criterion in Article I of the BWC irrelevant and preclude attempts inside or outside the BWC to heighten transparency in the biodefense area. However difficult, the global biosecurity concert should try to address this disconcerting trend by focusing attention on the biosecurity dangers of threat characterization research, emphasizing the importance of increasing biodefense transparency, and insisting on forms of effective oversight and accountability for all biodefense research.

Third, a global biosecurity concert could encourage and support collaborative biodefense research. The strength of the biodefense imperative means that biodefense will not wither and die as an activity of states. Creating bilateral, regional, or multilateral biodefense research activities, especially with respect to developing dual-purpose diagnostics and broad-spectrum countermeasures, which benefit both security and public health, could channel the biodefense imperative in productive directions. Cooperative scientific research on pathogens that cause naturally occurring infectious diseases has proved powerful, as the scientific collaboration that rapidly identified the SARS virus illustrates. Perhaps the same globalized scientific process can be useful for generating positive externalities for both security and public health from the biodefense imperative.

A global biosecurity concert could also prove useful for the challenge of supervising science for biosecurity purposes, especially with respect to identifying the types of scientific research that require heightened biosecurity scrutiny from governments, research institutions, and individual scientists. As we discussed in Chapter 3, efforts have been made to pinpoint techniques and experiments that raise biosecurity concerns, which efforts include codes of conduct for scientists doing biological research. Leading NGOs, scientific organizations, and individual scientists could effectively be integrated into this aspect of a concert's activities. A global biosecurity concert could also advance the objective of supervising science by pushing globally for baseline improvements in the protection of pathogens, research facilities, and pathogen transfers.

2. Infectious Diseases and a Global Biosecurity Concert

For public health, the IHR 2005 would serve as a center of governance gravity for a global biosecurity concert. As earlier chapters argued, the IHR 2005 constitutes a radically new international legal framework, and this framework has already become the centerpiece of global strategy for potential epidemic events. UN reform documents have stressed the importance of the new IHR (UN Secretary-General's High-level Panel on Threats, Challenges and Change 2004; UN Secretary-General 2005), and regional efforts on bioterrorism and epidemic threats also emphasize the IHR 2005 (Global Health Security Initiative 2005). In May 2006, the World Health Assembly urged WHO members to implement, on a voluntary basis, the IHR 2005 in light of the threat posed by avian influenza (WHO 2006c). This resolution also highlights the governance significance of the IHR 2005 because the regulations do not become legally binding on WHO members until June 2007.

Despite the IHR 2005's centrality to biosecurity governance, much work remains to be done to ensure that the opportunity presented by the new regulations is not wasted. Moving states toward compliance with the IHR 2005 will involve diplomatic efforts that include, but also go beyond, WHO. States, international organizations, and non-state actors should focus on, and support, rapid, effective implementation of the IHR 2005. Such implementation would serve global biosecurity much better than many of the decisions made at the Sixth Review Conference, such as pushing for universal BWC membership in the BWC or bringing CBM submission procedure into the electronic age. In keeping with the need for globalizing governance, non-state actors have responsibilities as well in advocating for and implementing the IHR 2005, particularly given how the IHR 2005 builds nongovernmental information into global surveillance. In short, across multiple fronts, a global biosecurity concert could make the IHR 2005 its lodestar for improving national and global public health surveillance and intervention capabilities.

The ability of surveillance improvements to produce synergy between security and public health objectives makes a concerted push on surveillance a robust way to integrate security and public health globally. A global biosecurity concert has to get beyond conceptual surveillance synergy and make headway against the surveillance gap that exists between developed and developing countries. Tackling intervention as a public health function will prove more difficult because creating and sustaining intervention synergies for defense against biological weapons and infectious diseases are more difficult tasks, as Chapter 5 examined. A global biosecurity concert could achieve progress by working toward the establishment of broadly applicable, dual-use intervention capabilities to create as much synergy as possible. This strategy makes sense particularly because the greatest biosecurity threats facing developing countries come from naturally occurring infectious diseases.

Serious attention to the public health needs of developing countries through the IHR 2005 can help states move beyond the stalemate in the BWC process caused by the clash between nonproliferation objectives and the duty to foster international cooperation in the biological sciences. The BWC intersessional meeting in 2009 on promoting capacity building in the fields of disease surveillance, detection, diagnosis, and containment of infectious diseases provides a prime opportunity to review progress on the implementation of the IHR 2005 and to develop strategies to strengthen implementation of the regulations.

3. Capacity Building, the Rule of Law, and a Global Biosecurity Concert

At the heart of the biological weapons and infectious disease tracks of a global biosecurity concert is the task of building biosecurity capacity at the national level. Much of the normative frameworks for biosecurity governance already exist through the BWC, IHR 2005, other treaties, Security Council mandates, and internationally recognized standards and best practices. What is often more lamented is the lack of effective implementation of existing obligations and responsibilities. Too much of the normative framework for biosecurity built multilaterally simply has not been internalized. An egregious example is the historical failure of BWC states parties to implement their BWC obligations in national legislation as required by the treaty.

As argued earlier, security and public health are not public goods without commitment and capacity within states to produce them. Passing a statute criminalizing biological weapons development without law enforcement capacity to administer and enforce the law does not improve biosecurity. Requiring higher standards for pathogen safety, transfer, and laboratory security is meaningless if personnel and facilities have no training, equipment, and resources to comply. Agreeing that surveillance and intervention need to be strengthened is easy; constructing improved and sustainable surveillance and intervention capacities is not. As one of us argued elsewhere, "Global health governance's biggest obstacle might not be unstructured plurality but the plurality of incapacity" (Fidler 2007b). The key test of a global biosecurity concert will be how effectively it contributes to the development of biosecurity capacities at the national and local level levels.

The capacity-building challenge will be a marker of a global biosecurity concert's ability to weave the integration of security and public health into national policies and laws. Such internalization is critical for embedding biosecurity in the rule of law. The process of empowering governments to act against biosecurity threats is incomplete without capacity to exercise that power in ways that respect individual rights and concepts of justice and foster transparency and accountability in the exercise of political power. When biosecurity crises hit, failure to internalize the normative frameworks and to build capacity will force governments to exercise broad emergency powers and ask rule of law questions later.

4. Collective Biosecurity Intervention

The Concert of Europe sought to provide the basis for European countries to intervene in the domestic affairs of countries experiencing revolts or rebellions as part of the Concert's effort to maintain the status quo. Other uses of the concert idea also contemplate concert members acting to prevent or respond to developments that threaten the concert's interests. For example, the proposal for a concert of democracies includes the right of the concert's members (1) to act to implement the "responsibility to protect" populations when other states fail to uphold this principle, and (2) to "become an alternative forum for the approval of the use of force in cases where the use of the veto at the Security Council prevented free nations from keeping faith with the aims of the UN Charter" (Ikenberry and Slaughter 2006, 26).

Similarly, a global biosecurity concert should be prepared to foster interventions in countries with respect to threats to biosecurity that arise. Such intervention should involve offers of security or public health assistance for countries struggling with biosecurity problems. The concert must also be willing to bring its collective political influence to bear on countries that deviate from the fundamental BWC norms or that fail to cooperate fully in addressing infectious disease epidemics. A global biosecurity concert could strive to create sufficiently deep and broad solidarity among states and non-state actors (e.g., multinational corporations) that collective interventions prove feasible.

Such biosecurity-related interventions occurred during the SARS outbreak when WHO confronted China's failure to cooperate transparently with WHO's containment efforts. The South African government faced concerted pressure to transform its policies on HIV/AIDS, which were contributing to a biosecurity crisis of the first order. Leading strategies for UN reform advocated increasing the Security Council's role in serious infectious disease events, and these strategies included recommendations that the Security Council mandate state cooperation with WHO in the investigation of significant outbreaks (UN Secretary-General 2005; UN Secretary-General's High-level Panel on Threats, Challenges and Change 2004). Countries hesitant or reluctant to confront the spread of avian influenza faced public and private sector pressures to act responsibly. The emerging global threat posed by the development and spread of extensively drug-resistant tuberculosis (XDR-TB) is putting some countries, especially South Africa, under increasing global health scrutiny. These events and ideas suggest that a global biosecurity concert could help create sufficient solidarity among state and non-state actors that would bring constructive and effective multilateral pressure to bear on states behaving in ways that threaten collective biosecurity.

Not surprisingly, the most difficult intervention context for the global biosecurity concern to manage involves activities that threaten the norms enshrined in the BWC. Existing and proposed mechanisms to address such activities have not proved successful in the past. No BWC state party has ever used the BWC's provision allowing states parties to bring allegations of violations to the Security Council (Article VI). The authority of the UN Secretary-General to investigate alleged uses of chemical and biological weapons has only been used to investigate chemical weapons incidents. The effort to craft a compliance mechanism through the BWC Protocol failed. Neither the Fifth nor Sixth BWC Review Conferences reached any decisions about strengthening compliance or investigatory strategies. As illustrated again at the Sixth Review Conference, the established pattern involves states parties leveling accusation of BWC violations at each other without providing evidence to substantiate the allegations. The strength of the biodefense imperative ensures that suspicions about BWC violations will continue and perhaps increase.

The difficulty of effective intervention into matters involving allegations of BWC violations should, thus, not be underestimated. Even so, a global biosecurity concert might make more headway than past approaches, which have focused on using or creating formal mechanisms (e.g., the Security Council, the BWC Protocol's proposed Organization for the Prohibition of Biological Weapons). Attempts to construct formalized approaches to potential BWC violations have not proved successful, and the nature of the biodefense imperative compounds the problem because it heightens the problem of establishing violations of the BWC. A global biosecurity concert, with a more flexible structure and dynamics, could approach concerns about BWC violations informally but iteratively across a number of diplomatic venues. This approach will not satisfy experts who believe that biosecurity needs formal BWC investigatory and compliance mechanisms, but, in the absence of any serious prospect that states will agree to such mechanisms, other strategies, however imperfect, are needed.

C. Concert Precursors and Precedents

The idea of a global biosecurity concert breaks with traditional approaches to biological weapons and infectious diseases, which centered on specific treaties or international organizations and operated independently of each other. A concert would use relevant treaties and organizations but seek to act beyond their formal, legal limitations to improve national, international, and global engagement with biosecurity challenges. As strange and abstract as the concert idea may seem, developments in biosecurity governance during the past decade point to precursors and precedents that lend support to a concert strategy.

We can begin with what happened to global health in the past ten years. As noted earlier, global health has experienced an explosion in new actors, approaches, financial resources, and activities. These developments give public health a greater political profile than it has ever had. Public health's new political importance was not produced by WHO fulfilling its functions as the UN specialized agency for international health. Paradoxically, public health's importance has grown as new actors, institutions, and initiatives challenged and sometimes diminished WHO's role in global health.

Although uncoordinated pluralism in global health causes problems, particularly in developing countries, the efforts reflect some unity in all the diversity. States, international organizations, and non-state actors have, for selfish and humanitarian reasons, decided to place greater political and economic emphasis on public health at home and abroad. Unity of purpose and diversity of effort are critical to achieving purposeful plurality through a global biosecurity concert. The governance trick is to harness the creativity and energy of the unity and diversity to serve the interests of human health more effectively. As discussed earlier, new ideas and strategies to harness the prohibition of global health endeavors are needed, and a global biosecurity concert should address these needs. For all its continued significance, WHO cannot shoulder these tasks by itself, even if states accorded WHO increasing authority and respect.

The proliferation of global health activities has helped usher in globalized forms of governance that biosecurity needs. A global biosecurity concert represents a middle way between the traditional international health model based in WHO and the relatively uncoordinated expansion of global health efforts now taking place. Policy desires to centralize, harmonize, and rationalize the proliferation of global health endeavors in WHO overestimate the potential capabilities of this intergovernmental entity and underestimate how significantly this proliferation has been the precursor for the development of radically different types of globalized governance for public health.

For all its troubling features, what happened between the Fifth and Sixth BWC Review Conferences can also be seen as a precursor for a global biosecurity concert. As the BWC process descended into crisis, governance initiatives on biological weapons increased in intensity and scope. The New Process agenda emerged from the BWC Protocol and Fifth Review Conference debacles as an effort to keep the BWC process alive, and this agenda helped illuminate just how far governance of the biological weapons problem had moved beyond the traditional arms control approach. The 2003 through 2005 intersessional meetings demonstrated that the BWC process needed to support governance trends the process did not generate, including the criminalization of biological weapons development and use, heightened supervision of the biological sciences, and emphasis on public health preparedness and response. The New Process agenda, combined with the outcome of the Sixth Review Conference, have made clear that the BWC is necessary but not sufficient to handle the challenges now facing the governance of the biological weapons threat.

Thus, the Security Council became directly involved, states launched initiatives and partnerships to advance biosecurity (e.g., Global Health Security Initiative [see later]), WHO integrated the threat of biological weapons into its global health agenda, and non-state actors became more engaged on biological weapons than ever before. Again, we see some unity amid the diversity in all this activity on biological weapons. Ironically, the BWC Protocol's death may have been one of the best things to happen in the new world of biological weapons governance because its demise has stimulated activities nationally, internationally, and globally—levels of activity never achieved by the traditional BWC process.

The involvement of more actors, institutions, and issues at each governance level with respect to biological weapons and naturally occurring infectious diseases enhances political interest, multiplies policy linkages, and creates a broader, more diverse constituency for biosecurity action. These linkages reflect both the multifaceted nature of public health and the broadening of how states view security as a policy pursuit. From this perspective, the proliferation of new governance initiatives related to biosecurity is more than a cacophony of unconnected concerns. The proliferation may be the prelude to something potentially more profound.

Some informal partnering arrangements that states have used for biosecurity purposes are also precedents for the biosecurity concert idea. From the concert perspective, one of the more interesting arrangements is the Global Health Security Initiative (GHSI). GHSI began in the immediate aftermath of the anthrax attacks in the United States among the Group of Seven (G7) countries plus Mexico, which agreed "to forge a new partnership to address the critical issue of protecting public health and security" (Ottawa Statement 2001). Since its establishment, GHSI partner states have agreed to take individual and collective actions to strengthen biosecurity against both biological weapons (e.g., through projects related to smallpox and anthrax) and naturally occurring infectious diseases (e.g., pandemic influenza preparedness). GHSI has established working groups, held workshops, and constructed new networks, such as the Emergency Contact Network and the Global Health Security Laboratory Network.

We argued earlier that a global biosecurity concert should emphasize the governance importance of the IHR 2005, and GHSI has already moved in this direction. GHSI (2005) strongly supported the IHR 2005, including a call for countries immediately to comply, on a voluntary basis, with the IHR 2005 before the regulations enter into force in June 2007. GHSI (2005) also supported efforts by its partner states and WHO to build capacity in epidemic alert and response in developing countries as part of activities designed to improve IHR 2005 implementation.

GHSI can be seen as a small-scale prototype of a global biosecurity concert. GHSI is pushing forward national, international, and global governance tasks related to preparation for biological attacks or outbreaks of epidemic infectious diseases. It has identified the IHR 2005 as a key instrument for advancing health security nationally and globally, and has focused on capacity building both within the partner countries and within developing countries. GHSI has also built new networks to enhance international cooperation on health security. It has supported and collaborated with WHO.

GHSI would form an important element of a global biosecurity concert. GHSI, on its own, is not sufficient for a global concert because its membership consists mainly of industrialized countries (the G7), and its activities do not include important aspects of contemporary biosecurity concern, particularly the criminalization of biological weapons development and use, regulation of the biological sciences, and managing the biodefense imperative. GHSI's strengths appear in those areas—public health surveillance and intervention—that bolster defenses against biological weapons and infectious diseases. Globalizing the governance partnership approach used by GHSI through replication and implementation in other regions of the world could contribute significantly to the workings of a global biosecurity concert.

D. Structuring a Global Biosecurity Concert

The current proliferation of initiatives connected to the security and public health aspects of biosecurity provides substantive ideas and practical precedents for the idea of a global biosecurity concert, but it does not, by itself, create the concert we have in mind. A "concert" implies something more organized than the collection of rather uncoordinated biosecurity governance activities presently underway or proposed. Such organization would aim to deepen and broaden the unity in the diversity present in biosecurity activities.

The concert idea does not, however, contemplate new legally binding treaties or intergovernmental organizations. A concert would involve strategic linkages of existing centers of normative authority and obligations that create the political leverage needed to make progress on biosecurity. These tasks could, of course, be achieved in diverse ways, but we offer one vision of structuring a global biosecurity concert.

Figure 7.1 depicts the structure for a global biosecurity concert we have in mind. The structure has a hierarchy determined by the key international agreements affecting biosecurity. At the top of the hierarchy sits the Security Council. The combination of its UN Charter authority in the security area and its growing involvement in biosecurity matters (e.g., Resolution 1540, viewing HIV/AIDS as a security threat, and recommendations of greater Security Council involvement in serious disease outbreaks) gives the Council preeminent stature in any concert arrangement.

The Security Council's responsibilities for maintaining international peace and security mean, however, that the Council cannot devote all its time to biosecurity. It should, however, establish a standing Committee on Biological Security with the mandate to oversee global efforts on biosecurity and to advise the Council on biosecurity problems emerging in the international system. A Committee on Biological Security would continue the work started by the 1540 Committee, but its jurisdiction should be broader than the matters covered in Resolution 1540.

The mandate for the Committee on Biological Security should include overseeing and coordinating activities under the BWC and the IHR 2005. This aspect of the concert structure reflects the normative and legal importance of the BWC and IHR 2005 in contemporary biosecurity governance and the need for the Security Council to monitor progress under both treaty regimes. Connecting the BWC, IHR 2005, and a Committee on Biological Security would require creating secretariat capabilities for the BWC, and this idea overlaps with proposals for the BWC states parties to create a small BWC secretariat at the Sixth Review Conference.

The next component of a concert structure would be regional biosecurity partnerships or initiatives, along the model of the GHSI. Some regional organizations have cooperative ventures on matters relating to biosecurity (e.g., enhanced regional infectious disease surveillance), but the Committee on Biological Security would push for regional initiatives or endeavors that addressed biological weapons and naturally occurring infectious diseases. The regional arrangements could be binding or nonbinding in nature and would report directly to the Committee on Biological Security on progress made within their regions on biosecurity governance tasks.

Underneath the regional partnerships or initiatives would be national interagency biosecurity focal points that would coordinate work with the regional efforts and the Committee on Biological Security and would be responsible for collecting data on and overseeing national-level activities on biosecurity governance. Governments may currently have different ministries involved in biosecurity tasks (e.g., defense ministries for biological weapons,

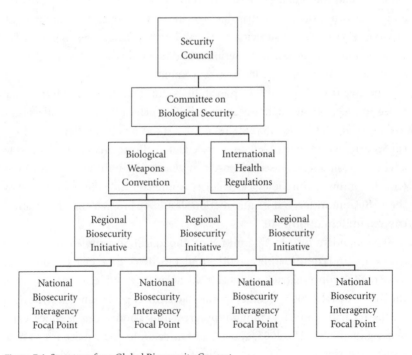

Figure 7.1 Structure for a Global Biosecurity Concert

health ministries for infectious diseases), but a concert strategy would emphasize closer national-level coordination through an interagency focal point mechanism.

A concert approach would also seek to involve relevant non-state actors at each level starting with the Committee on Biological Security, which would establish the precedent the regional initiatives and national interagency focal points should follow. This involvement recognizes the importance of non-state actors as both subjects and producers of biosecurity governance. Integrating non-state actors may help to produce more harmonization, especially through interfaces between regional efforts or consolidating work accomplished by the Committee on Biological Security.

The structure we have described is ambitious and raises feasibility issues, as do all governance ideas that deviate from the status quo. At the same time, a global biosecurity concert operating through this structure would draw on significant existing commitment, interest, and projects, making the concert idea and structure much more plausible than reviving the BWC Protocol or contemplating other expansive treaty projects would be. The idea of a Committee on Biological Security is not far-fetched given how the Security Council is now broadly engaged on biosecurity matters. Scaling-up or strengthening regional partnerships or initiatives is also not bizarre because regional organizations have already started down the path of improving regional biosecurity cooperation. Resolution 1540, the BWC, and the IHR 2005 already create the need for interagency cooperation and implementation at the national level, so the proposed concert structure again follows in the wake of prior governance developments.

The potential benefit of such a structure is how it would provide organization, transparency, and oversight to biosecurity activities undertaken by states, treaty regimes, intergovernmental organizations, and non-state actors. The structure would help move the current unstructured plurality toward purposeful plurality by deepening solidarity on biosecurity objectives while harnessing diverse efforts that contribute to bettering global biosecurity.

VI. CONCLUSION

This chapter explored the challenge of globalizing governance for biosecurity, which has cropped up at every turn in this book's analysis of biosecurity. The challenge is, thus, comprehensive and must be confronted. We examined conceptual aspects of the challenges's pervasiveness and complexities.

We identified difficulties created when the transnational problems of biological weapons and infectious diseases have to be addressed primarily by states interacting in anarchy. The transnational threats outstrip the capabilities of states and severely challenge traditional methods of collective action.

The critical normative and practical importance of globalizing governance for biosecurity has stimulated a wide range of initiatives designed to strengthen defenses against biological weapons, naturally occurring infectious diseases, or both. The chapter identified patterns that emerge from this activity at the levels of national, international, and global governance. The patterns reveal that the new worlds of biological weapons and public health governance will be more multifaceted and complicated than policy on biological weapons and infectious disease was when these were separate governance endeavors. In other words, the governance that will occur cannot be neatly packaged inside one or two treaty regimes that define the scope of the policies that states and non-state actors can pursue.

We argue that the complexity of the emerging governance politics is not chaos. Unity of purpose can be sensed in the diversity of governance operations. In this context, we described the needs discernable for the next phase of biosecurity governance in terms of a global biosecurity concert. The concert notion accepts the reality that governance will now and in the future have to involve many moving parts and pieces, some connected, others entirely unrelated. The concert idea seeks, however, to maximize the governance progress that this diversity of operations can achieve, especially progress on building sustainable biosecurity capacity at national governance levels. Using the involvement of the Security Council in biosecurity matters, the BWC and the IHR 2005 as centers of gravity, and the growth in regional biosecurity activities, a global concert approach could offer a practical and powerful way to create globalized governance to pursue the critical tasks of integrating security and public health, supervising science for biosecurity, and embedding biosecurity governance in the rule of law.

8 CONCLUSION

The Burden and Opportunity of Biosecurity in the Global Age

In this book, we examined the emergence of biosecurity as a critical policy area for national and international politics in the twenty-first century. Revolutionary changes have transformed the contexts for governance approaches to biological weapons and naturally occurring infectious diseases during the past thirty years, but particularly the changes that occurred during the last decade. The analysis found in these pages would have been both unnecessary and unthinkable before these revolutionary changes. In the late 1960s, the United States declared that infectious diseases had been conquered and unilaterally renounced offensive biological weapons. These developments narrowed the world of biosecurity to limited biodefense activities to protect military forces from biological attack. The past ten years have, however, witnessed events and experienced changes that shattered narrow conceptions of biosecurity and opened governance challenges that have few, if any, precedents to guide policy. Never before have states, including the most powerful, simultaneously treated biological weapons and infectious diseases as serious security threats.

We focused on the transformative events and forces that produced new governance worlds for countering the threats of biological weapons and naturally occurring infectious diseases. The problem of biological weapons has transcended, and rendered inadequate, the traditional arms control approach embodied in the Biological Weapons Convention (BWC). The biological weapons threat has forced states, intergovernmental organizations, and non-state actors to build more comprehensive and complex strategies to protect against the proliferation and use of biological weapons. Similarly, traditional approaches to infectious diseases proved inadequate as microbial dangers grew in scope and seriousness. These dangers prompted policy makers to engage in the securitization of public health and to embark on unprecedented efforts to remake global surveillance and intervention policies.

The emergence of radically new governance efforts on biological weapons and infectious diseases becomes even more important because, as argued throughout the book, these new governance worlds are interdependent. The traditional lack of connections between security and public health policy has vanished, leaving policy makers facing the task of weaving together strategies to address pathogenic threats regardless of their source or origin. This task—the integration of security and public health—constitutes a critical objective of the new world of biosecurity governance emphasized time and again in this book.

Pursuing the integration objective highlights other policy goals biosecurity governance must achieve: the supervision of science, embedding biosecurity governance in the rule of law, and globalizing governance. The need to supervise science as part of ensuring biosecurity radically transforms the relationship of science to policy on biological weapons and naturally occurring infectious diseases, and biosecurity governance has to manage this transformed relationship carefully. The objective concerning the rule of law emphasizes the normative significance of subjecting responses to the revolutionary changes of the last decade to the governance philosophy embodied in the rule of law. The integration, supervision, and rule of law tasks require globalized forms of governance because globalization permeates and shapes all aspects of biosecurity policy.

In addition to these central objectives, the new worlds of biological weapons and infectious disease governance create more specific policy challenges that policy makers from local to global levels must address. In terms of biological weapons, we highlighted the importance of managing four governance trends: the criminalization of biological weapons development and use, the regulation of the biological sciences, the development of the biodefense imperative, and creation of public health preparedness and response capabilities for biological attacks. For the securitization of public health, we explored the critical importance of improving public health infrastructures through strengthened surveillance and intervention capabilities.

We leavened our normative assertions about what biosecurity governance requires in the twenty-first century with examination of the difficulties these tasks confront. Integration of security and public health still faces skepticism and opposition by traditionalists in both fields who prefer to maintain separation between these policy areas. Supervising science for biosecurity requires careful balancing between security and public health interests, the practical challenges of which are enormous. Embedding biosecurity policies in the rule of law faces difficulties arising from not only the newness of contemporary challenges but also historical difficulties public health and security have experienced with rule of law disciplines. Globalizing governance is a task of such complexity that proposals for progress, such as our suggested global biosecurity concert, often seem unrealistic, simplistic, or naïve.

The more specific policy challenges biosecurity governance faces also experience complexities and obstacles that distort the clarity of their normative importance. Conceptually, criminalization of biological weapons development and use seems straightforward given how biological weapons are considered repugnant to the conscience of humanity. Criminalization has, however, proved enormously difficult to achieve effectively through international legal obligations in the BWC. Similarly, consensus exists that regulating science to ensure new developments, techniques, and technologies do not lead to biological weapons is prudent. How to regulate effectively remains problematical, as does the need to have such regulation harmonized globally to address the globalization of the biological sciences. Strengthening public health surveillance and intervention capacities as required for biosecurity is much easier recommended than achieved, and the world faces serious gaps in such capacities between developed and developing countries that must be addressed with alacrity.

Looming as a danger for the new worlds of biological weapons and public health governance is the renewed attention biodefense has received, particularly in the United States. Mismanagement of the biodefense imperative could adversely affect the ability of states, international organizations, and non-state actors to integrate security and public health effectively, supervise cutting-edge biological science appropriately, embed biosecurity governance in the rule of law, and globalize governance approaches to biosecurity threats. Excessive attention and resources devoted to biodefense could also produce a new kind of bio-deterrence in which states (and perhaps even non-state actors) balance each other's capabilities by competing to stay on the cutting edge of what is possible to accomplish with advances in the biological sciences.

This new form of bio-deterrence does not require the existence of stockpiles of biological weapons to create dangers for world politics. Our concept of the biodefense industrial complex expresses the concern that many arms control and public health experts have about reinvigorated biodefense functioning as a black hole that bends all biosecurity policies in its direction, undermining security and public health in the long run.

The scope of contemporary biosecurity governance, the intensity of the controversies it provokes, and the complexity of its general and specific policy challenges communicate collectively the burden that biosecurity policy represents for states and the international community in the twenty-first century. Just under forty years ago, most developed countries believed they had overcome the scourge of infectious diseases and celebrated the arms control breakthrough of the BWC. Seeing a day in the future when biological weapons and naturally occurring infectious diseases would simultaneously worry the great powers as serious security threats would have seemed, in the late 1960s, like bad science fiction. In 2007, seeing a day in the future when the malevolent manipulation of microbes and the potent evolutionary potential of the pathogenic world are minor matters in human affairs seems like pathetic science fiction. The burden of biosecurity will be neither lightly borne nor quickly set aside as an accomplished task.

For some, the burden of biosecurity remains a conglomeration of overblown worries cynically manipulated by those who benefit from the political attention and financial resources that accompany topics of policy hysteria. Growing threats in the realm of nuclear proliferation, the decaying situations in Iraq and Afghanistan, global conventional terrorism, China's rising military power, dependency on vulnerable oil supplies, global warming, and weak border controls over immigration at home are, in the minds of some, more important security matters than imagining the emergence of Islamic bioterrorists or fretting about bird flu being the second coming of the Great Influenza. We acknowledged throughout the book the ongoing controversies about how much danger biological weapons and infectious disease epidemics pose. Nor have we claimed that biosecurity constitutes the most important problem plaguing the planet today.

Complicating biosecurity policy making at virtually every turn is the relentless unease and uncertainties generated by the inability to assess with clarity the true nature of the risks. Questions swirl throughout the fog biosecurity generates: Will we ever experience Osama bio Laden? Will the avian influenza "go nuclear" and trigger a catastrophic pandemic? Will the thrill of pushing science deeper into nature's mysteries produce blowback through bioterrorism? Will expansion of the biodefense industrial complex accelerate the quickly shrinking opportunity developed countries have to help developing nations confront HIV/AIDS and other infectious disease scourges?

We believe that the burden of biosecurity, with all its uncertainties and competing policy agendas, must be taken seriously and shouldered with determination. This book explains the analytical reasons for our position, but we have personal motivations as well. Our individual scholarly and professional pursuits involved us in different aspects of security and public health before September 11th and the anthrax attacks. We recall palpable complacency about the terrorist and bioterrorist threats that existed before the tragedies of autumn 2001 shocked the world. The hubris-laden complacency that enervated public health for decades now appears like great folly in the wake of resurgent infectious diseases. Yet, we do not seem to learn unless another crisis again teaches hard lessons. Entirely predictable, and indeed predicted, epidemics, such as severe acute respiratory syndrome (SARS) and avian influenza, and natural disasters, such as hurricanes and tsunamis, still find rich and poor countries unprepared for the tragedies left in the wake of nature's fury.

Rejecting complacency and acknowledging the reality of the burden of biosecurity is not, of course, a strategy. How to structure and operate the new worlds of biological weapons and public health governance remains, and will remain, intensely controversial. As our notion of a global biosecurity concert suggests, we do not believe any easy fixes are available. The outcome of the Sixth BWC Review Conference demonstrated the complexities and difficulties facing efforts to address the biological weapons threat. The International Health Regulations (IHR) 2005 will not, by itself, keep the germs at bay. The IHR 2005 mandates core surveillance and intervention capabilities but provides no strategy or funds for the building of such capabilities, particularly in developing countries. Acknowledging these realities, the strategy of a global biosecurity concert is both more complicated and realistic than bolder visions of legally binding instruments of universal applicability.

Amid the burdens of biosecurity is, however, opportunity. As Chapter 7 noted, biosecurity endeavors by states, intergovernmental organizations, and non-state actors reveal unity of purpose in the diversity of activities taking place. The emerging features of biosecurity governance indicate a strengthening awareness of the need to confront the threat to security and human dignity posed by naturally occurring or intentionally manipulated microbes. This awareness presents the opportunity to develop, implement, and sustain new governance approaches to transnational problems. These new globalized approaches to governance can break new security and public health ground conceptually and practically while renewing faith in, and commitment to, the rule of law.

The opportunity of biosecurity in the global age is the challenge, in essence, of applied ideology. The world frequently appears united against some evil or in favor of some good. Too often such unity proves superficial, cynical, or utopian. Societies and states fail to apply their shared ideologies and shirk the heavy lifting required to achieve security and public health in ways that are sustainable and just. The policy earthquakes of the past decade have not destroyed the beliefs in the evil of biological weapons and the human dignity produced by public health. The new worlds of biological weapons and public health governance mean that commitment to these beliefs needs channeling into action through new strategies and policies. Harnessing renewed commitment and applying transformed strategies require the ability to appreciate change, the capability to innovate amid complexity and uncertainty, and a willingness to see opportunity, not in following the faded precedents of the past, but in the promise of imagining the future's potential.

ANNEX 1 U.S. GOVERNMENT SELECT AGENT LIST

HHS SELECT AGENTS AND TOXINS

Abrin

Cercopithecine herpesvirus 1 (Herpes B virus)

Coccidioides posadasii

Conotoxins

Crimean-Congo haemorrhagic fever virus

Diacetoxyscirpenol

Ebola virus

Lassa fever virus

Marburg virus

Monkeypox virus

Reconstructed replication competent forms of the 1918 pandemic influenza virus containing any portion of the coding regions of all eight gene segments (Reconstructed 1918 influenza virus)

Ricin

Rickettsia prowazekii

Rickettsia rickettsii

Saxitoxin

Shiga-like ribosome inactivating proteins

South American haemorrhagic fever viruses

    Flexal

    Guanarito

    Junin

Machupo

Sabia

Textrodotoxin

Tick-borne encephalitis complex (flavi) viruses

Central European tick-borne encephalitis

Far Eastern tick-born encephalitis

Kyasanur Forest disease

Omsk hemorrhagic fever

Russian spring-summer encephalitis

Variola major virus (Smallpox virus) and Variola minor virus (Alastrim)

Yersinia pestis

OVERLAP SELECT AGENTS AND TOXINS

Bacillus anthracis

Botulinum neurotoxins

Botulinum neurotoxin producing species of *Clostridium*

Brucella abortus

Brucella melitensis

Brucella suis

Burkholderia mallei (formerly *Pseudomonas mallei*)

Burkholderia pseudomallei (formerly *Pseudomonas pseudomallei*)

Clostridium perfringens epsilon toxin

Coccidioides immitis

Coxiella burnetii

Eastern equine encephalitis virus

Francisella tularensis

Hendra virus

Nipah virus

Rift Valley fever virus

Shigatoxin

Staphylococcal enterotoxins

T-2 toxin

Venezuelan equine encephalitis virus

USDA SELECT AGENTS AND TOXINS

African horse sickness virus

African swine fever virus

Akabane virus

Avian influenza virus (highly pathogenic)

Bluetongue virus (Exotic)

Bovine spongiform encephalopathy agent

Camelpox virus

Classical swine fever virus

Cowdria ruminantium (Heartwater)

Foot-and-mouth disease virus

Goat pox virus

Japanese encephalitis virus

Lumpy skin disease virus

Malignant catarrhal fever virus (Alcelaphine herpesvirus type 1)

Menangle virus

Mycoplasma capricolum/M.F38/*M. mycoides Capri* (contagious caprine
   pleuropneumonia)

Mycoplasma mycoides mycoides (contagious bovine pleuropneumonia)

Newcastle disease virus (velogenic)

Peste des petits ruminants virus

Rinderpest virus

Sheep pox virus

Swine vesicular disease virus

Vesicular stomatitis virus (Exotic)

USDA PLANT PROTECTION AND QUARANTINE (PPQ) SELECT AGENTS AND TOXINS

Candidatus Liberobacter africanus

Candidatus Liberobacter asiaticus

Peronosclerospora philippinensis

Ralstonia solanacearum race 3, biovar 2

Schlerophthora rayssiae var zeae

Synchytrium endobioticum

Xanthomonas oryzae pv. oryzicola

Xylella fastidiosa (citrus variegated chlorosis strain)

SOURCE: Centers for Disease Control and Prevention 2006a

Protocol for the Prohibition of the Use of Asphyxiating, Poisonous or Other Gases, and of Bacteriological Methods of Warfare. Geneva, 17 June 1925.

The undersigned Plenipotentiaries, in the name of their respective Governments:

[Here follow the names of Plenipotentiaries]

Whereas the use in war of asphyxiating, poisonous or other gases, and of all analogous liquids materials or devices, has been justly condemned by the general opinion of the civilized world; and

Whereas the prohibition of such use has been declared in Treaties to which the majority of Powers of the world are Parties; and

To the end that this prohibition shall be universally accepted as a part of International Law, binding alike the conscience and the practice of nations;

Declare:

That the High Contracting Parties, so far as they are not already Parties to Treaties prohibiting such use, accept this prohibition, agree to extend this prohibition to the use of bacteriological methods of warfare and agree to be bound as between themselves according to the terms of this declaration.

The High Contracting Parties will exert every effort to induce other States to accede to the present Protocol. Such accession will be notified to the Government of the French Republic, and by the latter to all Signatory and Acceding Powers, and will take effect on the date of the notification by the Government of the French Republic.

The present Protocol of which the French and English texts are both authentic, shall be ratified as soon as possible. It shall bear today's date.

The ratifications of the present Protocol shall be addressed to the Government of the French Republic, which will at once notify the deposit of such ratification to each of the Signatory and Acceding Powers.

The instruments of ratification and accession to the present Protocol will remain deposited in the archives of the Government of the French Republic.

The present Protocol will come into force for each Signatory Power as from the date of deposit of its ratification, and, from that moment, each Power will be bound as regards other Powers which have already deposited their ratifications.

In witness whereof the Plenipotentiaries have signed the present Protocol.

Done at Geneva in a single copy, the seventeenth day of June, One Thousand Nine Hundred and Twenty-Five.

Convention on the Prohibition of the Development, Production and Stockpiling of Bacteriological (Biological) and Toxin Weapons and on their Destruction. Opened for Signature at London, Moscow and Washington. 10 April 1972.

The States Parties to this Convention,

Determined to act with a view to achieving effective progress towards general and complete disarmament, including the prohibition and elimination of all types of weapons of mass destruction, and convinced that the prohibition of the development, production and stockpiling of chemical and bacteriological (biological) weapons and their elimination, through effective measures, will facilitate the achievement of general and complete disarmament under strict and effective international control.

Recognizing the important significance of the Protocol for the Prohibition of the Use in War of Asphyxiating, Poisonous or Other Gases, and of Bacteriological Methods of Warfare, signed at Geneva on June 17, 1925, and conscious also of the contribution which the said Protocol has already made, and continues to make, to mitigating the horrors of war,

Reaffirming their adherence to the principles and objectives of that Protocol and calling upon all States to comply strictly with them,

Recalling that the General Assembly of the United Nations has repeatedly condemned all actions contrary to the principles and objectives of the Geneva Protocol of June 17, 1925,

Desiring to contribute to the strengthening of confidence between peoples and the general improvement of the international atmosphere,

Desiring also to contribute to the realization of the purposes and principles of the Charter of the United Nations,

Convinced of the importance and urgency of eliminating from the arsenals of States, through effective measures, such dangerous weapons of mass destruction as those using chemical or bacteriological (biological) agents,

Recognizing that an agreement on the prohibition of bacteriological (biological) and toxin weapons represents a first possible step towards the achievement of agreement on effective measures also for the prohibition of the development, production and stockpiling of chemical weapons, and determined to continue negotiations to that end,

Determined, for the sake of all mankind, to exclude completely the possibility of bacteriological (biological) agents and toxins being used as weapons,

Convinced that such use would be repugnant to the conscience of mankind and that no effort should be spared to minimize this risk,

Have agreed as follows:

ARTICLE I

Each State Party to this Convention undertakes never in any circumstances to develop, produce, stockpile or otherwise acquire or retain:

1. Microbial or other biological agents, or toxins whatever their origin or method of production, of types and in quantities that have no justification for prophylactic, protective or other peaceful purposes;

2. Weapons, equipment or means of delivery designed to use such agents or toxins for hostile purposes or in armed conflict.

ARTICLE II

Each State Party to this Convention undertakes to destroy, or to divert to peaceful purposes, as soon as possible but not later than nine months after the entry into force of the Convention, all agents, toxins, weapons, equipment and means of delivery specified in Article I of the Convention, which are in its possession or under its jurisdiction or control. In implementing the provisions of this article all necessary safety precautions shall be observed to protect populations and the environment.

ARTICLE III

Each State Party to this Convention undertakes not to transfer to any recipient whatsoever, directly or indirectly, and not in any way to assist, encourage, or induce any State, group of States or international organizations to manufacture or otherwise acquire any of the agents, toxins, weapons, equipment or means of delivery specified in Article I of the Convention.

ARTICLE IV

Each State Party to this Convention shall, in accordance with its constitutional processes, take any necessary measures to prohibit and prevent the development, production, stockpiling, acquisition, or retention of the agents, toxins, weapons, equipment and means of delivery specified in Article I of the Convention, within the territory of such State, under its jurisdiction or under its control anywhere.

ARTICLE V

The States Parties to this Convention undertake to consult one another and to cooperate in solving any problems which may arise in relation to the objective of, or in the application of the provisions of, the Convention. Consultation and cooperation pursuant to this Article may also be undertaken through appropriate international procedures within the framework of the United Nations and in accordance with its Charter.

ARTICLE VI

1. Any State Party to this Convention which finds that any other State Party is acting in breach of obligations deriving from the provisions of the Convention may lodge a complaint with the Security Council of the United Nations. Such a complaint should include all possible evidence confirming its validity, as well as a request for its consideration by the Security Council.
2. Each State Party to this Convention undertakes to cooperate in carrying out any investigation which the Security Council may initiate, in accordance with the provisions of the Charter of the United Nations, on the basis of the complaint received by the Council. The Security Council shall inform the States Parties to the Convention of the results of the investigation.

ARTICLE VII

Each State Party to this Convention undertakes to provide or support assistance, in accordance with the United Nations Charter, to any Party to the Convention which so requests, if the Security Council decides that such Party has been exposed to danger as a result of violation of the Convention.

ARTICLE VIII

Nothing in this Convention shall be interpreted as in any way limiting or de-tracting from the obligations assumed by any State under the Protocol for the Prohibition of the Use in War of Asphyxiating, Poisonous or Other Gases, and of Bacteriological Methods of Warfare, signed at Geneva on June 17, 1925.

ARTICLE IX

Each State Party to this Convention affirms the recognized objective of effec-tive prohibition of chemical weapons and, to this end, undertakes to continue negotiations in good faith with a view to reaching early agreement on effective measures for the prohibition of their development, production and stockpil-ing and for their destruction, and on appropriate measures concerning equip-ment and means of delivery specifically designed for the production or use of chemical agents for weapons purposes.

ARTICLE X

1. The State Parties to this Convention undertake to facilitate, and have the right to participate in, the fullest possible exchange of equipment, materi-als and scientific and technological information for the use of bacterio-logical (biological) agents and toxins for peaceful purposes. Parties to the Convention in a position to do so shall also cooperate in contributing indi-vidually or together with other States or international organizations to the further development and application of scientific discoveries in the field of bacteriology (biology) for the prevention of disease, or for other peaceful purposes.

2. This Convention shall be implemented in a manner designed to avoid ham-pering the economic or technological development of States Parties to the Convention or international cooperation in the field of peaceful bacterio-logical (biological) activities, including the international exchange of bac-teriological (biological) agents and toxins and equipment for the process-ing, use or production of bacteriological (biological) agents and toxins for peaceful purposes in accordance with the provisions of the Convention.

ARTICLE XI

Any State Party may propose amendments to this Convention. Amendments shall enter into force for each State Party accepting the amendments upon their acceptance by a majority of the States Parties to the Convention and thereafter for each remaining State Party on the date of acceptance by it.

ARTICLE XII

Five years after the entry into force of this Convention, or earlier if it is requested by a majority of Parties to the Convention by submitting a proposal to this effect to the Depositary Governments, a conference of States Parties to the Convention shall be held at Geneva, Switzerland, to review the operation of the Convention, with a view to assuring that the purposes of the preamble and the provisions of the Convention, including the provisions concerning negotiations on chemical weapons, are being realized. Such review shall take into account any new scientific and technological developments relevant to the Convention.

ARTICLE XIII

1. This Convention shall be of unlimited duration.
2. Each State Party to this Convention shall in exercising its national sovereignty have the right to withdraw from the Convention if it decides that extraordinary events, related to the subject matter of the Convention, have jeopardized the supreme interests of its country. It shall give notice of such withdrawal to all other States Parties to the Convention and to the United Nations Security Council three months in advance. Such notice shall include a statement of the extraordinary events it regards as having jeopardized its supreme interests.

ARTICLE XIV

1. This Convention shall be open to all States for signature. Any State which does not sign the Convention before its entry into force in accordance with paragraph 3 of this Article may accede to it at any time.
2. This Convention shall be subject to ratification by signatory States. Instruments of ratification and instruments of accession shall be deposited with the Governments of the United States of America, the United Kingdom of Great Britain and Northern Ireland and the Union of Soviet Socialist Republics, which are hereby designated the Depositary Governments.
3. This Convention shall enter into force after the deposit of instruments of ratification by twenty-two Governments, including the Governments designated as Depositaries of the Convention.
4. For States whose instruments of ratification or accession are deposited subsequent to the entry into force of this Convention, it shall enter into force on the date of the deposit of their instruments of ratification or accession.

5. The Depositary Governments shall promptly inform all signatory and acceding States of the date of each signature, the date of deposit of each instrument of ratification or of accession and the date of the entry into force of this Convention, and of the receipt of other notices.

6. This Convention shall be registered by the Depositary Governments pursuant to Article 102 of the Charter of the United Nations.

ARTICLE XV

This Convention, the English, Russian, French, Spanish and Chinese texts of which are equally authentic, shall be deposited in the archives of the Depositary Governments. Duly certified copies of the Convention shall be transmitted by the Depositary Governments to the Governments of the signatory and acceding States.

ANNEX 4   PROVISIONS CONNECTED TO HUMAN RIGHTS IN THE INTERNATIONAL HEALTH REGULATIONS (2005)

Article	Subject Matter
3.1	The IHR 2005 shall be implemented with full respect for the dignity, human rights, and fundamental freedoms of persons.
23.2	On the basis of evidence of a public health risk, states parties may apply additional health measures to travelers, including the least intrusive and invasive medical examination that would achieve the public health objective of preventing the international spread of disease.
23.3	No medical examination, vaccination, prophylaxis, or health measures shall be carried out on travelers without their prior express informed consent, except in situations in which compulsory measures are warranted.
23.4	Travelers to be vaccinated or offered prophylaxis shall be informed of any risk associated with vaccination or non-vaccination and with the use or non-use of prophylaxis.
23.5	Any medical examination, medical procedure, vaccination or other prophylaxis that involves a risk of disease transmission shall be performed or administered only in accordance with established national or international safety guidelines and standards.
31.1	Invasive medical examination, vaccination or other prophylaxis shall not be required of any traveler except in circumstances specified in the IHR 2005.

31.2   States parties may implement compulsory health measures against travelers if there is evidence of an imminent public health risk. Any compulsory medical examination shall be the least invasive and intrusive examination that would achieve the public health objective.

32   In implementing health measures, states parties shall treat travelers with respect for their dignity, human rights, and fundamental freedoms and minimize any discomfort or distress associated with such measures, including by treating all travelers with courtesy and respect; taking into consideration the gender, sociocultural, ethnic, or religious concerns of travelers; and providing for adequate food and water, accommodation and clothing, baggage protection, medical treatment, means of communication, and other appropriate assistance to travelers who are quarantined, isolated, or subject to medical examinations or other procedures for public health purposes.

42   Health measures undertaken under the IHR 2005 shall be initiated and completed without delay, and applied in a transparent and nondiscriminatory manner.

43.2   Additional health measures that provide the same or greater levels of health protection than WHO recommendations or that are otherwise prohibited by the IHR 2005 shall not be more invasive or intrusive to persons than reasonably available alternatives that would achieve the appropriate level of health protection.

45.1   States parties must protect confidentiality of personally identifiable information received or collected under the IHR 2005.

45.2   In disclosing and processing personal data for purposes of assessing and managing a public health risk, states parties and WHO must ensure that such data are processed fairly and lawfully, relevant to the public health purpose, accurate and kept up to date, and kept no longer than necessary.

45.3   WHO must provide an individual who requests his or her personal data with access to it and to correct such data when necessary.

SOURCE: Fidler 2005c, 368

LIST OF REFERENCES

Acharya, A. 1999. A Concert of Asia? *Survival*, 41(3): 84–101.

Aglionby, J. 2007. Indonesia Agrees to Share Bird Flu Samples. *Financial Times,* February 17, p. 7.

Aglionby, J., and Jack, A. 2007a. Indonesia Withholds Genetic Samples of Bird Flu. *Financial Times USA,* February 6, p. 1.

Aglionby, J., and Jack, A. 2007b. Indonesia Accuses WHO of Misusing Flu Sample. *Financial Times,* February 8, p. 9.

Alberts, B., and Fineberg, H. V. 2003. Letter to U.S. Attorney General John Ashcroft, August 15, at http://www.fas.org/sgp/news/2003/08/nas081503.pdf

American Civil Liberties Union. 2002. The Model State Emergency Health Powers Act, January 1, at http://www.aclu.org/privacy/medical/14857res20020101.html

Antiterrorism and Effective Death Penalty Act. 1996. Public Law 104-132, 110 *U.S. Statutes* 1214.

Aristotle. 1947. *Nicomachean Ethics.* In *Introduction to Aristotle,* R. McKeon, ed. New York: Random House, pp. 300–543.

Artemisinin Project. 2006. *About the Artemisinin Project,* at http://www.artemisinin-project.org/

Arthur, C. 2001. GM Researchers Created Virus "As Dangerous as TB." *The Independent,* July 24.

Asia-Pacific Economic Cooperation (APEC). 2006. *APEC Symposium on Enchancing Surveillance on Emerging Infectious Diseases Enhances Cooperation,* April 6, at http://www.apec.org/apec/news___media/2006_media_releases/060406_prc_eid_symposium.html

Assessment of National Implementation of the Biological and Toxin Weapons Convention (BTWC). 2006. BWC/CONF.VI/WP.3, October 20.

Australia Group. 2006. *The Australia Group: An Introduction,* at http://www
.australiagroup.net/en/intro.html

Background Information Document on the History and Operation of the Confidence-Building Measures. 2006. BWC/CONF.VI.INF.3 (Prepared by the Secretariat), September 28.

Background Information Document on the Status of Universality of the Convention. 2006. BWC/CONF.VI/INF.5 (Prepared by the Secretariat), September 28.

Baker, M., and Fidler, D. P. 2006. Global Public Health Surveillance under New International Health Regulations. *Emerging Infectious Diseases,* 12: 1058–1065.

Barenblatt, D. 2004. *A Plague upon Humanity: The Hidden History of Japan's Biological Warfare Program.* New York: HarperCollins.

Barletta, M., Sands, A., and Tucker, J. B. 2002. Keeping Track of Anthrax: The Case for a Biosecurity Convention. *Bulletin of the Atomic Scientists,* 58(3): 57–62.

Barry, J. 2004. *The Great Influenza: The Epic Story of the Deadliest Plague in History.* New York: Penguin Books.

Bartlett, C. L. R., Kickbusch, I., and Coulombier, D. 2006. Cultural and Governance Influence on Detection, Identification and Monitoring of Human Disease, Foresight Project—Infectious Diseases: Preparing for the Future (Paper D4.3), at http://www.foresight.gov.uk/Previous_Projects/Detection_and_Identification_of_Infectious_Diseases/Reports_and_Publications/Final_Reports/Index.html

Beauchamp, D. E. 1999. Public Health as Social Justice. In *New Ethics for the Public's Health,* D. E. Beauchamp and B. Steinbock, eds. Oxford: Oxford University Press, pp. 101–109.

Bergen, P., and Garrett, L. 2005. *Report of the Working Group on State Security and Transnational Threats.* Princeton Project on National Security Working Paper, at http://www.wws.princeton.edu/ppns/conferences/reports/fall/SSTT.pdf

Berkelman, R., and Hughes, J. 1993. The Conquest of Infectious Disease: Who Are We Kidding? *The Annals of Internal Medicine,* 119: 426–428.

Biological Weapons Act. 1989. 18 *United States Code* §175 *et seq.*

Biological Weapons Convention. April 10, 1972. Convention on the Prohibition of the Development, Production and Stockpiling of Bacteriological (Biological) and Toxin Weapons and on Their Destruction. 11 *International Legal Materials* 309 (1972).

Biosafety and Biosecurity. 2006. BWC/CONF.VI.WP.2 (Working Paper Submitted by Germany on behalf of the European Union), October 20.

Bioterrorism Week. 2004. Researchers Accidentally Exposed to Deadly Live Bacterium Anthrax. *Bioterrorism Week,* July 5, p. 6.

Brandt, A. M. 1985. *No Magic Bullet: A Social History of Venereal Disease in the United States Since 1880.* Oxford: Oxford University Press.

Branswell, H. 2007. Poor Countries Insisting on Bird Flu Rules: They Want Fair Share of Vaccines. *Hamilton Spectator,* February 12, p. A05.

British Medical Association. 1999. *Biotechnology Weapons and Humanity.* London: Harwood Academic.

British Medical Association. 2004. *Biotechnology, Weapons and Humanity II.* London: British Medical Association.

BWC Sixth Review Conference Final Report. 2006. Final Report of the Sixth Review Conference of the States Parties to the Convention on the Prohibition of the Development, Production and Stockpiling of Bacteriological (Biological) and Toxin Weapons and on Their Destruction, December 8.

Calain, P. 2007a. Exploring the International Arena of Global Public Health Surveillance. *Health Policy and Planning,* 22: 2–12.

Calain, P. 2007b. From the Field Side of the Binoculars: A Different View on Global Public Health Surveillance. *Health Policy and Planning,* 22: 13–20.

Canadian Program on Genomics and Global Health. 2006. *DNA for Peace: Reconciling Biodevelopment and Biosecurity.* Toronto: University of Toronto, at http://www.utoronto.ca/jcb/home/documents/DNA_Peace.pdf

Carr, E. H. 1939. *The Twenty Years' Crisis, 1919–1939: An Introduction to the Study of International Relations.* London: Macmillan.

Carus, S. W. 2000. *Bioterrorism and Biocrimes: The Illicit Use of Biological Agents in the 20th Century.* April 2000 revision. Washington, D.C.: National Defense University and Center on Counterproliferation Research.

Cass, R. A. 2001. *The Rule of Law in America.* Baltimore: Johns Hopkins University Press.

Cello, J., Paul, A. V., and Wimmer, E. 2002. Chemical Synthesis of Poliovirus cDNA: Generation of Infectious Virus in the Absense of Natural Template. *Sciencexpress,* July 11, at http://www.sciencemag.org/cgi/reprint/1072266v1.pdf

Center for Arms Control and Non-Proliferation. 2006. BWC Observer: Key Issues, at http://www.bwc06.org/key-issues/

Center for Arms Control and Non-Proliferation. 2007. Federal Funding for Biological Weapons Prevention and Defense, Fiscal Years 2001 to 2008, at http://www.armscontrolcenter.org/policy/biochem/fy08_biodefense_funding/

Center for Biosecurity. 2005a. *Botulism Frequently Asked Questions,* retrieved May 15, 2006, from http://www.upmc-biosecurity.org/pages/agents/botulism/botulism_faq_2005.html

Center for Biosecurity. 2005b. *Plague Frequently Asked Questions,* retrieved May 15, 2006, from http://www.upmc-biosecurity.org/pages/agents/plague/plague_faq_2005.html

Center for Biosecurity. 2005c. *Tularemia Frequently Asked Questions,* retrieved May 15, 2006, from http://www.upmc-biosecurity.org/pages/agents/plague/plague_faq_2005.html

Center for Biosecurity. 2005d. *Hemorrhagic Fever Viruses Frequently Asked Questions,*

retrieved May 15, 2006, from http://www.upmc-biosecurity.org/pages/agents/
vhf/vhf_faq_2005.html

Center for Biosecurity. 2005e. *Smallpox Frequently Asked Questions*, retrieved May
15, 2006, from http://www.upmc-biosecurity.org/pages/agents/smallpox/
smallpox_faq_2005.html

Centers for Disease Control and Prevention (CDC). 2001a. *Facts About Botulism*, at
http://www.bt.cdc.gov/agent/botulism/factsheet.asp

Centers for Disease Control and Prevention (CDC). 2001b. Updated Guidelines for
Evaluating Public Health Surveillance Systems: Recommendations from the
Guidelines Working Group. *Morbidity and Mortality Weekly Report*, 50: 1–36.

Centers for Disease Control and Prevention (CDC). 2003. *Key Facts About Tularemia*,
at http://www.bt.cdc.gov/agent/tularemia/facts.asp

Centers for Disease Control and Prevention (CDC). 2004. *Viral Hemorrhagic Fevers
Fact Sheet*, at http://www.cdc.gov/ncidod/dvrd/spb/mnpages/dispages/vhf.htm

Centers for Disease Control and Prevention (CDC). 2005. *Frequently Asked Questions
About Plague*, at http://www.bt.cdc.gov/agent/plague/faq.asp

Centers for Disease Control and Prevention (CDC). 2006a. *HHS and USDA Select
Agents and Toxins*, at http://www.cdc.gov/od/sap/docs/salist.pdf

Centers for Disease Control and Prevention. 2006b. *BioSense*, at http://www.cdc
.gov/BioSense/

Center for Law and the Public's Health. 2006. *The Model State Public Health Emergency Powers Act*, at http://www.publichealthlaw.net/Resources/Modellaws.
htm#MSEHPA

Center for Public Integrity. 2006. *Bush's AIDS Initiative: Too Little Choice, Too
Much Ideology*, November 30, at http://www.publicintegrity.org/aids/report
.aspx?aid=800

Chang, I. 2003. Fear of SARS, Fear of Strangers. *New York Times*, May 21, p. A31.

Chemical Weapons Convention. September 3, 1992. Convention on the Prohibition
of the Development, Production, Stockpiling and Use of Chemical Weapons and
on Their Destruction. 1974 *United Nations Treaty Series* 317.

Chen, L. 2004. *Health as a Human Security Priority for the 21st Century*. Paper for
Human Security Track III of the Helsinki Process, December 7, at http://www
.helsinkiprocess.fi/netcomm/ImgLib/24/89/LCHelsinkiPaper12%5B1%5D.6.04
.pdf

Chyba, C. F. 2001. Biological Security in a Changed World. *Science*, 293: 2349.

Chyba, C. F. 2002. Toward Biological Security. *Foreign Affairs*, 81(3): 122–136.

Cohen, J. 2006. The New World of Global Health. *Science*, 311: 162–167.

Cohen, H. W., Gould, R. M., and Sidel, V. W. 2004. The Pitfalls of Bioterrorism Preparedness: The Anthrax and Smallpox Experiences. *American Journal of Public
Health*, 94: 1667–1671.

Committee on Advances in Technology and the Prevention of Their Application to Next Generation Biowarfare Threats. 2006. *Globalization, Biosecurity, and the Future of the Life Sciences.* Washington, D.C.: National Academies Press.

Committee on Smallpox Vaccination Program Implementation. 2005. *The Smallpox Vaccination Program: Public Health in an Age of Terrorism.* Washington, D.C.: National Academies Press.

Connolly, C. 2006. Bush Budget Would Cut Popular Health Programs. *Washington Post,* February 14, p. A03.

Department of Health and Human Services. 2005. Control of Communicable Diseases (Proposed Rule), 42 Code of Federal Regulations, Parts 70 and 71. 70 Federal Regulations (November 30), pp. 71892–948.

Department of Homeland Security. 2004. *Fact Sheet: Department of Homeland Security Appropriations Act of 2005,* October 18, at http://www.dhs.gov/xnews/releases/press_release_0541.shtm

Department of Homeland Security. 2005. Fact Sheet: National Biodefense Analysis and Countermeasures Center, February 24, at http://www.dhs.gov/xnews/releases/press_release_0627.shtm

Deudney, D. 1990. The Case Against Linking Environmental Degradation and National Security. *Millennium: Journal of International Studies,* 19: 461–476.

Diamond, J. 1997. *Guns, Germs, and Steel: The Fates of Human Societies.* New York: W. W. Norton.

Doe v. Rumsfeld. 2004. 341 F.Supp.2d (D.C. District Court), October 27, p. 1.

Douhet, G. 1921. *The Command of the Air.* D. Ferrari, trans. Washington, D.C.: Office of Air Force History, 1983.

Dunne, T. 2001. Liberalism. In *The Globalization of World Politics: An Introduction to International Relations,* J. Baylis and S. Smith, eds. Oxford: Oxford University Press, pp. 162–181.

Dunne, T., and Schmidt, B. 2001, Realism. In *The Globalization of World Politics: An Introduction to International Relations,* J. Baylis and S. Smith, eds. Oxford: Oxford University Press, pp. 141–161.

Enhancement of the Confidence-Building Measures (CBM) Process. 2006. BWC/CONF.VI/WP.4 (Submitted by France on Behalf of the European Union), October 20.

Environmental Protection Agency (EPA) Office of Inspector General. 2005. *EPA Needs to Fulfill Its Designated Responsibilities to Ensure Effective BioWatch Program.* Report No. 2005–P-00012, March 23.

European Centers for Disease Prevention and Control (ECDC). 2006. *About the ECDC,* at http://www.ecdc.eu.int/

Fee, E., and Brown, T. M. 2001. Preemptive Biopreparedness: Can We Learn Anything from History? *American Journal of Public Health,* 91: 721–726.

Feldbaum, H., Lee, K., and Patel, P. 2006. The National Security Implications of HIV/AIDS. *PLoS Medicine*, 3(6): e171.

Fidler, D. P. 1997. The Globalization of Public Health: Emerging Infectious Diseases and International Relations. *Indiana Journal of Global Legal Studies*, 5: 11–51.

Fidler, D. P. 2000. *International Law and Public Health: Materials on and Analysis of Global Health Jurisprudence*. Ardsley, N.Y.: Transnational Publishers.

Fidler, D. P. 2003a. Public Health and National Security in the Global Age: Bioterrorism, Infectious Diseases, and *Realpolitik*. *George Washington International Law Review*, 35: 787–856.

Fidler, D. P. 2003b. Disease and Globalized Anarchy: Theoretical Perspectives on the Pursuit of Global Health. *Social Theory & Health*, 1: 21–41.

Fidler, D. P. 2005a. Health as Foreign Policy: Between Principle and Power. *Whitehead Journal of Diplomacy and International Relations*, 6: 179–194.

Fidler, D. P. 2005b. *Health and Foreign Policy: A Conceptual Overview*. London: Nuffield Trust.

Fidler, D. P. 2005c. From International Sanitary Conventions to Global Health Security: The New International Health Regulations. *Chinese Journal of International Law*, 4: 325–392.

Fidler, D. P. 2007a. A Pathology of Public Health Securitism: Approaching Pandemics as Security Threats. In *Governing Global Health: Challenge, Response, Innovation*, A. Cooper, J. Kirton, and T. Schrecker, eds. Aldershot: Ashgate, pp. 41–64.

Fidler, D. P. 2007b. Architecture amidst Anarchy: Global Health's Quest for Governance. *Journal of Global Health Governance*, 1, at http://diplomacy.shu.edu/academics/global_health/journal/index.html

Fidler, D. P., and Gostin, L. O. 2006. The New International Health Regulations: An Historic Development for International Law and Public Health. *Journal of Law, Medicine & Ethics*, 34: 85–94.

Fink Committee on Research Standards and Practices to Prevent the Destructive Application of Biotechnology. 2004. *Biotechnology Research in an Age of Terrorism*. Washington, D.C.: National Academies Press.

Foresight Nanotech Institute. 2006. *Foresight Guidelines for Responsible Nanotechnology Development*, at http://www.foresight.org/guidelines/current.html#Regulation

Garrett, L. 2000. *Betrayal of Trust: The Collapse of Global Public Health*. New York: Hyperion.

Garrett, L. 2005a. *HIV and National Security: Where are the Links?* New York: Council on Foreign Relations.

Garrett, L. 2005b. The Next Pandemic? *Foreign Affairs*, 84(4): 3–23.

Garrett, L. 2006. Unless We Act Now, Bird Flu May Win. *International Herald Tribune*, February 26, at http://www.iht.com/articles/2006/02/26/opinion/

edgarrett.php

Garrett, L. 2007. The Challenge of Global Health. *Foreign Affairs,* 86(1): 14–38.

General Accounting Office. 2006. *Global Health: Spending Requirement Presents Challenges for Allocating Prevention Funds under the President's Emergency Plan for AIDS Relief.* GAO-06-395, April 6.

Geneva Protocol. June 17, 1925. Geneva Protocol for the Prohibition of the Use in War of Asphyxiating, Poisonous or Other Gases, and of Bacteriological Methods of Warfare. 94 *League of Nations Treaty Series* 65.

German Overseas Institute. 2006. Workshop on Defining and Shaping the Architecture for Global Health Governance, February 22–24.

Gillis, J. 2006. White House Admits Lag in Bioterror Effort. *Washington Post,* April 7, p. A11.

Glasser, S. B., and Grunwald, M. 2005. The Steady Buildup to a City's Chaos: Confusion Reigned at Every Level of Government. *Washington Post,* September 11, p. A01.

Global Health Security Initiative (GHSI). 2005. *Sixth Ministerial Meeting on Health Security and Bioterrorism,* November 18, at http://www.g7.utoronto.ca/health/rome2005.html

Global Pathogen Surveillance Act. 2005. Senate Bill 2170, December 22.

Goldblat, J., and Bernaure, T. 1991. *The Third Review of the Biological Weapons Convention: Issues and Proposals.* United Nations Institute for Disarmament Research (UNIDIR) Research Paper No. 9. New York: United Nations.

Goodman, N. M. 1971. *International Health Organizations and Their Work,* 2nd ed. London: Churchill Livingstone.

Goodman, R. A. et al. 2006. Law and Public Health at CDC. *Morbidity and Mortality Weekly,* 55 (Supp.): 29–33.

Gostin, L. O. 2000. *Public Health Law: Power, Duty, Restraint.* Berkeley: University of California Press and Milbank Memorial Fund.

Gostin, L. O. 2004. *The AIDS Pandemic: Complacency, Injustice, and Unfulfilled Expectations.* Chapel Hill: University of North Carolina Press.

Gostin, L. O. 2006. Federal Executive Power and Communicable Disease Control: CDC Quarantine Regulations. *Hastings Center Report,* March/April: 10–11.

Gostin, L. O., Berkman, B., and Fidler, D. P. 2006. *Comments on Department of Health and Human Services, Control of Communicable Diseases (Proposed Rule), 42 CFR Parts 70 and 71 (November 30, 2005),* at http://www.publichealthlaw.net/Resources/BTlaw.htm

Grotto, J., and Tucker, J. B. 2006. *Biosecurity: A Comprehensive Action Plan.* Washington, D.C.: Center for American Progress.

Guillemin, J. 2005. *Biological Weapons: From the Invention of State-Sponsored Programs to Contemporary Bioterrorism.* New York: Columbia University Press.

Haas, E. 1964. *Beyond the Nation-State: Functionalism and International Organizations.* Stanford, CA: Stanford University Press.

Hamdan v. Rumsfeld. 2006. 126 S. Ct. 2749.

Hamdi v. Rumsfeld. 2004. 542 U.S. 507.

Harland, C. B., and Woodward, A. 2006. A Model Law: The Biological and Toxin Weapons Crimes Act—An Act to Implement Obligations under the 1972 Biological and Toxin Weapons Convention and the 1925 Geneva Protocol. *International Review of the Red Cross,* 87: 573–586.

Hart, J. 2006. The Soviet Biological Weapons Program. In *Deadly Cultures: Biological Weapons Since 1945,* M. Wheelis, L. Rózsa, and M. Dando, eds. Cambridge, MA: Harvard University Press, pp. 132–156.

Helsinki Process. 2005. *Empowering People at Risk: Human Security Priorities for the 21st Century.* Working Paper for the Helsinki Process—Report of the Track on Human Security, at http://www.helsinkiprocess.fi/netcomm/ImgLib/53/164/hp_track3_report.pdf

Heritage Foundation. 2002. *The Model State Emergency Health Powers Act: An Assault on Civil Liberties in the Name of Homeland Security,* June 10, at http://www.heritage.org/Research/HealthCare/HL748.cfm

Hinsley, F. H. 1967. *Power and the Pursuit of Peace.* Cambridge: Cambridge University Press.

Hirschler, B. 2005. Frist Calls for New "Manhattan Project" to Fight Bioterror. *Reuters,* January 27.

Holsti, O. R. 1995. Theories of International Relations and Foreign Policy: Realism and Its Challengers. In *Controversies in International Relations Theory: Realism and the Neoliberal Challenge,* C. W. Kegley, Jr., ed. New York: St. Martin's Press, pp. 35–65.

Homer Dixon, T. F. 1999. *Environment, Scarcity, and Violence.* Princeton, N.J.: Princeton University Press.

Howard-Jones, N. 1950. Origins of International Health Work. *British Medical Journal,* May 6: 1032–1037.

Howard-Jones, N. 1975. *The Scientific Background of the International Sanitary Conferences 1851–1938.* Geneva: World Health Organization.

Human Rights Watch. 2005. *The Less They Know, The Better: Abstinence-Only HIV/ AIDS Programs in Uganda,* March, at http://www.hrw.org/reports/2005/uganda0305/index.htm

Ikenberry, G. J., and Slaughter, A.-M. 2006. *Forging a World of Liberty Under Law: U.S. National Security in the 21st Century* (Final Report of the Princeton Project on National Security). Princeton, N.J.: Princeton University, Woodrow Wilson School of Public and International Affairs.

Institute of Medicine Committee on Microbial Threats to Health in the 21st Century. 2003. In *Microbial Threats to Health: Emergence, Detection, and Response,*

M. S. Smolinski, M. A. Hamburg, and J. Lederberg, eds. Washington, D.C.: National Academies Press.

International Committee of the Red Cross (ICRC). 2004a. *Biotechnology, Weapons, and Humanity: Introduction,* at http://www.icrc.org/web/eng/siteeng0.nsf/ iwpList515/89A6AC62FB0A19DAC1256E21004C25C6

International Committee of the Red Cross (ICRC). 2004b. *Responsibilities of Actors in the Life Sciences to Prevent Hostile Use,* January 20, at http://www.icrc.org/ Web/Eng/siteeng0.nsf/iwpList515/7358E6A439390A02C1256E21004E1195

International Convention for the Suppression of Terrorist Bombings. January 9, 1998. *International Legal Materials,* 37: 249–260.

International Covenant on Civil and Political Rights. December 19, 1966. 999 *United Nations Treaty Series* 171.

International Finance Facility for Immunization (IFFIm). 2007. At http://www .iff-immunisation.org/

International Health Regulations (IHR). July 25, 1969. 764 *United Nations Treaty Series* 3.

International Health Regulations (IHR). May 23, 2005. *Revision of the International Health Regulations,* WHO Doc. WHA58.3.

International Sanitary Regulations (ISR). May 25, 1951. 175 *United Nations Treaty Series* 215.

Interpol. 2006a. *The Bioterrorism Threat: Strengthening Law Enforcement,* at http:// www.interpol.int/Public/BioTerrorism/default.asp

Interpol. 2006b. *Biocriminalization,* at http://www.interpol.int/Public/BioTerrorism /bioC/default.asp

Interpol. 2006c. *Interpol's Model Legislation to Prohibit Biocrimes and to Promote Biosafety and Biosecurity (Draft),* retrieved April 3, 2006, from http://www.interpol .int/Public/BioTerrorism/modellegislation/biocriminalizationact.pdf

Jew Ho v. Williamson. 1900. 103 F. 10 (Circuit Court Northern District California).

Joint Centre for Bioethics. 2006. *Call for World Scientists' Network to Keep Vigil on Biotechnology Misuse,* February 26, at http://www.utoronto.ca/jcb/home/news_ bioterrorism.htm

Kahn, L. 2007. Government Oversight and the Life Sciences. *Bulletin of the Atomic Scientists (Online),* at http://www.thebulletin.org/columns/laura-kahn/ 20070109 .html

Kash, J. C. et al. 2006. Genomic Analysis of Increased Host Immune and Cell Death Responses Induced by 1918 Influenza Virus. *Nature,* 433: 578–581.

Kaul, I., Conceição, P., Le Goulven, K., and Mendoza, R. U. 2003a. How to Improve the Provision of Global Public Goods. In *Providing Global Public Goods: Managing Globalization,* I. Kaul, P. Conceição, K. Le Goulven, and R. U. Mendoza, eds. Oxford: Oxford University Press, pp. 21–58.

Kaul, I., Conceição, P., Le Goulven, K., and Mendoza, R. U et al., eds. 2003b. *Providing Global Public Goods: Managing Globalization.* New York: Oxford University Press.

Kaul, I., Grunberg, I., and Stern, M. A., eds. 1999. *Global Public Goods: International Cooperation in the 21st Century.* New York: Oxford University Press.

Kelle, A. 2005a. *Securitization of International Public Health—Implications for Global Health Governance and the Biological Weapons Prohibition Regime,* Bradford Regime Review Paper No. 1, University of Bradford Department of Peace Studies, May, at http://www.brad.ac.uk/acad/sbtwc/regrev/Kelle_securitization.pdf

Kelle, A. 2005b. *Bioterrorism and the Securitization of Public Health in the United States of America—Implications for Public Health and Biological Weapons Arms Control,* Bradford Regime Review Paper No. 2, University of Bradford Department of Peace Studies, July, at http://www.brad.ac.uk/acad/sbtwc/regrev/Kelle_SecuritizationinUS.pdf

Kellman, B. 2001. Biological Terrorism: Legal Measures for Preventing Catastrophe. *Harvard Journal of Law & Public Policy,* 24: 417–488.

Kellman, B. 2006a. Notes from a BWC Gadfly. *Biosecurity and Bioterrorism,* 4(3): 231–236.

Kellman, B. 2006b. *Preventing Bio-Violence: The Need for International Legal Action.* Lecture presented to the Program on Science and Global Security, Princeton University, February 10.

Keohane, R. O., and Martin, L. 1995. The Promise of Institutionalist Theory. *International Security,* 20: 39–51.

Khoo, N., and Smith, M. L. 2002. The Future of American Hegemony in the Asia-Pacific: A Concert of Asia or a Clear Pecking Order? *Australian Journal of International Affairs,* 56(1): 65–81.

Kickbusch, I. 2003. Global Health Governance: Some Theoretical Considerations on the New Political Space. In *Health Impacts of Globalization: Towards Global Governance,* K. Lee, ed. Basingstoke: Palgrave Macmillan, pp. 192–203.

Kobasa, D. et al. 2007. Aberrant Innate Immune Response in Lethal Injection of Macaques with the 1918 Influenza Virus. *Nature,* 445: 319–323.

Koplow, D. 2003. *Smallpox: The Fight to Eradicate a Global Scourge.* Berkeley: University of California Press.

Korematsu v. United States. 1944. 323 U.S. 214.

Kunreuther, H. 2002. Risk Analysis and Risk Management in an Uncertain World. *Risk Analysis,* 22: 655–664.

Lam, C., Franco, C., and Schuler, A. 2006. Billons for Biodefense: Federal Agency Biodefense Funding, FY2006–FY2007. *Biosecurity and Bioterrorism,* 4(2): 113–127.

Lancet, The. 2006. HIV Prevention Policy Needs an Urgent Cure. *The Lancet,* 367: 1213.

Lawler, A. 2005. Boston University Under Fire for Pathogen Mishap. *Science,* 307: 501.

Lazzarini, Z., Goodman, R. A., and Dammers, K. S. 2007. Criminal Law and Public Health Practice. In *Law in Public Health Practice,* R. A. Goodman, W. Lopez, G. W. Matthews, M. A. Rothstein, and K. L. Foster, eds. Oxford: Oxford University Press, pp. 136–167.

Lee, K., and Fidler, D.P. 2007. Avian and Pandemic Influenza: Progress and Problems with Global Health Governance. *Global Public Health,* 2(3): 215–34.

Lee, K., and Zwi, A. 2003. A Global Political Economy Approach to AIDS: Ideology, Interests, and Implications. In *Health Impacts of Globalization: Towards Global Governance.* K. Lee ed. Basingstoke: Palgrave Macmillan, pp. 13–32.

Leitenberg, M. 2004. *The Problem of Biological Weapons.* Stockholm: Swedish National Defense College.

Leitenberg, M. 2005. *Assessing the Biological Weapons and Bioterrorism Threat.* Carlisle, PA: U.S. Army War College.

Leitenberg, M., Leonard, J., and Spretzel, R. 2004. Biodefense Crosses the Line. *Politics and the Life Sciences,* 22: 1–2.

Lengel, A., and Warrick, J. 2006. FBI is Casting a Wider Net in Anthrax Attacks. *Washington Post,* September 25, p. A1.

Lipton, E., and Johnson, K. 2001. A Nation Challenged: The Anthrax Trail: Tracking Bioterror's Tangled Course. *New York Times,* December 26, p. A1.

Littlewood, J. 2005. *The Biological Weapons Convention: A Failed Revolution.* Aldershot: Ashgate.

MacPherson, K., and Sherman, T. 2005. Fumblers of Plague Told to Boost Biosafety: Missing Mice Underscore Growing Problem. *Star-Ledger,* September 16, p. 1.

Madison, J. 1865. *Letters and Other Writings of James Madison,* P. R. Fendall, ed. Philadelphia: Lippincott Press.

Mangels, J. 2006a. Plagued by Fear. *Cleveland Plain Dealer,* March 26.

Mangels, J. 2006b. Vials Reporting Missing and Feds Swarm In. *Cleveland Plain Dealer,* March 27.

Mangels, J. 2006c. Polygraph Expert Zeros in on Texas Tech Scientist. *Cleveland Plain Dealer,* March 28.

Mangels, J. 2006d. Polygraph Doesn't Lie—Or Does It? *Cleveland Plain Dealer,* March 29.

Mangels, J. 2006e. Prosecution Lays Waste to "Dr. Plague." *Cleveland Plain Dealer,* March 30.

Mangels, J. 2006f. Butler Tells His Story, and Jury Responds. *Cleveland Plain Dealer,* March 31.

Mangels, J. 2006g. Plagued by Fear. *Cleveland Plain Dealer,* April 2.

Markel, H., Gostin, L. O., and Fidler, D.P. Extensively Drug-Resistant Tuberculosis: An Isolation Order, Public Health Powers, and a Global Crisis. *Journal of the American Medical Association,* 298(1): 83–86.

Matthews, G. W., Abbott, E. B., Hoffman, R. E., and Cetron, M. S. 2007. Legal Authorities for Interventions in Public Health Emergencies. In *Law in Public Health Practice,* 2nd ed. R. Goodman, R. E. Hoffman, W. Lopez, G. W. Matthews, M. A. Rothstein, and K. L. Foster, eds. Oxford: Oxford University Press, pp. 262–283.

Mearsheimer, J. J. 1994/1995. The False Promise of International Institutions. *International Security,* 19: 5–49.

Meier, O. 2007. States Strengthen Biological Weapons Convention. *Arms Control Today* (January/Feb), at http://www.armscontrol.org/act/2007_01-02/News AnalysisBWC.asp

Meselson, M., and Robinson, J. 2004. A Draft Convention to Prohibit Biological and Chemical Weapons under International Criminal Law. *Fletcher Forum of World Affairs,* 28: 57–71.

Miller, J., Engelberg, S., and Broad, W. 2001. *Germs: Biological Weapons and America's Secret War.* New York: Simon & Schuster.

Model State Emergency Health Powers Act. 2001. Prepared by the Center for Law and the Public's Health, Georgetown and Johns Hopkins Universities, December 21, at http://www.publichealthlaw.net/MSEHPA/MSEHPA2.pdf

Moravcsik, A. 1997. Taking Preferences Seriously: A Liberal Theory of International Politics. *International Organization,* 51: 513–533.

Musto, D. F. 1986. Quarantine and the Problem of AIDS. *Milbank Quarterly,* 64 Suppl. 1: 97–117.

Myers, N. 1989. Environmental Security. *Foreign Policy,* No. 74: 23–41.

National Science Advisory Board for Biosecurity Charter. 2006. At http://www .biosecurityboard.gov/revised%20NSABB%20charter%20signed%20031606.pdf

Nature. 2007. Editorial: Safety Clause. *Nature,* 448:105–06.

Normile, D. 2004. Severe Acute Respiratory Syndrome: Lab Accidents Prompt Calls for New Containment Program. *Science,* 304:1223–1225.

Nuclear Threat Initiative. 2004. *New Tool Launched in Fight Against Infectious Disease Outbreaks: Expanded Global System Will Help Detect Potential Public Health Threats.* November 17, at http://www.nti.org/c_press/release_gphin_111704.pdf

Office of Homeland Security. 2002. *The National Strategy for Homeland Security.* Washington, D.C.: Office of Homeland Security.

Office of Inspector General of the Department of Energy. 2005. *Coordination of Biological Select Agent Activities at Department of Energy Facilities.* July, Doc. DOE/ IG-0695.

Office of Inspector General of the Department of Health and Human Services. 2004.

Summary Report on Select Agent Security at Universities. March, Doc. A-04–04–02000.

Olson, K. B. 1999. Aum Shinrikyo: Once and Future Threat? *Emerging Infectious Diseases,* 5: 513–516.

O'Neill, W. H. 1977. *Plagues and Peoples.* New York: Doubleday.

Open Letter to Elias Zerhouni. 2005. *Science Online,* March 4, at http://www.sciencemag.org/feature/misc/microbio/307_5714_1409c.pdf

Open Society Institute. 2005. *The OSI Seminar on the Global Governance of Health: Conference Report,* December 5–8.

Ottawa Statement. 2001. *Statement of the G7 Health Ministers' Meeting (Plus Mexico),* November 7, at http://www.g7.utoronto.ca/health/ottawa2001.html

Padilla v. Hanft. 2005. 423 F.3rd 386 (Fourth Circuit Court of Appeals).

Pearson, A. 2006. Modest Progress at the Sixth Review Conference, Biological Weapons Convention 2006, at http://www.bwc06.org

Pearson, G. 1998. The Vital Importance of the Web of Deterrence. Bradford Project on Strengthening the Biological and Toxin Weapons Convention (BTWC) Background Papers, May, at http://www.bradford.ac.uk/acad/sbtwc/other/webdet.html

Pearson, G. 2006. The Iraqi Biological Weapons Program. In *Deadly Cultures: Biological Weapons Since 1945,* M. Wheelis, L. Rózsa, and M. Dando, eds. Cambridge, MA: Harvard University Press, pp. 169–190.

Pearson, G., Sims, N., and Dando, M. 2006. *Strengthening the Biological Weapons Convention: Key Points for the Sixth Review Conference.* West Yorkshire, U.K.: University of Bradford, Department of Peace Studies.

Piller, C. 2003. Expert Cleared of Serious Charges in Bioterror Case. *New York Times,* December 2, p. 16.

Price-Smith, A. T. 2002. *The Health of Nations: Infectious Disease, Environmental Change, and Their Effects on National Security and Development.* Cambridge, MA: MIT Press.

(Product)[Red]. 2007. At http://www.joinred.com/default.asp

Project on Government Oversight. 2005. *(Bio)Shielding Industry,* October 20, at http://pogoblog.typepad.com/pogo/2005/10/bioshielding_in.html

ProMED-mail. 2006. *About ProMED-mail,* at http://www.promedmail.org/pls/promed/f?p=2400:1950:8463725126752208698

Rasul v. Bush. 2004. 542 U.S. 466.

Reuters. 2007. Indonesia, Baxter Sign Pact on Bird Flu Vaccine, February 7, at http://www.alertnet.org/thenews/newsdesk/JAK76679.html

Reynolds, A. 2005. WMD Doomsday Distractions. *Washington Times,* April 10, at http://washingtontimes.com/commentary/20050409-102738–7969r.htm

Rischard, J.-F. 2002. Global Issue Networks: Desperate Times Deserve Innovative Measures. *Washington Quarterly,* 26(1): 17–33.

Risse, G. B. 1988. Epidemics and History: Ecological Perspectives and Social Responses. In *AIDS: The Burdens of History,* E. Fee and D. M. Fox, eds. Berkeley: University of California Press, pp. 33–58.

Risse, G. B. 1992. Revolt Against Quarantine: Community Responses to the 1916 Polio Epidemic, Oyster Bay, New York. *Transactions and Studies of the College of Physicians of Philadelphia,* 14: 23–50.

Roberts, A., and Guelff, R. 2000. *Documents on the Laws of War,* 3rd ed. Oxford: Oxford University Press.

Rome Agreement Establishing the International Office of Public Health, December 9, 1907. Reprinted in N. M. Goodman, *International Health Organizations and Their Work,* 2nd ed., London: Churchill Livingstone, 1971, p. 101.

Ruppe, D. 2004. Proposed U.S. Biological Research Could Challenge Treaty Restrictions, Experts Charge. *Global Security Newswire,* June 30, at http://www.nti.org/d%5Fnewswire/issues/2004/6/30/8736549a%2D9948%2D4406%2Da795%2D99a92e47a15a.html

Ruppe, D. 2005. Experts Question Merit of Recent Smallpox Exercise. *Global Security Newswire,* March 9, at http://www.nti.org/d_newswire/issues/2005_3_9.html#77244457

Sachs, J. 2005. *The End of Poverty: Economic Possibilities for Our Time.* New York: Penguin.

Sachs, J. 2007. Beware False Tradeoffs, at http://www.foreignaffairs.org/special/global_health/sachs

Salerno, R. M., and Estes, D. P. 2003. *National Legislative Measures to Prevent the Proliferation of Biological Weapons.* Albuquerque: Sandia National Laboratories.

Secretariat Background Information Document. 2006. Background Information Document on Developments since the Last Review Conference in Other International Organizations Which May be Relevant to the Convention, BWC/CONF. VI/INF.2, September 28.

Security Council. 2000. *Security Council Holds Debate on Impact of AIDS on Peace and Security in Africa.* United Nations Information Service, January 11, at http://www.unis.unvienna.org/unis/pressrels/2000/sc1173.html.

Security Council. 2001. Resolution 1373 (2001), S/RES/1373, September 28.

Security Council. 2004. Resolution 1540 (2004), S/RES/1540, April 28.

Security Council. 2006. Resolution 1673 (2006), S/RES/1673, April 27.

Selection Bipartisan Committee to Investigate the Preparation for and Response to Hurricane Katrina. 2006. *A Failure of Initiative: The Final Report of the Select Committee to Investigate the Preparation of and Response to Hurricane Katrina.* Washington, D.C.: U.S. House of Representatives.

Shea, D. A., and Lister, S. A. 2003. *The BioWatch Program: Detection of Bioterrorism.* Congressional Research Service Report No. RL 32152, November 19.

Singh, J. A., Upshur, R., and Padayatchi, N. 2007. XDR-TB in South Africa: No Time for Denial or Complacency. *PLoS Medicine,* 4(1), at http://medicine.plosjournals. org/perlserv/?request=get-document&doi=10.1371/journal.pmed.0040050

Somerville, M., and Atlas, R. 2005. Ethics: A Weapon to Counter Bioterrorism. *Science,* 307: 1881–1882.

Stein, J. 2006. FBI Chief to Face Anthrax Questions at Hearing. *Congressional Quarterly Homeland Security Daily Briefing,* December 5.

Steinbruner, J., Harris, E. D., Gallagher, N., and Okutani, S. M. 2005. *Controlling Dangerous Pathogens: A Prototype Protective Oversight System.* College Park, Md.: Center for International and Security Studies.

Steinbruner, J., Harris, E. D., Gallagher, N., and Okutani, S. M. 2007. *Controlling Dangerous Pathogens: A Prototype Protective Oversight System.* College Park, Md.: Center for International and Security Studies.

Taubenberger, J. K., Reid, A. H., Lourens, R. M., Wang, R., Jin, G., and Fanning, T. G. 2005. Characterization of the 1918 Influenza Virus Polymerase Genes. *Nature,* 437: 889–893.

Trust for America's Health. 2003. *Ready or Not? Protecting the Public's Health in an Age of Bioterrorism,* at http://healthyamericans.org/state/bioterror/

Trust for America's Health. 2004. *Ready or Not? Protecting the Public's Health in an Age of Bioterrorism,* at http://healthyamericans.org/reports/bioterror04/

Trust for America's Health. 2005. *Ready or Not? Protecting the Public's Health from Disease, Disasters, and Bioterrorism, 2005,* at http://healthyamericans.org/ reports/bioterror05/

Trust for America's Health. 2006. *Ready or Not? Protecting the Public's Health from Disease, Disaster, and Bioterrorism, 2006,* at http://healthyamericans.org/ reports/bioterror06/

Tucker, J. B. 2004. The BWC New Process: A Preliminary Assessment. *Nonproliferation Review,* Spring: 26–39.

Tucker, J. B. 2007. The Sixth Review Conference of the Biological Weapons Convention: Success or Failure? Center for Nonproliferation Studies, January 4, at http://cns.miis.edu/pubs/week/070104.htm

Tumpey, T. M. et al. 2005. Characterization of the Reconstructed 1918 Spanish Influenza Pandemic Virus. *Science,* 310: 77–80.

Ullman, R. 1983. Redefining Security. *International Security,* 8(1): 129–153.

UNITAID. 2007. At http://www.unitaid.eu/en/

United Nations Charter. June 26, 1945. In *Blackstone's International Law Documents,* 6th ed. rev. M. D. Evans, ed. Oxford: Oxford University Press, 2003, pp. 8–26.

United Nations Convention against Torture and Other Forms of Cruel and Inhuman Treatment or Punishment. 1984.

United Nations Development Programme. 1994. *Human Development Report 1994.* New York: United Nations.

United Nations Secretary-General. 2004. Foreword by the United Nations Secretary-General. In United Nations Secretary-General's High-level Panel on Threats, Challenges and Change. *A More Secure World: Our Shared Responsibility.* New York: United Nations, 2004, pp. vii–x.

United Nations Secretary-General. 2005. *In Larger Freedom: Towards Development, Security, and Human Rights for All.* UN Doc. A/59/2005.

United Nations Secretary-General. 2006a. United Against Terrorism: Recommendations for a Global Counter-Terrorism Strategy, A/60/825, April 27.

United Nations Secretary-General. 2006b. Remarks to the Sixth Review Conference of the Biological Weapons Convention, November 20.

United Nations Secretary-General's High-level Panel on Threats, Challenges and Change. 2004. *A More Secure World: Our Shared Responsibility.* New York: United Nations.

United Nations Security Council. 2000. *Round-Up: Developments throughout Africa, Renewed Violence in Middle East Among Key Issues for Security Council in 2000,* UN Doc. SC/6987.

USA PATRIOT Act. 2001. Public Law 107-56, September 28.

U.S. Department of Health and Human Services. 2006a. Pandemic Planning Update II: A Report from Secretary Michael O. Leavitt, Washington, D.C., June 29.

U.S. Department of Health and Human Services. 2006b. Pandemic Planning Update: A Report from Secretary Michael O. Leavitt, Washington, D.C., March 13.

U.S. Leadership Against HIV/AIDS, Tuberculosis, and Malaria Act. 2003. Public Law 108-25.

U.S. Federal News. 2006. HHS Secretary Levitt, Adm. Agwunobi, and Others Speak on U.S. Participation in the World Health Assembly, May 22.

VERTIC. 2003. *Time to Lay Down the Law: National Legislation to Enforce the BWC.* London: VERTIC.

Wall Street Journal. 2006. Google Philanthropy Director To Take On Disease Outbreaks. *Wall Street Journal,* February 27, at http://online.wsj.com/article/SB114099876038683781.html

Warrick, J. 2006. The Secretive Fight Against Bioterror. *Washington Post,* July 30, p. A01.

Wassenaar Arrangement. 2006. *Introduction to the Wassenaar Arrangement on Export Controls for Conventional Arms and Dual-Use Goods and Technologies,* at http://www.wassenaar.org/introduction/index.html

Weapons of Mass Destruction Commission. 2006. *Weapons of Terror: Freeing the World of Nuclear, Biological and Chemical Arms.* Stockholm: Weapons of Mass Destruction Commission.

Weindling, P., ed. 1995. *International Health Organisations and Movements, 1918–1939.* Cambridge: Cambridge University Press.

Wendt, A. 1992. Anarchy is What States Make of It: The Social Construction of Power Politics. *International Organization,* 46: 391–425.

Wendt, A. 1999. *Social Theory of International Politics.* Cambridge: Cambridge University Press.

Wheelis, M., and Dando, M. 2003. Back to Bioweapons? *Bulletin of the Atomic Scientists,* 59: 40–46.

Wheelis, M., Rózsa, L., and Dando, M. Eds. 2006. *Deadly Cultures: Biological Weapons Since 1945.* Cambridge, MA: Harvard University Press.

White, H. 2006. Building Security in Asia. *Far Eastern Economic Review,* at http://rspas.anu.edu.au/gssd/analysis/White_FEERFutureSecurityAsiaDec06.pdf.

White House. 2002. *The National Security Strategy of the United States of America.* Washington, D.C.: The White House.

White House. 2003. *President Bush's State of the Union Address,* January 28, at http://www.whitehouse.gov/news/releases/2003/01/20030128–19.html

White House. 2005. *National Strategy for Pandemic Influenza.* Washington, D.C.: The White House.

White House. 2006a. *The National Security Strategy of the United States of America.* Washington, D.C.: The White House.

White House. 2006b. *Implementation Plan for the National Strategy for Pandemic Influenza.* Washington, D.C.: The White House.

Winslow, C.-E.-A. 1943. *The Conquest of Epidemic Disease: A Chapter in the History of Ideas.* Princeton, N.J.: Princeton University Press.

World Health Organization. July 22, 1946. Constitution of the World Health Organization. 14 *United Nations Treaty Series* 185.

World Health Organization. 2001. *Global Health Security: Epidemic Alert and Response,* WHO Doc. WHA54.14.

World Health Organization. 2002. *Global Defence Against the Infectious Disease Threat,* M. K. Kindhauser, ed. Geneva: WHO.

World Health Organization. 2005. *Donation of Three Million Treatments of Oseltamivir to WHO Will Help Early Response to an Emerging Influenza Pandemic.* Press Release, Aug. 24, at http://www.who.int/mediacentre/news/releases/2005/pr36/en/

World Health Organization. 2006a. *Global Outbreak Alert and Response Network,* at http://www.who.int/csr/outbreaknetwork/en/

World Health Organization. 2006b. *International Health Migration: A Challenge for Health Systems in Developing Countries: Report by the Secretariat.* WHO Doc. A59/18, May 4.

World Health Organization. 2006c. *Application of the International Health Regulations (2005)*. WHO Doc. WHA59.3, May 26, at http://www.who.int/gb/ebwha/pdf_files/WHA59/WHA59_2-en.pdf

World Health Organization. 2006d. Emergence of XDR-TB, September 5, at http://www.who.int/tb/features_archive/xdr-tb/en/index.html

World Health Organization. 2006e. *WHO Influenza Pandemic Draft Protocol for Rapid Response and Containment,* May 30, at http://www.who.int/csr/disease/avian_influenza/guidelines/protocolfinal30_05_06a.pdf

World Health Organization. 2007a. *Joint Statement from the Ministry of Health, Indonesia and the World Health Organization Regarding the Sharing of Avian Influenza Viruses and Pandemic Vaccine Production,* February 16, Statement WHO/2, at http://www.who.int/mediacentre/news/statements/2007/s02/en/index.html

World Health Organization. 2007b. *WHO Guidance on Human Rights and Involuntary Detention for XDR-TB Control,* January 24, at http://www.who.int/tb/xdr/involuntary_treatment/en/index.html

World Health Organization. 2007c. *Pandemic Influenza Preparedness: Sharing of Influenza Viruses and Access to Vaccines and Other Benefits.* WHO Doc. WHA60.28, May 23.

Yach, D., Leeder, S., Bell, J., and Kistnasamy, B. 2005. Global Chronic Diseases. *Science,* 307: 317.

INDEX

Abbott, E. B., 196
Acharya, A., 239
Afghanistan, 197, 260
Aglionby, J., 170, 172
Alberts, B., 77
American Civil Liberties Union, 199
anthrax: attacks of 2001, 5, 23, 25, 26–27,
     31, 36, 52, 53, 75, 88, 93–94, 99, 136,
     153, 180–81, 190, 196, 204, 252, 261; as
     biological weapon, 35–36, 39–40, 41, 45,
     92–93, 95–96, 168, 173, 184, 201, 215;
     vaccination for, 101, 166–67, 184
antibiotics, 26, 30, 33–34, 36, 37, 80, 87, 168,
     171; antimicrobial resistance to, 124,
     138, 141, 153, 157, 228
Antiterrorism and Effective Death Penalty
     Act, 57
antiviral drugs, 37, 80, 160, 169, 171, 174, 175,
     209, 210; Tamiflu, 161–62, 198, 215
Aristotle, 203
Artemisinin Project, 43
Arthur, C., 42
Ashcroft, John, 77
Asia-Pacific Economic Cooperation (APEC),
     230
Assessment of National Implementation
     of the Biological and Toxin Weapons
     Convention, 70
Atlantic Storm exercise, 180
Atlas, R., 85
Aum Shinrikyo cult, 40, 51
Australia Group, 229

Australian mousepox experiment, 42, 190
avian influenza, 1, 81, 138, 153, 212, 228, 248;
     threat of pandemic, 5, 10, 157, 158–59,
     170–73, 175, 198, 245–46, 260–61

Bacchus/BACUS, 94–95
Bacillus anthracis. See anthrax
Background Information Document on
     the History and Operation of the
     Confidence-Building Measures, 103
Background information Document on the
     Status of Universality of the Convention,
     104
Baker, M., 155
BARDA. *See* Biomedical Advanced Research
     and Development Authority
Barenblatt, D., 46
Barletta, M., 84, 229
Barry, J., 133
Bartlett, C. L. R., 232
Beauchamp, D. E., 208
Bell, J., 8, 150
Bergen, P., 6
Berkelman, R., 133
Berkman, B., 200
Bernaure, T., 56
Bill and Melinda Gates Foundation, 16, 175,
     176
biodefense, 19, 36, 46–47, 87–99, 195, 206,
     229, 258; Bacchus/BACUS, 94–95; and
     bioterrorism, 94–97; and BWC, 33–34,
     54, 55–56, 58, 59–60, 87–88, 90, 91–95,